MFK
FISHER

The

Gastronomical

Me

NORTH POINT PRESS
Farrar, Straus and Giroux
New York

Published in Canada by HarperCollins*CanadaLtd*
Printed in the United States of America
Originally published in 1943 by Duell, Sloan & Pearce
This edition first published in 1989 by North Point Press
Designed by David Bullen
Seventh printing, 1997

LIBRARY OF CONGRESS CATALOGING-IN-PUBLICATION DATA
Fisher, M. F. K. (Mary Frances Kennedy), 1908–1992
  The gastronomical me / M. F. K. Fisher.
     p.   cm.
  Reprint. Originally published: New York: Duell,
  Sloan & Pearce, © 1943.
  1. Gastronomy.   I. Title.
TX633.F518   1989
641'.01'3—dc19   88-32967

North Point Press
A division of Farrar, Straus and Giroux
New York

For Anne Kennedy Kelly

Contents

Foreword

People ask me: Why do you write about food, and eating and drinking? Why don't you write about the struggle for power and security, and about love, the way others do?

They ask it accusingly, as if I were somehow gross, unfaithful to the honor of my craft.

The easiest answer is to say that, like most other humans, I am hungry. But there is more than that. It seems to me that our three basic needs, for food and security and love, are so mixed and mingled and entwined that we cannot straightly think of one without the others. So it happens that when I write of hunger, I am really writing about love and the hunger for it, and warmth and the love of it and the hunger for it . . . and then the warmth and richness and fine reality of hunger satisfied . . . and it is all one.

I tell about myself, and how I ate bread on a lasting hillside, or drank red wine in a room now blown to bits, and it happens without my willing it that I am telling too about the people with me then, and their other deeper needs for love and happiness.

There is food in the bowl, and more often than not, because of what honesty I have, there is nourishment in the heart, to feed the wilder, more insistent hungers. We must eat. If, in the face of that dread fact, we can find other nourishment, and tolerance and compassion for it, we'll be no less full of human dignity.

There is a communion of more than our bodies when bread is broken and wine drunk. And that is my answer, when people ask me: Why do you write about hunger, and not wars or love?

M.F.K.F.

To be happy you must have taken the measure of your powers,
tasted the fruits of your passion, and learned your place in the world.

SANTAYANA

The

Gastronomical

Me

The Measure
of My Powers

1912

The first thing I remember tasting and then wanting to taste again is the grayish-pink fuzz my grandmother skimmed from a spitting kettle of strawberry jam. I suppose I was about four.

Women in those days made much more of a ritual of their household duties than they do now. Sometimes it was indistinguishable from a dogged if unconscious martyrdom. There were times for This, and other equally definite times for That. There was one set week a year for "the sewing woman." Of course, there was Spring Cleaning. And there were other periods, almost like festivals in that they disrupted normal life, which were observed no matter what the weather, finances, or health of the family.

Many of them seem odd or even foolish to me now, but probably the whole staid rhythm lent a kind of rich excitement to the housebound flight of time.

With us, for the first years of my life, there was a series, every summer, of short but violently active cannings. Crates and baskets and lug-boxes of fruits bought in their prime and at their cheapest would lie waiting with opulent fragrance on the screened porch, and a whole battery of enameled pots and ladles and wide-mouthed funnels would appear from some dark cupboard.

All I knew then about the actual procedure was that we had delightful picnic meals while Grandmother and Mother and the cook worked with a kind of drugged concentration in our big dark kitchen, and were tired and cross and at the same time oddly triumphant in their race against summer heat and the processes of rot.

Now I know that strawberries came first, mostly for jam. Sour red cherries for pies and darker ones for preserves were a little later, and then came the apricots. They were for jam if they were very ripe, and the solid ones were simply "put up." That, in my grandmother's language, meant cooking with little sugar, to eat for breakfast or dessert in the winter which she still thought of in terms of northern Iowa.

She was a grim woman, as if she had decided long ago that she could thus most safely get to Heaven. I have a feeling that my Father might have liked to help with the cannings, just as I longed to. But Grandmother, with that almost joyfully stern bowing to duty typical of religious women, made it clear that helping in the kitchen was a bitter heavy business forbidden certainly to men, and generally to children. Sometimes she let me pull stems off the cherries, and one year when I was almost nine I stirred the pots a little now and then, silent and making myself as small as possible.

But there was no nonsense anyway, no foolish chitchat. Mother was still young and often gay, and the cook too . . . and with Grandmother directing operations they all worked in a harried muteness . . . stir, sweat, hurry. It was a pity. Such a beautifully smelly task should be fun, I thought.

In spite of any Late Victorian asceticism, though, the hot kitchen sent out tantalizing clouds, and the fruit on the porch lay rotting in its crates, or readied for the pots and the wooden spoons, in fair glowing piles upon the juice-stained tables. Grandmother, saving always, stood like a sacrificial priestess in the steam, "skimming" into a thick white saucer, and I, sometimes permitted and more often not, put my finger into the cooling froth and licked it. Warm and sweet and odorous. I loved it, then.

A Thing Shared

1918

Now you can drive from Los Angeles to my Great-Aunt Maggie's ranch on the other side of the mountains in a couple of hours or so, but the first time I went there it took most of a day.

Now the roads are worthy of even the All-Year-Round Club's boasts, but twenty-five years ago, in the September before people thought peace had come again, you could hardly call them roads at all. Down near the city they were oiled, all right, but as you went farther into the hills toward the wild desert around Palmdale, they turned into rough dirt. Finally they were two wheel-marks skittering every which way through the Joshua trees.

It was very exciting: the first time my little round brown sister Anne and I had ever been away from home. Father drove us up from home with Mother in the Ford, so that she could help some cousins can fruit.

We carried beer for the parents (it exploded in the heat), and water for the car and Anne and me. We had four blowouts, but that was lucky, Father said as he patched the tires philosophically in the hot sun; he'd expected twice as many on such a long hard trip.

The ranch was wonderful, with wartime crews of old men and loud-voiced boys picking the peaches and early pears all day, and singing and rowing at night in the bunkhouses. We couldn't go near them or near the pen in the middle of a green alfalfa field where a new prize bull, black as thunder, pawed at the pale sand.

We spent most of our time in a stream under the cottonwoods, or with Old Mary the cook, watching her make butter in a great churn between her mountainous knees. She slapped it into pats, and put them down in the stream where it ran hurriedly through the darkness of the butter-house.

She put stone jars of cream there, too, and wire baskets of eggs and lettuces, and when she drew them up, like netted fish, she would shake the cold water onto us and laugh almost as much as we did.

Then Father had to go back to work. It was decided that Mother would stay at the ranch and help put up more fruit, and Anne and I would go home with him. That was as exciting as leaving it had been, to be alone with Father for the first time.

He says now that he was scared daft at the thought of it, even though our grandmother was at home as always to watch over us. He says he actually shook as he drove away from the ranch, with us like two suddenly strange small monsters on the hot seat beside him.

Probably he made small talk. I don't remember. And he didn't drink any beer, sensing that it would be improper before two unchaperoned young ladies.

We were out of the desert and into deep winding canyons before the sun went down. The road was a little smoother, following streambeds under the live oaks that grow in all the gentle creases of the dry tawny hills of that part of California. We came to a shack where there was water for sale, and a table under the dark wide trees.

Father told me to take Anne down the dry streambed a little way. That made me feel delightfully grown-up. When we came back we held our hands under the water faucet and dried them on our panties, which Mother would never have let us do.

Then we sat on a rough bench at the table, the three of us in the deep green twilight, and had one of the nicest suppers I have ever eaten.

The strange thing about it is that all three of us have told other people that same thing, without ever talking of it among ourselves until lately. Father says that all his nervousness went away, and he saw us for the first time as two little brown humans who were fun. Anne and I both felt a subtle excitement at being alone for the first time with the only man in the world we loved.

(We loved Mother too, completely, but we were finding out, as Father was too, that it is good for parents and for children to be alone now and then with one another . . . the man alone or the woman, to sound new notes in the mysterious music of parenthood and childhood.)

That night I not only saw my Father for the first time as a person. I saw the golden hills and the live oaks as clearly as I have ever seen them since; and I saw the dimples in my little sister's fat hands in a way that still moves me because of that first time; and I saw food as something beautiful to be shared with people instead of as a thrice-daily necessity.

I forget what we ate, except for the end of the meal. It was a big round peach pie, still warm from Old Mary's oven and the ride over the desert. It was deep, with lots of juice, and bursting with ripe peaches picked that noon. Royal Albertas, Father said they were. The crust was the most perfect I have ever tasted, except perhaps once upstairs at Simpson's in London, on a hot plum tart.

And there was a quart Mason jar, the old-fashioned bluish kind like Mexican glass, full of cream. It was still cold, probably because we all knew the stream it had lain in, Old Mary's stream.

Father cut the pie in three pieces and put them on white soup plates in front of us, and then spooned out the thick cream. We ate with spoons too, blissful after the forks we were learning to use with Mother.

And we ate the whole pie, and all the cream . . . we can't remember if we gave any to the shadowy old man who sold water

. . . and then drove on sleepily toward Los Angeles, and none of us said anything about it for many years, but it was one of the best meals we ever ate.

Perhaps that is because it was the first conscious one, for me at least; but the fact that we remember it with such queer clarity must mean that it had other reasons for being important. I suppose that happens at least once to every human. I hope so.

Now the hills are cut through with superhighways, and I can't say whether we sat that night in Mint Canyon or Bouquet, and the three of us are in some ways even more than twenty-five years older than we were then. And still the warm round peach pie and the cool yellow cream we ate together that August night live in our hearts' palates, succulent, secret, delicious.

The Measure
of My Powers

I know a beautiful honey-colored actress who is a gourmande, in a pleasant way. She loves to cook rich hot lavish meals. She does it well, too.

She is slender, fragile, with a mute otherworldly pathos in her large azure eyes, and she likes to invite a lot of oddly assorted and usually famous people to a long table crowded with flowers, glasses, dishes of nuts, bowls of Armenian jelly and Russian relishes and Indian chutney, and beer and wine and even water, and then bring in a huge bowl of oxtail stew with dumplings. She has spent days making it, with special spices she found in Bombay or Soho or Honolulu, and she sits watching happily while it disappears. Then she disappears herself, and in a few minutes staggers to the table with a baked Alaska as big as a washtub, a thing of beauty, and a joy for about fifteen minutes.

But this star-eyed slender gourmande has a daughter about eight or nine, and the daughter *hates* her mother's sensuous dishes. In fact, she grows spindly on them. The only way to put meat on her bones is to send her to stay for a week or two with her grandmother, where she eats store ice cream for lunch, mashed potatoes for supper, hot white pap for breakfast.

"*My* daughter!" the actress cries in despair and horror. I tell her there is still hope, with the passage of time. But she, perhaps because of her beauty, pretends Time is not.

The truth is, I think, that small children have very sensitive palates. A little pepper is to them what a highly spiced curry is to us. They can stand sweetness best, perhaps, but anything sour or spiced is actually painful to them.

The ability of an adult to enjoy a subtle goulash or a red-hot enchilada or even a well-hung bird is due partly to his dulled taste buds, calloused by other such delightful ordeals and the constant stupefaction of alcohol and cigaret smoke. Young humans, not yet tough, can taste bland delight in dishes that would sicken older men.

On the other hand, it is wrong to think that children with any spirit and intelligence welcome complete monotony. I know that, because I remember most clearly a cook we had when I was about nine, named Ora.

My grandmother, who oddly seems to have been connected with whatever infantine gastronomy I knew, spent the last thirty years of her life dying of some obscure internal ailment until a paralytic stroke finished her in four days. She was a vigorous woman, tight with repressed emotions, and probably had a "nervous stomach." She spent a lot of time at sanatoria, often genuinely ill, and when she was with us we had to follow her dietary rules, probably to our benefit: no fried things or pastries, no oils, no seasonings.

Grandmother, a handsome dignified old lady, had been told by her doctors to belch whenever she felt like it, which she did . . . long voluptuous Gargantuan belches, anywhere and any time at all, which unless you knew Grandmother would have led you to believe that our table was one of fabulous delights. And once, for a few weeks, it was. That was during Ora's sojourn in our kitchen.

Ora was a spare gray-haired woman, who kept herself to herself in a firm containment. She took her afternoons and Sundays off without incident or comment, and kept her small hot room as neat as her person. The rest of the time she spent in a kind of ecstasy in the kitchen.

She loved to cook, the way some people love to pray, or dance, or fight. She preferred to be let alone, even for the ordering of food, and made it clear that the meals were her business. They were among the best I have ever eaten . . . all the things we had always accepted as food, but presented in ways that baffled and delighted us.

Grandmother hated her. I don't know any real reasons, of course, after such a long time, but I think it was because Ora was not like the friendly stupid hired girls she thought were proper for middle-class kitchens. And then Ora did things to "plain good food" that made it exciting and new and delightful, which in my poor grandmother's stern asceticism meant that Ora was wrong.

"Eat what's set before you, and be thankful for it," Grandmother said often; or in other words, "Take what God has created and eat it humbly and without sinful pleasure."

Most of the things Ora brought to the table Grandmother professed to be unable to touch. Her belches grew uncompromisingly louder, and she lived on rice water and tomatoes stewed with white bread.

"The girl is ruining you," she would say to Mother when Monday's hash appeared in some new delicious camouflage. But the bills were no larger, Mother must confess.

"The children will be bilious before another week," Grandmother would remark dourly. But we were healthier than ever.

"Their table manners are getting worse," Grandmother observed between belches. And that was true, if you believed as she and unhappy millions of Anglo-Saxons have been taught to believe, that food should be consumed without comment of any kind but above all without sign of praise or enjoyment.

My little sister Anne and I had come in Ora's few weeks with us to watch every plate she served, and to speculate with excitement on what it would taste like. "Oh, *Mother*," we would exclaim in a kind of anguish of delight. "There are little stars, all made of pie crust! They have seeds on them! Oh, how beautiful! How good!"

Mother grew embarrassed, and finally stern; after all, she had been raised by Grandmother. She talked to us privately, and told us how unseemly it was for little children to make comments about food, especially when the cook could hear them. "You've never behaved this way before," she said, thereby admitting the lack of any reason to, until then.

We contented ourselves with silent glances of mutual bliss and, I really think, an increased consciousness of the possibilities of the table.

I was very young, but I can remember observing, privately of course, that meat hashed with a knife is better than meat mauled in a food-chopper; that freshly minced herbs make almost any good thing better; that chopped celery tastes different from celery in the stalk, just as carrots in thin curls and toast in crescents are infinitely more appetizing than in thick chunks and squares.

There were other less obvious things I decided, about using condiments besides salt and pepper, about the danger of monotony . . . things like that. But it is plain that most of my observations were connected in some way with Ora's knife.

She did almost everything with it, cut, and carved, and minced, and chopped, and even used it to turn things in the oven, as if it were part of her hand. It was a long one, with a bright curved point. She brought it with her to our house, and called it her French knife. That was one more thing Grandmother disliked about her; it was a wicked affectation to have a "French" knife, and take it everywhere as if it were alive, and spend all the spare time polishing and sharpening it.

We had an old woman named Mrs. Kemp come to the house every Saturday morning, to wash Grandmother's beautiful white hair and sometimes ours, and she and Grandmother must have talked together about Ora. Mrs. Kemp announced that she would no longer come through the kitchen to keep her appointments.

She didn't like "that girl," she said. Ora scared her, always sitting so haughty sharpening that wicked knife.

So Mrs. Kemp came in the front door, and Anne and I kept our tongues politely silent and our mouths open like little starved birds at every meal, and Grandmother belched rebelliously, and I don't remember what Mother and Father did, except eat of course.

Then, one Sunday, Ora didn't come back with her usual remote severity from her day off. Mother was going to have a baby fairly soon, and Grandmother said, "You see? That girl is way above herself! She simply doesn't want to be in the house with a nurse!"

Grandmother was pleased as Punch, and that night for supper we probably had her favorite dish, steamed soda crackers with hot milk.

The next day, though, we found that Ora, instead of leaving her mother after a quiet pleasant Sunday in which the two elderly women had gone to church and then rested, had cut her into several neat pieces with the French knife.

Then she ripped a tent thoroughly to ribbons. I don't know how the tent came in . . . maybe she and her mother were resting in it. Anyway, it was a good thing to rip.

Then Ora cut her wrists and her own throat, expertly. The police told Father there wasn't a scratch or a nick in the knife.

Mrs. Kemp, and probably Grandmother too, felt righteous. "I just *felt* something," Mrs. Kemp would say, for a long time after Ora left.

I don't know about Father and Mother, but Anne and I were depressed. The way of dying was of only passing interest to us at our ages, but our inevitable return to ordinary sensible plain food was something to regret. We were helpless then, but we both learned from mad Ora, and now we know what to do about it, because of her.

The Measure
of My Powers

1919–1927

The first thing I cooked was pure poison. I made it for Mother, after my little brother David was born, and within twenty minutes of the first swallow she was covered with great itching red welts. The doctor came, soda compresses were laid on, sedatives and mild physic were scattered about, and all subsided safely . . . except my feeling of deep shock and hurt professional pride. As the nurse, Miss Faulck, pointed out, I should have been content to let well enough alone.

The pudding was safe enough: a little round white shuddering milky thing I had made that morning under the stern eye of Miss Faulck and whoever it was that succeeded mad Ora in the kitchen. It had "set" correctly. It was made according to the directions for Invalid Cookery in Mother's best recipe book, and I had cleaned my fingernails until tears filled my eyes before I touched so much as the box of cornstarch.

Then, in the middle of the afternoon, when the pudding slid with a chill plop into the saucer, I knew that I could not stand to present it, my first culinary triumph, in its naked state. It was obscenely pure, obscenely colorless.

A kind of loyalty to Ora rose in me, and without telling Miss Faulck I ran into the back yard and picked ten soft ripe blackberries. I blew off the alley-dust, and placed them gently in a perfect circle around the little pudding. Its cool perfection leaped into sudden prettiness, like Miss America when the winning ribbon is hung across her high-breasted symmetry.

And even a little while later, when Mother lay covered with compresses and Miss Faulck pursed her lips and David howled for a meal he couldn't have because he might drink hive-juice, Mother smiled at my shocked anxious confusion, and said, "Don't worry, sweet. . . . it was the loveliest pudding I have ever seen."

I agreed with her in spite of the despair.

I can't remember ever learning anything, that is, I don't hear Mother's voice saying to me, "Now this is a teaspoon, and this is the way you sift flour, and warm eggs won't make mayonnaise . . ." But evidently I loved to cook, and she taught me several things without making them into lessons, because in the next few years I knew how to make white sauce, and cup cakes with grated orange rind in them. (Father was always very complimentary about them, and Anne and I loved to save ours until the rest of the family had left the table, and then cover them with cream and sugar and eat them with a spoon.)

I could make jelly rolls, too, which seems odd now; I don't think I've even tasted one since I was about ten, much less had any interest in putting one together.

I loved to read cookbooks (unlike my feeling for jelly roll that passion has grown stronger with the years), and inevitably I soon started to improve on what I had read. Once I made poor Anne share my proud misery with something I called Hindu Eggs. I was sure I had read about it in Fanny Farmer; all you did was add curry powder to a white sauce and pour it over sliced hardboiled eggs.

When Mother said she and Father would be away one night, and I might get supper alone, I hid the gleam in my eye when she told me to put the sauce and the eggs in a casserole, and be sure to drink milk, and open a jar of plums or something for dessert.

"Yes, Mother, I know I can do it," I said smoothly, and the word *Hindu* danced sensuously in my mind, safely unsaid until Mother was out of the house.

The casserole was handsome, too, when Anne and I sat down to it in exciting solitude at the big table. Anne admired me, there was no doubt of it . . . and I admired myself. The rich brown sauce bubbled and sent out puffs of purely Oriental splendor. I sat in Father's place, and served each of us generously.

The first bite, and perhaps the next two or three, were all right; we were hungry, and in a hurry to feel the first warmth in our little bellies. Then Anne put down her fork. She beat me to it, so I continued to hold mine, determined like any honest cook to support my product.

"It's too hot, it burns," my little sister said, and gulped at her milk.

"Blow on it," I instructed. "Mother's not here."

We blew, and I ate three more bites to Anne's dutiful one. The heat seemed to increase. My influence over Anne must have been persuasive as well as autocratic in those far days, because she ate most of what was on her plate before the tears started rolling down her round brown cheeks.

I ate all mine, proudly, but inside I was cold with the new knowledge that I had been stupid. I had thought I remembered a recipe when I didn't, and I had used curry without knowing anything about it, and when the sauce looked boringly white I had proceeded to make it richly darker with probably five tablespoonfuls of the exotic powder.

I ate all I could, for fear Father would see how much we threw into the garbage pail, and then after my sweet forgiving little sister helped me straighten the kitchen we went upstairs and, with the desperate intuition of burned animals, sat on the edge of the bathtub for a long time with our mouths full of mineral oil. She never said anything more about it, either; and the next morning there were only a few blisters, just inside our lips.

When I was eleven we all moved to the country. We had a cow, and chickens, and partly because of that and partly because Grandmother had died we began to eat more richly.

We had chocolate puddings with chopped nuts and heavy cream. The thought of them makes me dizzy now, but we loved them. And lots of butter: I was good at churning, and learned very well how to sterilize the wooden churn and make the butter and then roll it into fine balls and press it into molds. I liked that. And we could have mayonnaise, rich yellow with eggs and oil, instead of the boiled dressing Grandmother's despotic bowels and stern palate called for.

Mother, in an orgy of baking brought on probably by all the beautiful eggs and butter lying around, spent every Saturday morning making cakes. They were piled high with icings. They were filled with crushed almonds, chopped currants, and an outrageous number of calories. They were beautiful. Saturday afternoons they sat cooling, along with Mother and the kitchen after the hectic morning, and by Sunday night they were already a pleasant if somewhat bilious memory.

After about a year of this luscious routine, Mother retired more or less permanently to the front part of the house, perhaps with half an eye on the bathroom scales, but before she gave up cooking, I learned a lot about cakes from her. The fact that I have never made one since then—at least, the kind with many layers and fillings and icings and all that—has little to do with the gratitude I have often felt for knowing how to measure and sift and be patient and not be daunted by disappointment.

Mother, like all artists, was one-sided. She only cooked what she herself liked. She knew very little about meats, so I gradually learned all that myself. She hated gravies, and any sauces but "white sauce" (probably a hangover from Grandmother's training), so I made some hideous mistakes with them. And there was always an element of surprise, if not actual danger, in my meals; the Hindu eggs had warned me but not curbed my helpless love of anything rare or racy.

But in spite of all that, I was the one who got dinner on the cook's off-night. I improved, there is no doubt about it, and it was taken for granted that I would step into the kitchen at the drop of a hat.

Perhaps Anne would have liked a chance at having all the family's attention for those few hours. If so she never got it. The stove, the bins, the cupboards, I had learned forever, make an inviolable throne room. From them I ruled; temporarily I controlled. I felt powerful, and I loved that feeling.

I am more modest now, but I still think that one of the pleasantest of all emotions is to know that I, I with my brain and my hands, have nourished my beloved few, that I have concocted a stew or a story, a rarity or a plain dish, to sustain them truly against the hungers of the world.

The First Oyster

1924

The intramural complexities of the faculty at Miss Huntingdon's School for Girls have become much clearer to me since I left there, but even at sixteen I knew that Mrs. Cheever's social position was both uncomfortable and lonely.

She had her own office, which was certainly more than any snobbish Latin teacher could boast. She was listed as part of the school's administration in the discreet buff and sepia catalog; I cannot remember now just what her title was, except that it implied with high-sounding ambiguity that she was the housekeeper without, of course, using that vulgar word itself.

She was a college graduate, even though it was from some domestic-science school instead of Smith or Mount Holyoke.

She was, above all, a lady.

She was almost a super-lady, mainly because it was so obvious that the rest of the faculty, administration as well as teachers, considered her a cook. When she stepped occasionally after dinner into the library, where I as an honor Sophomore was privileged to carry demitasses to the Seniors and the teachers on alternate Wednesday nights, I could see that she was snubbed almost as thoroughly as her well-fed colleagues snubbed the school nurse, one notch below the housekeeper on the social scale but also a colleague as far as the catalog went.

No malicious, inverted, discontented boarding-school teacher on God's earth, however, could snub the poor nurse as much as Mrs. Cheever could. Her coarsely genteel face under its Queen Mary coiffure expressed with shocking clarity the loathing she felt for that gentle ninny who dealt out pills and sticking plasters, and all the loneliness and bitter social insecurity of her own position showed in the way Mrs. Cheever stood proudly alone in the crowded library, smiling with delicacy and frightful pleasure at the nurse, whose hand trembled clumsily as she sipped at her little coffee cup and tried to look like a college graduate.

The two women studiously spoke to no one, mainly because no one spoke to them. Perhaps once or twice, long since, the nurse may have said a timid nothing to the housekeeper, but Mrs. Cheever would have bitten out her own tongue before loosening it in charity toward a sister outcast.

Once it almost looked as if she would have a friend on the faculty, when a new gym teacher came. So often athletic people were not exactly . . . that is, they seldom had M.A.'s, even if they seemed really quite ladylike at times. And Mrs. Cheever felt sure that the new colleague would be as scornful as she was herself of all the pretentious schoolma'ams, with their airs and graces.

But after the first week, during which the little gym teacher stood shyly by the housekeeper for coffee, or nibbled in her room on the pink grapes and small frosted cakes that Mrs. Cheever sent her, the other women discovered that not only was she from Barnard . . . *summa cum laude, parbleu!* . . . but that she had the most adorable little cracked voice, almost like a boy's. It was perfect with her hair, so short and boyish too, and by the end of the second week three of the teachers were writing passionate notes to her, and Mrs. Cheever once more stood magnificently alone on her occasional visits to the library after dinner.

Perhaps loneliness made her own food bitter to her, because Mrs. Cheever was an obvious dyspeptic. The rest of us, however:

Miss Huntingdon herself, remote and saint-like; Miss Blake, her shadow, devoted, bewigged, a skin-and-bone edition of Krafft-Ebing; all the white women of the school, fat, thin, frantic or calm, and all the Filipino servants, pretty little men-dolls as mercurial as monkeys, and as lewd; all the girls, who felt like victims but were really the raison d'être of this strange collection within the high walls . . . Mrs. Cheever fed us four times a day with probably the best institutional food in America.

She ran her kitchens with such skill that in spite of ordinary domestic troubles like flooded basements and soured cream, and even an occasional extraordinary thing like the double murder and hara-kiri committed by the head-boy one Good Friday, our meals were never late and never bad.

There were about seventy boarders and twenty-five women, and for morning-recess lunch a pack of day-girls, and most of us ate with the delicacy and appreciation of half-starved animals. It must have been sickening to Mrs. Cheever to see us literally wolfing her well-planned, well-cooked, well-served dishes. For in spite of doing things wholesale, which some gastronomers say is impossible with any finesse, the things we ate at Miss Huntingdon's were savory and interesting.

Mrs. Cheever, for instance, would get a consignment of strange honey from the Torrey pine trees, honey which only a few people in the world were supposed to have eaten. I remember it now with some excitement, as a grainy greenish stuff like some I once ate near Adelboden in the Bernese Alps, but then it was to most of us just something sweet and rather queer to put on hot biscuits. Tinned orange marmalade would have done as well.

At Thanksgiving she would let the Filipinos cover the breakfast tables with dozens of odd, beautiful little beasts they had made from vegetables and fruits and nuts, so that the dining room became for a while amazingly funny to us, and we were allowed to make almost as much noise as we wanted while we ate forbidden things like broiled sausage and played with the crazy toys. The boys would try not to laugh too, and even Mrs. Cheever would incline her queenly topknot less scornfully than usual when spoken to.

Saturday noons we could eat sandwiches and cocoa or pink punch on the hockey field, and have ice cream from the soda fountain in the village if we told Mrs. Cheever between eight and nine that morning. I sometimes went without it, or got another girl to order for me, simply because I could not bear to go into the little office and have the housekeeper look at me. She made me feel completely unattractive, which is even worse at sixteen than later.

She would sit stiffly at her desk, waiting for orders with an expression of such cold impersonal nausea on her face that I could hardly believe the gossip that she had made a fat sum weekly by charging us almost double what the drug store got for its cartons of ice cream and its incredibly sweet sauces.

She would make precise notations on a sheet of paper while we mumbled our orders, and sometimes even suggested in her flat clear voice that salted pecans might be better than strawberry syrup on chocolate-ice-cream-with-butterscotch-sauce. Her expression of remote anguish never changed, even when she reminded us, with her eyes resting coldly on a bulging behind or a spotty chin, that we were limited to one pint apiece.

It was for festivals like Easter and Old Girls' Day, though, that she really exercised her talents. Now I can see that she must have filled many hours of snubbed isolation in plans for our pleasure, but then I only knew that parties at Miss Huntingdon's School for Girls were really fun, mostly because the food was so good. Mrs. Cheever, callously ignored by the girls except for a few minutes each Saturday morning, and smiled at condescendingly by her unwilling colleagues with university degrees, turned our rare bats into what could truly be called small gastronomic triumphs . . . and the more so because they were what they were within high walls.

Old Girls' Day, for instance, meant to all but the Seniors, who had to be nice to the returning alumnae, that we spent a long gray warm June day on the sand and the rocks, and that we could wear our full pleated gym bloomers and *no stockings*, and take pictures of each other with our Brownies, and, best of all, that at half past noon a procession of house-boys would come down the cliffs from the school with our lunch for us in big baskets.

There would be various things, of course, like pickles and napkins and knives and probably sandwiches and fruit, although how Mrs. Cheever managed it with the school full of hungry shrieking postgraduates is more than I can guess. Perhaps she even sent down devilled eggs to make it a real picnic.

I don't remember, because all that we thought about then, or could recall now if we ever dared to think at all of those days, were the hot crisp fried halves of young chickens, stiff and tempting. We could have all we wanted, even three or four, and we could eat with our fingers, and yell, and gobble. It was wonderful.

There must have been chaperones, but they seemed not to exist down there in the warmth and the silly freedom, and when a stately figure stood for an instant on the cliff top, wrapped fussily in an afternoon gown for the Old Girls, and looked down at us with her face set in a sour chill smile, we waved our greasy drumsticks hilariously up at her, and cried,

Miss-is Chee-ver
Miss-is Chee-ver
Miss-is Chee-ver
Rah-ah-ah-ah,

almost as if she were a whole basketball game between the Golds and the Purples. For one moment, at least, in the year, we were grateful to her for our deliciously full mouths.

She did her conscientious best to be sensible in her menus, and fed us better garden things and fresher cream and milk than most of us have eaten since, but there must have been a dreadful impatience in her for such pap, so that occasionally she would give us the Torrey pine-honey for breakfast, or have the Chinese cook put chives over the Friday fish instead of a cream sauce.

Once, for the Christmas Party, she served Eastern oysters, fresh oysters, oysters still in their shells.

Nothing could have been more exotic in the early twenties in

Southern California. The climate was still considered tropical, so that shellfish imported alive from the East were part of an oil-magnate's dream, or perhaps something to be served once or twice a year at Victor Hugo's, in a private room with pink candleshades and a canary. And of course any local molluscs were automatically deemed inedible, at least by *nice* people.

The people, that Christmas Party night, were indeed nice. We wore our formals: skirts not less than eight nor more than fifteen inches from the floor, dresses of light but not bright colors and of materials semi-transparent or opaque, neck-lines not more than three inches below the collar bone and sleeves long or elbow-length. We all passed the requirements of the catalog, but with such delectable additions as long chiffon scarves twined about our necks in the best Nita-Naldi-bronchitic manner, or great artificial flowers pinned with holiday abandon on our left shoulders. Two or three of the Seniors had fox furs slung nonchalantly about them, with the puffy tails dangling down over their firmly flattened young breasts in a most fashionable way.

There may even have been a certain amount of timid make-up in honor of Kris Kringle and the approaching libertinage of Christmas vacation, real or devoutly to be hoped for, but fortunately the dining room was lighted that night by candles only.

Mrs. Cheever had outdone herself, although all we thought then was that the old barn had never looked so pretty. The oblong tables, usually in ranks like dominoes in their box, were pushed into a great horseshoe, with a little table for Miss Huntingdon and Miss Blake and the minister and the president of the trustees in the middle, and a sparkling Christmas tree, and . . . yes! . . . a space for dancing! And there were candles, and the smells of pine branches and hot wax, and place cards all along the outer edge of the horseshoe so that the Freshmen would not sit in one clot and the other groups in theirs.

We marched once around the beautiful room in the flickering odorous candlelight, singing, "God Rest You Merry, Gentlemen" or some such thing to the scrapings of the assistant violin instructor and two other musicians, who in spite of their trousers had been accurately judged unable to arouse unseemly longings in our cloistered hearts.

Then we stood by the chairs marked with our names, and waited for the music to stop and Miss Huntingdon and the minister to ask the blessings in their fluty voices. It was all very exciting.

When I saw that I was to sit between a Senior and a Junior, with not a Freshman in sight, I felt almost uplifted with Christmas joy. It must mean that I was Somebody, to be thus honored, that perhaps I would even be elected to the Altar Guild next semester. . . .

I knew enough not to speak first, but could not help looking sideways at the enormous proud nose of Olmsted, who sat at my left. She was president of the Seniors, and moved about the school in a loose-limbed dreamy way that seemed to me seraphic. Inez, the Junior, was less impressive, but still had her own string of horses in Santa Barbara and could curse with great concentration, so many words that I only recognized *damn* and one or two others. Usually she had no use for me, but tonight she smiled, and the candlelight made her beady eyes look almost friendly.

The grace done with, we pulled our chairs in under the unaccustomed silkiness of our party-dress bottoms with less noise than usual, and the orchestra flung itself into a march. The pantry doors opened, and the dapper little house-boys pranced in, their smooth faces pulled straight and their eyes snapping with excitement.

They put a plate in front of each of us. We all looked mazily at what we saw, and waited with mixed feelings until Miss Huntingdon had picked up her fork (where, I wonder now, did Mrs. Cheever even find one hundred oyster forks in a California boarding school?), before we even thought of eating. I heard Inez mutter under her breath, several more words I did not recognize except as such, and then Olmsted said casually, "How charming! Blue Points!"

There was a quiet buzz . . . we were being extremely well-bred, all of us, for the party . . . and I know now that I was not the only Westerner who was scared shaky at the immediate prospect of eating her first raw oyster, and was putting it off for as long as possible.

I remembered hearing Mother say that it was vulgar as well as extremely unpleasant to do anything with an oyster but swallow it as quickly as possible, without *thinking*, but that the after-taste was rather nice. Of course it was different with tinned oysters in turkey dressing: they could be chewed with impunity, both social and hygienic, for some reason or other. But raw, they must be swallowed whole, and rapidly.

And alive.

With the unreasoning and terrible persnicketiness of a sixteen-year-old I knew that I would be sick if I had to swallow anything in the world alive, but especially a live oyster.

Olmsted picked up one deftly on the prongs of her little fork, tucked it under her enormous nose, and gulped. "Delicious," she murmured.

"Jesus," Inez said softly. "Well, here goes. The honor of the old school. Oi!" And she swallowed noisily. A look of smug surprise crept into her face, and she said in my ear, "Try one, Baby-face. It ain't the heat, it's the humidity. Try one. Slip and go easy." She cackled suddenly, watching me with sly bright eyes.

"Yes, do," Olmsted said.

I laughed lightly, tinklingly, like Helen in *Helen and Warren*, said, "Oh, I *love* Blue Points!" and got one with surprising neatness into my mouth.

At that moment the orchestra began to play, with sexless abandon, a popular number called, I think, "Horses." It sounded funny in Miss Huntingdon's dining room. Olmsted laughed, and said to me, "Come on, Kennedy. Let's start the ball rolling, shall we?"

The fact that she, the most wonderful girl in the whole school, and the most intelligent, and the most revered, should ask me to dance when she knew very well that I was only a Sophomore, was so overwhelming that it made even the dreamlike reality that she had called me Kennedy, instead of Mary Frances, seem unimportant.

The oyster was still in my mouth. I smiled with care, and stood up, reeling at the thought of dancing the first dance of the evening with the senior-class president.

The oyster seemed larger. I knew that I must down it, and was equally sure that I could not. Then, as Olmsted put her thin hand on my shoulder blades, I swallowed once, and felt light and attractive and daring, to know what I had done. We danced stiffly around the room, and as soon as a few other pairs of timid girls came into the cleared space by the tree, headed toward Miss Huntingdon's table.

Miss Huntingdon herself spoke to me by name, and Miss Blake laughed silently so that her black wig bobbled, and cracked her knuckles as she always did when she was having a good time, and the minister and Olmsted made a little joke about Silent Sophomores and Solemn Seniors, and I did not make a sound, and nobody seemed to think it strange. I was dumb with pleasure at my own importance . . . practically the Belle of the Ball I was! . . . and with a dawning gastronomic hunger. Oysters, my delicate taste buds were telling me, oysters are *simply marvelous*! More, more!

I floated on, figuratively at least, in Olmsted's arms. The dance ended with a squeaky but cheerful flourish, and the girls went back to their seats almost as flushed as if they were returning from the arms of the most passionate West Point cadets in white gloves and coats.

The plates had been changed. I felt flattened, dismayed, as only children can about such things.

Olmsted said, "You're a funny kid, Kennedy. Oh, green olives!" when I mumbled how wonderful it had been to dance with her, and Inez murmured in my ear, "Dance with me next, will you, Baby-face? There are a couple of things boys can do I can't, but I can dance with you a damn sight better than that bitch Olmsted."

I nodded gently, and smiled a tight smile at her, and thought that she was the most horrible creature I had ever known. Perhaps I might kill her some day. I was going to be sick.

I pushed back my chair.

"Hey, Baby-face!" The music started with a crash, and Inez put her arms surely about me, and led me with expert grace around and around the Christmas tree, while all the candles fluttered in time with my stomach.

"Why don't you talk?" she asked once. "You have the cutest little ears I ever saw, Baby-face . . . like a pony I had, when I was in Colorado. How do you like the way I dance with you?"

Her arm tightened against my back. She was getting a crush on me, I thought, and here it was only Christmas and I was only a Sophomore! What would it be by April, the big month for them? I felt somewhat flattered, because Inez was a Junior and had those horses in Santa Barbara, but I hated her. My stomach felt better.

Miss Huntingdon was watching me again, while she held her water glass in her white thin fingers as if it had wine in it, or the Holy Communion. She leaned over and said something to Miss Blake, who laughed silently like a gargoyle and cracked her knuckles with delight, not at what Miss Huntingdon was saying but that she was saying anything at all. Perhaps they were talking about me, saying that I was nice and dependable and would be a good Senior president in two more years, or that I had the cutest ears. . . .

"Relax, kid," Inez murmured. "Just pretend . . ."

The pantry door swung shut on a quick flash of gray chiffon and pearls, almost at my elbow, and before I knew it myself I was out of Inez' skillful arms and after it. I had to escape from her; and the delightful taste of oyster in my mouth, my new-born gourmandise, sent me toward an unknown rather than a known sensuality.

The thick door shut out almost all the sound from the flickering, noisy dining room. The coolness of the pantry was shocking, and Mrs. Cheever was even more so. She stood, queenly indeed in her beautiful gray evening dress and her pearls and her snowy hair done in the same lumpy rhythm as Mary of England's, and her face was all soft and formless with weeping.

Tears trickled like colorless blood from her eyes, which had always been so stony and now looked at me without seeing me at all.

Her mouth, puckered from years of dyspepsia and disapproval, was loose and tender suddenly, and she sniffed with vulgar abandon.

She stood with one arm laid gently over the scarlet shoulders of the fat old nurse, who was dressed fantastically in the ancient costume of Saint Nicholas. It became her well, for her formless body was as generous as his, and her ninny-simple face, pink-cheeked and sweet, was kind like his and neither male nor female. The ratty white wig sat almost tidily on her head, which looked as if it hardly missed its neat black-ribboned nurse's cap, and beside her on the pantry serving table lay the beard, silky and monstrous, ready to be pulled snug against her chins when it was time to give us all our presents under the Christmas tree.

She looked through me without knowing that I stood staring at her like a paralyzed rabbit. I was terrified, of her the costumed nurse and of Mrs. Cheever so hideously weeping and of all old women.

Mrs. Cheever did not see me either. For the first time I did not feel unattractive in her presence, but rather completely unnecessary. She put out one hand, and for a fearful moment I thought perhaps she was going to kiss me: her face was so tender. Then I saw that she was putting oysters carefully on a big platter that sat before the nurse, and that as she watched the old biddy eat them, tears kept running bloodlessly down her soft ravaged cheeks, while she spoke not a word.

I backed toward the door, hot as fire with shock and the dread confusion of adolescence, and said breathlessly, "Oh, excuse me, Mrs. Cheever! But I . . . that is, *all* the Sophomores . . . on behalf of the Sophomore Class I want to thank you for this beautiful, this *simply marvelous* party! Oysters . . . and . . . and everything . . . It's all *so* nice!"

But Mrs. Cheever did not hear me. She stood with one hand still on the wide red shoulders of the nurse, and with the other she put the oysters left from the Christmas Party on a platter. Her eyes were smeared so that they no longer looked hard and hateful, and as she watched the old woman eat steadily, voluptuously, of the fat cold molluscs, she looked so tender that I turned anxiously toward the sureness and stability of such small passions as lay in the dining room.

The pantry door closed behind me. The orchestra was whipping through "Tales from the Vienna Woods," with the assistant violin instructor doubling on the artificial mocking bird. A flock of little Filipino boys skimmed like monkeys into the candlelight, with great trays of cranberry sauce and salted nuts and white curled celery held above their heads, and I could tell by their faces that whatever they had seen in the pantry was already tucked far back behind their eyes, perhaps forever.

If I could still taste my first oyster, if my tongue still felt fresh and excited, it was perhaps too bad. Although things are different now, I hoped then, suddenly and violently, that I would never see one again.

The Measure
of My Powers

1927

That year I graduated from boarding school, and my parents, occupied by three younger children and perhaps an unusual flurry of deaths-and-taxes . . . I don't remember . . . did not really know what to do with me.

My mother had gone gracefully through finishing school, a long well-chaperoned stay in Europe, and even more than the required number of hearts. Then, in the correct time, she had married . . . a starved-looking country-newspaper editor instead of one of the plump-cheeked rising young thises-and-thats she might have chosen from, but still it was marriage. My many cousins, on her side of the family at least, followed much the same pattern, and after school made debuts and married.

It was different with the "other side": my father's mother, as well as his father, had graduated from college. It took her eight years to do it, because she went a year and then had a baby for a year until four sons and a Bachelor of Arts were behind her. All her boys went through college, too, and my father's nieces were going as a matter of course.

But at home there was an almost invisible feeling of resentment between my parents about it. If Father would mention casually, and I am sure innocently, that So-and-so's wife was a college graduate, Mother would be huffy.

She would be huffy in such a subtle delicate way that I don't think Father noticed it very often: her right foot would tap in the small rapid tapping that only my mother can do, impossible to imitate, and she would take pains to show that she was better educated, farther traveled, more widely read than So-and-so's wife . . . all of it true, usually. In fact, she made it quite clear, to me at least, that So-and-so's wife was a "so-and-so" too, and that college educations might be fine for women who could get no other advantages, *but* . . .

The odd thing was that Mother never seemed to realize that the "advantages" she referred to with such bland satisfaction were as lacking in my life as in any other benighted female's who wanted to go to a university: I had never traveled more than a twelve-hour trip home from school for vacations; I lived in the country outside a very small California town; I had almost no friends there, because I had been away a long time and grown very shy and rather snobbish; I was as sexless as a ninety-year-old nun, in spite of a few timid dreams that Ronald Colman would see me someplace and say, "That's the girl I must have in my next picture!"

And there I was suddenly, big, moody, full of undirected energies of a thousand kinds. Father and Mother, panicky, decided to put me in one of the large universities in Los Angeles, where I would "be near home" until . . . until some miracle happened, I suppose.

But to be near home was the one thing I could not tolerate just then. I fought against it as instinctively as a person on the operating table fights against ether. The time had come for me to leave, and leave I must, strong always with the surety that I could return to my dear family.

I lived through two months or so of learning to play bridge because I was told I'd be a complete social failure if I didn't, and of sorority rushing parties at which other girls whispered to me that if I ate the lettuce under my so-called salad I would be blackballed. Then, probably because I was so obviously miserable, my father and mother reversed all their protective tactics, gave me a large letter of credit, and with carefully hidden anguish put me on the train for a semester in Illinois with my cousin . . . one of the many times they have thus astonished me, and perhaps themselves.

I went as far as Chicago with my Uncle Evans, Mother's brother. He was a quietly worldly man, professorial at times but always enjoyably so, who knew more about the pleasures of the table than anyone I had yet been with.

Before Prohibition he had loved to drink beer and good whiskey, and May wine in the spring, enough to sing and sometimes weep a little, for he was very sentimental. But as soon as alcohol was illegal, he stopped drinking it; he was a teacher of law, and too honest to preach what he did not practice. He was rare.

Personally I regret his honesty, because I think he would have been a fine man to drink with, and by the time I knew how to, and the country could, it was too late. He had been killed by a drunken driver.

But, the summer I was nineteen and went away to a new land, I started out with him, and learned for the first time that a menu is not something to be looked at with hasty and often completely phony nonchalance.

I must have been a trial, or at least a bore, on that trip. I was horribly self-conscious; I wanted everybody to look at me and think me the most fascinating creature in the world, and yet I died a small hideous death if I saw even one person throw a casual glance at me. In the dining car, which was an unusually good one rather the way the Broadway Limited was to be later, with an agreeable smooth dash to it, I would glance hastily at the menu and then murmur the name of something familiar, like lamb chops.

"But you know what lamb chops taste like," my uncle would say casually. "Why not have something exciting? Why not order . . . uh . . . how about Eastern scallops? Yes," he would go on before I could do more than gulp awkwardly, "we will have scallops tonight, Captain, and I think an avocado cocktail with plenty of fresh lime juice . . ." and so forth.

My uncle was so quiet about it that he made me feel free and happy, and those dinners with him are the only things I remember about the long hot filthy trip.

Then, when we got to Chicago, his son met us. Bernard was by far the brainiest member of our generation in the family, on Mother's side, and I was much in awe of him. He may even have been of me, for other reasons of course, but he never showed it. The minute I saw his solemn young face under its big brow I forgot all the ease that being with my uncle had brought me, and when we went into a station restaurant for dinner and my uncle asked me what I would like to eat, I mumbled stiffly, "Oh, anything . . . anything, thank you."

(That was an excellent restaurant: a rather small room with paneled walls and comfortable chairs and old but expert waiters. It was in the Union Station, I think. I went back years later, and found it had a good wine list and a good chef. It was like coming full circle, to find satisfaction there where I first started to search for it.)

"Anything," I said, and then I looked at my uncle, and saw through all my *gaucherie*, my really painful wish to be sophisticated and polished before him and his brilliant son, that he was looking back at me with a cold speculative somewhat disgusted look in his brown eyes.

It was as if he were saying, "You stupid uncouth young ninny, how dare you say such a thoughtless thing, when I bother to bring you to a good place to eat, when I bother to spend my time and my son's time on you, when I have been so patient with you for the last five days?"

I don't know how long all that took, but I knew that it was a very important time in my life. I looked at my menu, really looked with all my brain, for the first time.

"Just a minute, please," I said, very calmly. I stayed quite cool, like a surgeon when he begins an operation, or maybe a chess player opening a tournament. Finally I said to Uncle Evans, without batting an eye, "I'd like iced consommé, please, and then sweetbreads *sous cloche* and a watercress salad . . . and I'll order the rest later."

I remember that he sat back in his chair a little, and I knew that he was proud of me and very fond of me. I was too.

And never since then have I let myself say, or even think, "Oh, anything," about a meal, even if I had to eat it alone, with death in the house or in my heart.

The Measure
of My Powers

1927–1928

The winter of 1927–1928 was one of conscious gourmandise for me, or perhaps gluttony would be the word.

The small college my cousin Nan and I went to was riddled with tradition and poverty. The Underground Railway still tunnelled under the fine old houses and the stately avenues of tall elm trees, and rats ran healthily in their own tunnels through the walls of the big brick dormitory where we lived. I remember that the wing with my room in it was leaning away from the main building, so that I had six-inch blocks under one side of my bed, my desk, and my fairly modern (that is, post-Civil War) bureau.

The meals were bad. We ate them ravenously, because classes were almost a two-mile walk from the Hall, and by the time we had sprinted home for lunch we were hungry indeed. By the time we had walked back and then to the Hall again for dinner we were frankly starved, and would joyfully have wolfed down boiled sawdust.

The only actual thing I can remember about any meals but breakfast is that once I walked by mistake through the back lot of the Hall, and passed a pile taller than I was of empty gallon cans labeled Parsnips.

Breakfasts, every Sunday morning, consisted of all we could hold of really delicious hot cinnamon rolls. We had to eat them by a certain time . . . undoubtedly a dodge to get us up for church. Nan and her roommate Rachel and I used to dress in our church clothes, eat cinnamon rolls until we were almost sick, and then go back to bed. By mid-afternoon we were indigestibly awake, and the day usually ended in homesick mopes, misunderstandings, and headaches.

It all seems incredibly stupid now, but was natural then.

Quite often Rachel and Nan and I would invent some excuse . . . a birthday or a check from home or an examination passed . . . and would go to The Coffee and Waffle Shop, where we could have four waffles and unlimited coffee or a five-course meal for forty cents. Then we would go to the theatre and eat candy; there were still small companies playing *Smilin' Through* and *Seventh Heaven* then, or traveling magicians. And after the show we'd have another waffle, or two or three cups of hot chocolate.

On dates, which were limited because we were Freshmen, we drank chocolate or coffee and almost always ate chili beans. We would sit out in the cars, no matter how cold it was, and drink and eat. Then we would go back to the dance or the Hall. Everybody did that, and I suppose everybody smelled of chili powder and onions, so we never noticed it.

Now and then visiting relatives or kind family friends would invite us either to The Colonial Inn or to their homes. The food was always divine; that was the word we used, and we really meant it, after days of meals at the Hall. There were fine cooks in that part of Illinois, most of them colored, and I regret that I knew so little then about the way they handled chickens and hams and preserves and pickles.

Always for dessert there was pie *and* ice cream, on separate plates but to be eaten in alternating bites. Sometimes there were two kinds of pie, pumpkin and mince, with homemade eggnog ice cream, rich enough to make your teeth curl.

Most of the people who went to the college were poor. There were a few boys with raccoon coats and flasks, but all we really knew about the drinking that had the nation worried was what we read in *College Humor*.

The dates I liked best were with a twenty-year-old Irish edition of Jimmy Durante named Cleary, who divided his passion between football and James Branch Cabell, with practically none left over for me.

I used to sit with surprising docility through country high-school football games he was refereeing, so cold that when I stood up my ankles would bend without my knowing it, and whereas now I think I would really die under such conditions without at least a few drags at the schnapps bottle, then I felt quite happy with a little lukewarm coffee after our side had lost. Cleary was said to drink a little . . . any man full of forward passes and Cabellian double-talk needs to . . . but I never saw liquor while I was feeling my first freedom, with him or the other people I dated in Illinois. That is probably surprising.

So is the fact that Nan and Rachel and I never finished the first year there at that college, and that we all left without burst appendixes, ulcers, or any such minor banes as adiposity, dyspepsia, or spots.

I shudder wholeheartedly and without either affectation or regret at what and how we ate, nine tenths of the time we were there, and remember several things with great pleasure: Mr. Cleary, of course; the dishes of pickled peaches like translucent stained glass, at the Inn when we were taken there for Sunday dinner; best of all, probably, the suppers Nan and Rachel and I would eat in their room.

Now I think we ate them the way puppies chew grasstops. They probably saved our lives.

We would buy ginger ale, rolls, cream cheese, anchovy paste, bottled "French" dressing, and at least six heads of the most beautiful expensive lettuce we could find in that little town where only snobs ate anything but cabbage, turnips, and parsnips for the winter months.

We would lock the door, and mix the cheese and anchovy together and open the ginger ale. Then we would toast ourselves solemnly in our toothbrush mugs, loosen the belts on our woolen bathrobes, and tear into that crisp cool delightful lettuce like three starved rabbits.

Now and then one or another of us would get up, go to a window and open it, bare her little breasts to the cold sweep of air, and intone dramatically, "Pneu-mo-*o-o-onia*!" Then we would all burst into completely helpless giggles, until we had laughed enough to hold a little more lettuce. Yes, that was the best part of the year.

Sea Change

1929–1931

I

In 1929 the stock market crashed, and I got married for the first time and traveled into a foreign land across an ocean. All those things affected me, and the voyage perhaps most.

Everyone knows, from books or experience, that living out of sight of any shore does rich and powerfully strange things to humans. Captains and stewards know it, and come after a few trips to watch all passengers with a veiled wariness.

On land, the tuggings of the moons can somewhat safely be ignored by men, and left to the more pliant senses of women and seeds and an occasional warlock. But at sea even males are victims of the rise and fall, the twice-daily surge of the waters they float on, and willy-nilly the planetary rhythm stirs them and all the other voyagers.

They do things calmly that would be inconceivable with earth beneath them: they fall into bed and even into love with a poignant desperate relish and a complete disregard for the land-bound proprieties; they weep after one small beer, not knowing why; they sometimes jump overboard the night before making port. And always they eat and drink with a kind of concentration which, according to their natures, can be gluttonous, inspired, or merely beneficent.

Sometimes, if people make only one short voyage, or are unusually dull, they are not conscious of sea change, except as a feeling of puzzlement that comes over them when they are remembering something that happened, or almost happened, on board ship. Then for a few seconds, they will look like children listening to an old dream.

Often, though, and with as little volition, people will become ship addicts, and perjure themselves with trumpery excuses for their trips. I have watched many of them, men and women too, drifting in their drugged ways about the corridors of peacetime liners, their faces full of a contentment never to be found elsewhere.

(I know only one person who ever crossed the ocean without feeling it, either spiritually or physically. His name is Spittin Stringer, because he spits so much, and he went from Oklahoma to France and back again, in 1918, without ever getting off dry land. He remembers several places I remember too, and several French words, but he says firmly, "We must of went different ways. I don't rightly recollect no water, never.")

The sea change in me was slow, and it continues still. The first trip, I was a bride of some eleven nights, and I can blame on the ocean only two of the many physical changes in me: my smallest fingers and toes went numb a few hours after we sailed, and stayed so for several days after we landed, which still happens always; and I developed a place on the sole of my left foot about as big as a penny, which has to be scratched firmly about five times a week, a few minutes after I have gone to bed, whether I am on land or sea. The other changes were less obvious, and many of them I do not know, or have forgotten.

For a while, several years later, I mistrusted myself alone at sea. I found myself doing, or perhaps only considering doing, many things I did not quite approve of. I think that may be true of most women voyaging alone; I have seen them misbehave, subtly or coarsely, not wanting to, as if for a few days more than the decks beneath them had grown unstable. Then, as land approached and they felt nearer to something they loved, or at least recognized, their eyes cleared, as if they were throwing off an opiate, coming into focus again.

Yes, I have been conscious of that, and mistrusted it, so that I usually acted so stiffly virginal as to frighten even myself when for many reasons I had to go alone to America or back to France or Switzerland. I think that by now I am old enough, though, to know why such things happen, or at least how to cope with the ramifications and complexities of loneliness, which is by now my intimate and, I believe, my friend.

The first time I was with my husband I was shy, and surrounded with that special and inviolable naïveté of a new bride, so that Al and I walked about, and ate, and talked, almost without contact with the rest of the ship. That seemed natural to us.

I remember now that there were two young Jewish medical students going to Glasgow who eyed us often at meals. They looked nice, but it never occurred to me to speak to them or even smile, and I am sure that such an idea would have shocked them, because of the connubial glow that enfolded me.

Al bandied a few words of Princetonian Greek with a priest returning to Athens, and now and then we bought Martinis for a seedy English major who was going back to mythical clubs in London after an equally mythical and important lecture tour. He was unpleasant, in a vague way, and after he asked me to lead him, one night when we were dancing, I dismissed him with faint repugnance and no regret from my dream-filled life.

Al and I, partly because it fitted our budgets and mostly because it was the exciting, adventurous, smart thing to do, were traveling in what was called Student Third, on the *Berengaria*. I would quite frankly hate it now, but then it was part of the whole perfect scheme of things—even the one time I felt squeamish, from sloshing around in a wooden tub full of hot sea water right over the screws.

It seemed strange to find "Victoria and Albert" painted in the bottom of the throne-like toilets, when I knew British royalty could not be represented on the stage.

And in spite of my rosy daze I knew that the food was bad . . . heavy and graceless. People in the low stuffy dining hall ate hungrily of it, even when it was called Yorkshire Pudding with blasphemous misrepresentation. But I plucked happily at the baskets of grapes and beribboned goodies that bulged out the walls of our minute cabin, and sniffed at the wilting flowers from well-meaning relatives, and beamed at the blue September water that washed past our single porthole.

Occasionally I pinched my little fingers, but they were still asleep . . . like me.

II

The next time I went on the ocean I was alone. It was two years later, and my family felt that it was time for me to be in California again for a few weeks.

My mother, who believed in the "niceness" of the Cunard Line almost as firmly as she approved of the Forsyte Saga, sent me a passage to New York from Cherbourg on one of the lesser liners, which at that time were trying to appeal to the democratic spirit by abolishing classes and selling only Cabin and Tourist tickets. I was Tourist.

The month was May, and we took almost twelve days instead of nine. There were about eighty passengers instead of a thousand, too, and down in the bowels, where my cabin was, no attempt was made to ventilate after the portholes were firmly closed for the duration. It was miserable, and I thought of my first trip, so gay and airy, and of my husband whom I still loved dearly.

If I stayed below I felt stuffy (I was still too young to admit I felt damnably sick), so I walked miles every day, clutching at ropes put up along the deck and talking into the wind with a man named Thames Williamson who had written a couple of good books and felt as mournful as I at the slow but irrevocable approach of the American shore-line.

I can remember nothing about the food except that it was inferior to the *Berengaria*'s, and that I ate almost none of it in spite of the fact that my cabin, this time, was as empty of hothouse grapes as it was of my dear Al.

The sub-assistant purser, a small pale youth, had seen that I was assigned to his little table, the first meal out, and I was too naïve and shy to change things. But my total and obvious disinterest in him or any other male, and my exaggerated primness at finding myself alone in the middle of the ocean, soon reduced him to a state of dyspeptic boredom. Once he asked me to join him and the other officers for a drink, where I don't know, but my thank-you-no was so firm that he hardly dared mumble good-evenings to me for the rest of the trip.

I was desperately lonely, but I didn't know what to do about it. Besides the purser and Mr. Williamson there were some harried but attractive university people named Stewart, the only other people in Tourist Class, I think. He was returning from a sabbatical. They had two little children with flower-faces. I talked shyly a few times with Mrs. Stewart, but when I dared go alone to the grim smoking room, ostentatiously carrying a book, and they smiled at me, I hurried away to bed.

Once their little girl, who was about four, looked at me as I plodded along the sloping deck in the morning, and asked, "Why don't you just get a pan and womm-up, the way my mother does? It's much easier." I knew it would be, but I felt that if I unloosened enough to be sick, the way my body wanted to be, and scared and lonely, the way my heart felt, I'd never be able to stand the rest of the summer! I'd never be able to get off the boat in New York.

As it was I arrived, impregnably friendless, some fifteen pounds thinner and looking very chic. There were two groups of relatives who had never met before, Al's and mine, waiting protectively for me. They stood around the dock for six hours, with increasing politeness, while I proved to a suspicious customs man that the trunkful of old stained woolen underwear Al had saved from Cody, Wyoming, for skiing and then decided to save a few more years for something else did not have diamonds in the seams.

Now and then one or another of my unrelated relatives would say, "Well, there's nothing like a sea trip!"

Finally, when the customs man was either worn out or convinced, my cousin Weare Holbrook, who had given up writing the Great American Novel to be a professional humorist on the *Herald Tribune* and who at that time wore a beautiful red beard, took all of us except the inspector to a Schrafft's, where we ate strawberry shortcake.

And I dared at last be violently and thoroughly seasick all the way to Chicago. . . .

III

Near the end of that summer I went back to France, convinced to my own bitter satisfaction that I did not agree with my family about at least one thing: my mother's theory, generously supported with tickets and traveling allowances, that it does wives and husbands good to take long vacations from each other.

I was willing then, as now, to admit that not all wives were like me, but I have never profited from being away from men I have truly loved, for more than a few days. I think that when two people are able to weave that kind of invisible thread of understanding and sympathy between each other, that delicate web, they should not risk tearing it. It is too rare, and it lasts too short a time at best. . . .

I took my sister Norah with me. She was about thirteen, I think . . . a quiet thoughtful child, potentially beautiful but too tall and clumsy then, and somewhat given to exchanges of quotations from Ruskin with her pure-minded schoolmaster.

My parents did not know what to do with her; she was far ahead of her class in public school, and too dreamily sensitive to be put into any distant and probably hockey-mad private school. So, in one of their more inspired inconsistencies, my Father and Mother stopped calling me unstable, scatterbrained, and profligate long enough to tuck a letter of credit, several trunk checks, and Norah's hand in mine, and wish us Godspeed for another year or so. Fortunately Norah liked me almost as much as I did her.

That was before trains were air-conditioned, of course, but we had a compartment. We dressed just long enough to change stations in Chicago, and the rest of that August trip we spent lying on our berths, covered only with perspiration and a light coat of cinders, drinking ice-cold milk, and eating fruit a few minutes faster than it could rot in two large baskets that had been sent us.

As we got nearer New York, I fought a constant sense of uncertainty; there had always been cousins or parents or Al, before, to see that trains and boats left correctly with me even more correctly on them, and suddenly I was alone with a large child and tickets and baggage. . . .

A few hours out of New York I added to my secret panic by getting a steel splinter in one eye. That meant leaving Norah in a hotel bedroom while I went to an emergency hospital.

The doctor was an old Frenchman, from Dijon, where Al and I had been living! I had a quiet cry on his sere but willing shoulder, and after convincing him that when the boat sailed that night I'd be on it, even as blind as most of the other passengers but for a different reason, he took out the splinter, filled my eye full of opiates and me full of brandy, and gave me several addresses to Dijonnais I already knew.

The day passed agreeably. I could have handled several more judiciously spaced brandies with enthusiasm, but Prohibition still existed, and even if I had known how to go alone to New York speakeasies I would not have left Norah. So we shopped at De Pinna's and ate iced melon in a tea-room, and I frightened only a few people by having one eye that gushed steadily.

That night our cousin Bernard, the bright one in the family who has always seen me at my worst, in railroad stations and such, took us to dinner at a place in Brooklyn hung with life preservers and fish nets. The view, which twinkled foggily through my flow of tears, was lovely, and we ate a rather elaborate prix-fixe meal containing either steak or chicken, I am sure. I decided then, once and for all, that I would never again willingly try to eat in the same room with a dance orchestra, and except for one night in Paris at the Ritz, several years later, I don't think it has happened.

Our ship was a completely characterless and classless matron, English of course, since my mother had bought the tickets. Our cabin, thanks to the depression, was almost empty of "steamer baskets," but to our snobbish horror we found that what had been labeled Sofa on the deck plan was already well occupied by a woman, and that hanging in front of the porthole was her canary in a cage. The agent who had promised us the cabin to ourselves was in California; the ship was already shuddering in the river: we responded chillingly to the other passenger's sleepy goodnight and went to bed.

She turned out to be a small polite Englishwoman, and I cannot remember ever seeing her wash her teeth or dress or undress. She was always neatly in bed, or gone . . . and her canary was even more circumspect; I don't believe that he made either a sound or a dropping during the whole voyage.

Norah solved any nautical problems she might have had by sleeping almost continually until we got to Cherbourg.

I was consumed by a need to get there, get home, get back to Dijon and the arms of my love, and what sea change I felt took the form of refusing a few invitations to the bar and always speaking in French to Norah when she made her few sleepwalking appearances at table.

I thought the French was to get her used to it, but probably it was a childish wish to hide from the people around me . . . a kind of refusal to identify my real self with this interminable voyage home. It embarrassed nobody; Norah was too drowsy to pay any attention to me, and the other people at our table were thick quiet Flemish farmers.

I don't know what they were doing at that time of year in the middle of the Atlantic. I never saw them except at meals, and they never saw me at all. They ate several kinds of cheese at every meal, but especially at breakfast . . . which is absolutely the only thing I can remember about food, that trip. I have since learned to enjoy a breakfast of cheese and beer very much myself, especially if I have drunk too much the night before. (I know a Swiss surgeon who always eats freely of cheese if he has drunk much wine at a meal. He calls it a prophylactic [!] and says that it makes sure that in case of an emergency his hand and his eye are steady. It is, apparently, as if the concentrated and fermented curd acts as a sponge for alcohol. I wonder.)

And then the little yellow bird sighted Land's End through the porthole and burst into song, and his mistress began to chatter to us in a high laughing voice. Norah opened her eyes, so brown and deep. And there on the pilot boat outside Cherbourg was Al, fantastically handsome in the peasant boots and black corduroy suit he loved, with his hair too long. "Is he a poet?" lady passengers whispered to Norah on the boat train. And I ate and ate of the good bread, and laughed and put my head on his shoulder right in the restaurant car, knowing he was.

The Measure
of My Powers

1929–1930

Paris was everything that I had dreamed, the late September when we first went there. It should always be seen, the first time, with the eyes of childhood or of love. I was almost twenty-one, but much younger than girls are now, I think. And I was wrapped in a passionate mist.

Al and I stayed on the Quai Voltaire. That was before the trees were cut down, and in the morning I would stand on our balcony and watch him walk slowly along by the book stalls, and wave to him if he looked up at me. Then I would get into bed again.

The hot chocolate and the rich croissants were the most delicious things, there in bed with the Seine flowing past me and pigeons wheeling around the gray Palace mansards, that I had ever eaten. They were really the first thing I had tasted since we were married . . . tasted to remember. They were a part of the warmth and excitement of that hotel room, with Paris waiting.

But Paris was too full of people we knew.

Al's friends, most of them on the "long vac" from English universities, were full of *Lady Chatterley's Lover* and the addresses of quaint little restaurants where everybody spoke in very clipped, often newly acquired British accents and drank sparkling Burgundy.

My friends, most of them middle-aged women living in Paris on allowances from their American husbands "because of the exchange," were expensive, generous, foolish souls who needed several champagne cocktails at the Ritz Bar after their daily shopping, and were improving their French by reading a page a week of Maurois's *Ariel*. Al and I got out as soon as we politely could, or a little sooner, not downcast, because we knew we would come back.

On the way to Dijon we had lunch in the courtyard of the old post hotel in Avallon. We were motoring down with two large soft Chicago women who were heading for Italy, mainly, it seemed, because they "simply couldn't sit *five minutes* in a restaurant in Rome" without being subtly assaulted by lovesick Army officers. "Italians *appreciate* mature women," they said, their chaste bosoms heaving with a kind of innocent yearning lechery I have often noticed in American females of their class.

I remember that once on the road, when the chauffeur got out to look at a wheel, his coat flapped open as he bent over. Both of our companions squeaked at what they saw, and hustled out of the car. They asked a question in dreadful Italian, and whipped back the lapels of their own traveling suits. And then the fat shifty-looking driver and the two elegant middle-aged women stood in the dust, their eyes fixed on one another's magic enameled Fascist Party pins, so carefully hidden until now, and the three of them solemnly saluted, chins out, just like Mussolini in the newsreels.

Al and I were oddly embarrassed, and did not look at each other.

The hotel in Avallon, because of its ancient location on the Paris-Lyons post road, had inevitably been taken over by a noted chef, with all the accompanying *chi-chi*. I went back there several times in the next few years, because it was convenient and the redecorated bedrooms were comfortable. The kitchen wall into the courtyard had been replaced by an enormous window, I remember, and the swanky motorists who stopped there for lunch and the modern water closets could watch the great cook and his minions moving like pale fish behind the glass.

The food was not bad but not very good, when you knew what it might have been under such a once-famous man. But that September noon in 1929, when Al and I ate in the courtyard with the two kind silly women and felt ourselves getting nearer and nearer to Dijon, one important thing happened.

We were hungry, and everything tasted good, but I forget now what we ate, except for a kind of soufflé of potatoes. It was hot, light, with a brown crust, and probably chives and grated Parmesan cheese were somewhere in it. But the great thing about it was that it was served alone, in a course all by itself.

I felt a secret justification swell in me, a pride such as I've seldom known since, because all my life, it seemed, I had been wondering rebelliously about potatoes. I didn't care much for them, except for one furtive and largely unsatisfied period of yearning for mashed potatoes with catsup on them when I was about eleven. I almost resented them, in fact . . . or rather, the monotonous disinterest with which they were always treated. I felt that they *could* be good, if they were cooked respectfully.

At home we had them at least once a day, with meat. You didn't say Meat, you said Meat-and-potatoes. They were mashed, baked, boiled, and when Grandmother was away, fixed in a casserole with cream sauce and called, somewhat optimistically, O'Brien. It was shameful, I always felt, and stupid too, to reduce a potentially important food to such a menial position . . . and to take time every day to cook it, doggedly, with perfunctory compulsion.

If I ever had my way, I thought, I would make such delicious things of potatoes that they would be a whole meal, and never would I think of them as the last part of the word Meat-and-. And now, here in the sunny courtyard of the first really French restaurant I had ever been in, I saw my theory proved. It was a fine moment.

We stayed at the Cloche in Dijon for a few days, mainly because it was the biggest and best-known place in town. We knew too little yet to appreciate its famous cellars, and found the meals fairly dull in the big grim dining room. Later we learned that once a year, in November for the Foire Gastronomique, it recaptured for those days all its old glitter. Then it was full of gourmets from every corner of France, and famous chefs twirled saucepans in its kitchens, and wine buyers drank Chambertins and Cortons and Romanée-Contis by the *cave*-ful.

But for us it was not the place to be, and while Al was blissfully submerging himself in the warm safe bath of University life, filling out scholarly questionnaires and choosing his own library corner for writing (which he soon exchanged for a quiet table at the Café de Paris), I hopped in and out of fiacres looking for a flat to live in.

The streets were narrow and crooked, in the district around the Faculté, and at that time of year rich with a fruity odor of cellars, dog dirt, and the countless public urinals needed in a wine town. In all the little squares yellowing chestnut leaves fell slowly down, and fountains spouted. I felt very happy when I started out, with a discreetly small dictionary in one hand and the University list of approved boarding houses in the other. The horse wore a straw hat with red crocheted gloves for his ears sticking out of the crown, and there were cafés everywhere, so that even if I took only one quick dismayed glance at the next place on the list, my driver had time for a drink and remained cheerful.

When I remember now how tired I got, and how discouraged, I think I should have joined him at least once out of every four or five times.

The house we were to live in for the next two years, and where a part of me will always be, was the first one I saw. It was near the Faculté . . . it was perfect. But I didn't know that until I had seen a few of the others on the list.

It was a real Burgundian townhouse, in two parts, one on the street and the other at the back, beyond a deep narrow courtyard.

A covered stairway zigzagged up one side of the court, connecting the two halves floor by floor, and the rooms I looked at were on the top, in the back part. There was a narrow deep room with a big bed and an armoire in it, and another even narrower room with a couch and a desk and shelves. There was a little closet off the stairs, with running cold water in a tiny washbowl and a one-burner gas plate. There was a big window in each room, looking down into the hard gray little court, and there was steam heat. The bedroom was papered in mustard and black stripes, about eight inches wide, with a wide band of American beauty roses around the ceiling; the smaller one was in several shades of purple and lavender, with brown accents . . . a more feminine décor, the landlady pointed out.

In the little closet were all the necessities . . . a potty, a kidney-shaped pan on legs . . . but down in the court there was also a real toilet, with a pitcher of water and a neat pile of newspapers beside it. You pulled a handle which flapped back the bottom of the toilet, and you could look right down into the gurgling waters of the ancient Dijon sewer. (I learned that later, of course.)

There was also a bathroom, on the ground floor, and the landlady assured me that for seven francs, or six if we used our own soap, a bath could be drawn at only a few hours' notice.

The entrance to the whole place was a normal-sized door cut in the great double door that once had let carriages into the courtyard, under the front half of the house, and on one side was the bathroom and on the other, in what probably had once been the doorkeeper's room, was the dining room. There, the landlady told me, we would eat well, three times a day, with her husband, her stepson, one or two carefully selected students, and herself.

I bowed myself into my fiacre, not knowing what a jewel I thus nonchalantly toyed with.

Three or four hours later, after looking at a dozen places without water, without heat, certainly without bath, but all with a dank smell which I had not caught in the house on Petit-Potet, I hurried back as fast as the weary hack would pull me. It was the opening of a new session at the Faculté . . . Dijon was probably teeming with students all more sensible than I . . . I was a fool. Central heating, a real toilet, a nice smell. . . .

It was growing dark when I pulled myself for the last time out of the fiacre. I banged on the little door in the big door, and someone shrieked harshly to come in. Madame Biarnet darted from the kitchen, which lay just beyond the dining room, under the first rise of the staircase. She had on a filthy apron, and I could hear someone rattling pans and chopping and beating.

Madame pushed her hennaed hair back from her forehead, assured me that I had the air well fatigued, and said that the rooms were still free. I almost cried. I gave her all the money I had, even without getting Al's opinion first, and said haltingly that we would arrive the next noon.

"We?" she said, with a sharp mocking voice that I was to know very well, and grow fond of.

"Yes . . . my husband . . . I am married."

She laughed loudly. "All right, all right, bring your friend along," she said, but there was nothing mean about her voice.

"'Voir, 'tite 'zelle," she called hurriedly and disappeared into the kitchen as I closed the door and climbed wearily into the fiacre. But before we could start, she came shrieking out onto the narrow sidewalk, with a scrawled piece of wrapping paper in her hand, a receipt for what I had paid her.

I turned back to smile at her as we drove off. She was standing with one foot over the high doorsill, hands rolled in her apron, watching me with a mixture of affection and innate scorn which I soon learned she felt for all creatures, but mostly humans.

II

The next night, after we had moved and arranged about having Al's trunks of books sent from the station, I looked up the word anniversary in my dictionary and told Madame that it was our first one. "Impossible," she shouted, glaring at me, and then roaring with laughter when I said, "Month, not year." We would like to go to a nice restaurant to celebrate, I said.

She ripped a piece of paper off a package on the wine-stained tablecloth, scrawled on it with a pencil stub she always seemed to have somewhere about her, and said, "Here . . . you know where the Ducal Palace is? The Place d'Armes? You will see a sign there, the Three Pheasants. Give this to Monsieur Ribaudot."

And she laughed again, as if I were amusing in an imbecilic way. I didn't mind.

We changed our clothes in the unfamiliar rooms. The lights were on wires with weighted pulleys, so that by sliding them up or down you could adjust their distance from the ceiling, and there was a kind of chain running through the socket of each one, which regulated the power of the light. There were fluted glass shades like pie-pans, with squares of brown and purple sateen over them, weighted at each corner with a glass bead. The shadows in the unfamiliar corners, and on our faces, were dreadful in those mauve and mustard chambers.

But we felt beautiful. We put on our best clothes, and tiptoed down the wide stone stairs and past the lighted dining room, with a great key in Al's pocket and our hearts pounding . . . our first meal alone together in a restaurant in France.

First we went up the Rue Chabot-Charny to the Café de Paris, by the theatre. It was Al's first love, and a faithful one. He worked there almost every day we lived in Dijon, and grew to know its waiters, the prostitutes who had their morning cards-and-coffee there, its regular patrons and the rolling population of stock-actors and singers who were playing at the theatre across the street. It was warm in winter, and cool and fresh as any provincial café could be in the summer. I liked it as soon as I walked shyly into it, that first night.

We were very ignorant about French apéritifs, so Al read from a sign above the cash desk when the waiter came, and said, "The Cocktail Montana, please." The waiter looked delighted, and dashed to the bar. After quite a while he brought a large tumbler, rimmed with white sugar, and filled with a golden-pink liquid. There were two straws stuck artfully on the frosted glass, one on Al's side and one on mine.

Al was a little embarrassed that he had not ordered clearly for both of us, but as it turned out, anything else would have been a disaster: the Cocktail Montana whipped up by the Café de Paris was one of the biggest, strongest, loudest drinks I ever drank.

We learned later that a traveling cowboy, stranded from a small Yankee circus, offered to teach its priceless secret to the café owner for free beer, promising him that Americans for miles around would flock to buy it . . . at nine francs a throw, instead of the one franc fifty ordinary drinks cost there. Of course, there were no Americans to flock; the few who stopped in Dijon sipped reverently of rare wines at the Three Pheasants or the Cloche, and would have shuddered with esthetic and academic horror at such a concoction as we took turns drinking that night.

We enjoyed it immensely (we even had it once or twice again in the next two years, in a kind of sentimental loyalty), and walked on toward the Ducal Palace feeling happier than before.

We saw the big gold letters, Aux Trois Faisans, above a dim little café. It looked far from promising, but we went in, and showed Madame Biarnet's scribbled note to the man behind the bar. He laughed, looked curiously at us, and took Al by the arm, as if we were deaf and dumb. He led us solicitously out into the great semicircular *place*, and through an arch with two bay trees in tubs on either side. We were in a bare beautiful courtyard. A round light burned over a doorway.

The man laughed again, gave us each a silent little push toward the light, and disappeared. We never saw him after, but I remember how pleased he seemed to be, to leave his own café for a minute and direct such obviously bemazed innocents upstairs to Ribaudot's. Probably it had never occurred to him, a good Burgundian, that anyone in the world did not know exactly how to come from any part of it straight to the famous door.

The first meal we had was a shy stupid one, but even if we had never gone back and never learned gradually how to order food and wine, it would still be among the important ones of my life.

We were really very timid. The noisy dark staircase; the big glass case with dead fish and lobsters and mushrooms and grapes piled on the ice; the toilet with its swinging door and men laughing and buttoning their trousers and picking their teeth; the long hall past the kitchens and small dining rooms and Ribaudot's office; then the dining room . . . I grew to know them as well as I know my own house now, but then they were unlike any restaurant we had ever been in. Always before we had stepped almost from the street to a table, and taken it for granted that somewhere, discreetly hidden and silenced, were kitchens and offices and storage rooms. Here it was reversed, so that by the time we came to the little square dining room, the raison d'être of all this light and bustle and steam and planning, its quiet plainness was almost an anticlimax.

There were either nine or eleven tables in it, to hold four people, and one round one in the corner for six or eight. There were a couple of large misty oil paintings, the kind that nobody needs to look at, of Autumn or perhaps Spring landscapes. And there were three large mirrors.

The one at the end of the room, facing the door, had a couple of little signs on it, one recommending some kind of cocktail which we never ordered and never saw anyone else drink either, and the other giving the price by carafe and half-carafe of the red and white *vin du maison*. As far as I know, we were the only people who ever ordered that: Ribaudot was so famous for his Burgundian cellar that everyone who came there knew just what fabulous wine to command, even if it meant saving for weeks beforehand. We did not yet know enough.

We went into the room shyly, and by luck got the fourth table, in a corner at the far end, and the services of a small bright-eyed man with his thinning hair waxed into a rococo curlicue on his forehead.

His name was Charles, we found later, and we knew him for a

long time, and learned a great deal from him. That first night he was more than kind to us, but it was obvious that there was little he could do except see that we were fed without feeling too ignorant. His tact was great, and touching. He put the big menus in our hands and pointed out two plans for us, one at twenty-two francs and the other, the *diner de luxe au prix fixe*, at twenty-five.

We took the latter, of course, although the other was fantastic enough . . . a series of blurred legendary words: *pâté truffé Charles le Téméraire, poulet en cocette aux Trois Faisans, civet à la mode bourguignonne* . . . and in eight or nine courses. . . .

We were lost, naturally, but not particularly worried. The room was so intimate and yet so reassuringly impersonal, and the people were so delightfully absorbed in themselves and their plates, and the waiter was so nice.

He came back. Now I know him well enough to be sure that he liked us and did not want to embarrass us, so instead of presenting us with the incredible wine book, he said, "I think that Monsieur will enjoy trying, for tonight, a carafe of our own red. It is simple, but very interesting. And may I suggest a half-carafe of the white for an appetizer? Monsieur will agree with me that it is not bad at all with the first courses. . . ."

That was the only time Charles ever did that, but I have always blessed him for it. One of the great wines, which I have watched other people order there through snobbism or timidity when they knew as little as we did, would have been utterly wasted on us. Charles started us out right, and through the months watched us with his certain deft guidance learn to know what wine we wanted, and why.

That first night, as I think back on it, was amazing. The only reason we survived it was our youth . . . and perhaps the old saw that what you don't know won't hurt you. We drank, besides the astounding Cocktail Montana, almost two litres of wine, and then coffee, and then a little sweet liqueur whose name we had learned, something like Grand Marnier or Cointreau. And we ate the biggest, as well as the most exciting, meal that either of us had ever had.

As I remember, it was not difficult to keep on, to feel a steady avid curiosity. Everything that was brought to the table was so new, so wonderfully cooked, that what might have been with sated palates a gluttonous orgy was, for our fresh ignorance, a constant refreshment. I know that never since have I eaten so much. Even the thought of a prix-fixe meal, in France or anywhere, makes me shudder now. But that night the kind ghosts of Lucullus and Brillat-Savarin as well as Rabelais and a hundred others stepped in to ease our adventurous bellies, and soothe our tongues. We were immune, safe in a charmed gastronomical circle.

We learned fast, and never again risked such surfeit . . . but that night it was all right.

I don't know now what we ate, but it was the sort of rich winy spiced cuisine that is typical of Burgundy, with many dark sauces and gamy meats and ending, I can guess, with a soufflé of kirsch and glacé fruits, or some such airy trifle.

We ate slowly and happily, watched over by little Charles, and the wine kept things from being gross and heavy inside us.

When we finally went home, to unlock the little door for the first time and go up the zigzag stairs to our own room, we wove a bit perhaps. But we felt as if we had seen the far shores of another world. We were drunk with the land breeze that blew from it, and the sure knowledge that it lay waiting for us.

III

The dining room at the Biarnets' was just large enough for the round table, six or eight chairs, and a shallow kind of cupboard with a deerhead over it and two empty shell-cases marked *Souvenir de Verdun* on the top. It was an ugly little room, spotted and stuffy, with a cluster of mustard and spice pots on the dirty checked table-cloth. But it was pleasant while Madame was in it. Her wonderful honest vulgarity made us alive too, and after a meal, when she finally stopped pestering the cook and stretched her tired piano-teacher hands out across the cloth, her talk was good.

She was always late for meals; her pupils were for the most part young or stupid, and she was too much interested in even the dullest of them to send them off at the strike of the hour. Instead, she pounded out do-re-mis on the big piano under our rooms so long and so violently that from pure exhaustion the children grasped their rhythmic monotony before she let them go home. Then she came running down to the dining room, the lines deep in her red face.

She was usually two courses behind us, but caught up with our comparatively ponderous eating almost before we could wipe our lips or drink a little wine, which on her instruction Monsieur Biarnet kept well watered in our tumblers. She ate like a mad woman, crumbs falling from her mouth, her cheeks bulging, her eyes glistening and darting about the plates and cups and her hands tearing at chunks of meat and crusts of bread. Occasionally she stopped long enough to put a tiny bite between the wet delicate lips of her little terrier Tango, who sat silently on her knees through every meal.

Under and around and over the food came her voice, high and deliberately coarse, to mock her prissy husband's Parisian affectations. She told jokes at which her own lusty laughter sounded in the hot air before ours did, or proved that Beethoven and Bach were really Frenchmen kidnapped at birth by the Boches. She became excited about the last war, or the lying-in of a step-daughter by one of her three other marriages, or the rising prices, and talked in a frantic stream of words that verged on hysteria and kept us tense and pleasurably horrified.

We were hypnotized, Al and I and any other transient diners whose extra francs were so irresistible. Madame glanced at our faces as if we were her puppets, her idiotic but profitable puppets. Her eyes, amicably scornful, appraised us, felt the stuff of our clothes, weighed the gold in our rings, and all the time she saw to it that we ate better than any other *pensionnaires* in town, even if she did make more money out of us than any other landlady.

Her reputation was a strange one, and everyone in Dijon knew her as the shrewdest bargainer, the toughest customer who ever set foot in the markets. One of her husbands had been a pawn-broker . . . but gossip said that she taught him everything he ever knew. She was supposed to be wealthy, of course, and I think she was.

She drove herself cruelly, and looked younger than many women half her age, except for the hardness in her finely modeled mouth when it was still. She supervised the cooking, gave music lessons, played in the pit for visiting musical shows, and if the leading man pleased her slept with him . . . gossip again . . . and did all the marketing.

I was to learn, a couple of years later, that collecting enough food for even two people in a town the size of Dijon meant spending two or three days a week scuttling, heavily laden, from the big market to the *charcuterie* around the block, to the *primeur's*, to the milk-shop. And Madame's system was even more complicated by her passion for economizing.

Storekeepers automatically lowered their prices when they saw her coming, but even so she would poke sneeringly at the best bananas, say, and then demand to be shown what was in reserve. Up would come the trapdoor to the cellar, and down Madame would climb, with the poor little fruit man after her. She would tap and sniff knowingly at the bunches hanging in the coolness, and then, on her hands and knees, pull off the greenish midgets that grow along the step at the bottom of the great clusters.

They were worthless: the man had to admit he gave them to his children to play house with. Into the black string bag they went, for a magnanimous twenty centimes or so . . . and in a few days we would have them fixed somehow with cream (at half-price because it was souring) and kirsch (bought cheaply because it was not properly stamped and Madame already knew too much about the wine merchant's private life). They would be delicious.

And while she was in the cellar she would pick up a handful of bruised oranges, a coconut with a crack in it, perhaps even some sprouting potatoes.

The little fruit man shook his head in an admiring daze, when she finally dashed out of the shop.

She sometimes wore several diamond rings left to her by her late husbands, and when she was playing at the music hall she had her hair freshly tinted and waved. The rest of the time, in the daily hysterical routine, her appearance meant nothing to her if it involved spending money. She had an old but respectable fur coat, but scuttled around town in two or three or four heavy sweaters rather than wear it out, and when even they did not hold off the dank Dijon cold, she simply added more layers of underwear.

"Eugénie," her husband said one day, in his precise pettish voice, rolling his eyes waggishly, "it is hardly seemly that a woman of your age go around looking as if she were about to produce twins."

Jo, his gentle effeminate son, flushed at the ugly reference to human reproduction. He was used to enduring in stiff silence his stepmother's vulgarities, but could usually trust his father to behave like a member of the upper classes to which they both so earnestly aspired.

Madame looked quickly at them. Two men, her eyes seemed to say, but neither one a man. . . .

She screamed with laughter. "Twins! No fear, Paul! The Dijonnais would never blame *you* for twins. If anything but a little gas should raise my belly, there would be more horns in this room than those on the deer's head!"

Her eyes were screwed into little points, very bright and blue under the tangled hair. She was cruel, but we had to laugh too, and even Monsieur Biarnet grinned and stroked his little moustache.

He accepted his advancing years grudgingly, and floated from one unmentioned birthday to the next on an expensive flood of "virility" tonics. Of course, the labels said Rheumatism, Grippe, Gout, but we saw around him an aura of alarm: Eugénie stayed so *young.* . . . In spite of his Royalist leanings and his patent embarrassment at her robust vulgarity, he knew she had more life in her eyelashes than he in his whole timid snobbish body. He took refuge in wincing at her Burgundian accent, and raising his dainty son to be a gentleman.

Madame had a hard time keeping cooks in the house. They found it impossible to work with her, impossible to work at all. She was quite unable to trust anyone else's intelligence, and very frank in commenting on the lack of it, always in her highest, most fish-wifish shriek. Her meals were a series of dashes to the kitchen to see if the latest slavey had basted the meat or put the coffee on to filter.

She could keep her eyes on the bottle that way, too. All her cooks drank, sooner or later, in soggy desperation. Madame took it philosophically; instead of hiding the supply of wine, she filled up the bottles with water as they grew empty, and told us about it loudly at the table, as one more proof of human imbecility.

"Poor fools," she said, her strong flushed face reflective and almost tender. "I myself . . . what would I be if I'd spent my life in other people's swill? The only cook I ever had that didn't take to the bottle ate so much good food that her feet finally bent under when she walked. I'd rather have them stagger than stuff."

Madame herself drank only in Lent, for some deeply hidden reason. Then she grew uproarious and affectionate and finally tearful on hot spiced *Moulin à Vent*, in which she sopped fried pastries called *Friandises de Carême*. They immediately became very limp and noisy to eat, and she loved them: a way to make long soughings which irritated her husband and satisfied her bitter insistence that we are all beasts.

She let the little dog Tango chew soft bits from the dripping crullers in her big fine hands, and they both grew more loving, until finally poor Biarnet flounced from the room, *L'Action Française* tucked under his arm.

Madame loved boarders; they amused her, and brought in regular money which became with her magnificent scrimpings a fat profit every month. When Al and I came we were the only ones, but in the next few months, before she had rented the house with us in it to the Rigagniers, there were probably twenty people who came and went, most of them foreigners.

Monsieur Biarnet, who resented having paying strangers at his table, but had little to say about it in the face of his wife's pecuniary delight in them, only put his foot down, and then lightly, about Germans. He loathed them. They made him choke. He would starve himself rather than be polite to them, he said.

Madame shrugged. "We all must eat. Who knows? Someday they may come to Dijon as bosses, and then we'll be glad we were decent to them."

So there were a few who ate with us now and then. They never stayed long. Paul Biarnet really won, because he was so loath-somely, so suavely polite, so overpoweringly the tight-lipped French courtier, that the poor baby–Boches soon found other places to eat. Madame grinned affectionately and rather proudly, and soon refilled the empty chairs with pretty Rumanian girls, or large heavy Czechs.

She liked to have at least one safely attractive female at the table; it kept Paul's small pretentious mind off his various aches and grouses, and made it easier for her to continue her own robust and often ribald life. I did very well . . . I was young and amusing, and at the same time safely and obviously in love with my husband. Monsieur Biarnet made himself truly charming to me, and even Jo, now and then, would flutter from his sexless dream world long enough to make a timid joke with me. It was good for my French, and pleased Madame. Life would have been hell if it hadn't.

We used to sit there at the table, after the noon dinner or on Sundays, and talk about the private lives of ghosts and archbishops and such. Occasionally, the cook would hiccup.

"You hear that?" Madame would interrupt herself. Then she would shout toward the kitchen, "*Imbécile!!*"

We would go on talking, cracking little wizened delicious nuts that had been picked up off the cellar floor of some helplessly hypnotized merchant. We would be pleasantly full of good food, well cooked, and seasoned with a kind of avaricious genius that could have made boiled shoe taste like milk-fed lamb *à la mode printanière.*

Maybe it *was* boiled shoe . . . but by the time Madame got through with it, it was nourishing and full of heavenly flavor, and so were all the other courses that she wrung daily, in a kind of maniacal game, from the third-rate shops of Dijon and her own ingenuity.

She would look at us, as we sat there cozily in the odorous little room, and while she told us the strange story of one of her pupils who ran off with a priest, her mind was figuring what each of us had paid her for the good meal, and how much profit she had made.

"*Imbécile!*" she would scream ferociously at another helpless hiccup from the kitchen. And when we finally left, she would dart to the sink, and we would hear her say, gently, "Girl, you're tired. Here's enough cash for a seat at the movie. Finish the dishes and then go there and rest your feet. And don't bring home any soldiers."

Then Madame would laugh loudly and, if it were Sunday, go to her little salon and play parts of a great many things by Chopin . . . all tenderness and involuted passion.

To Feed
Such Hunger

After Christmas the foreign students changed, at the University in Dijon. The hungry Poles with too-bright eyes, who lived through the warmer months on international fellowships and pride in unlisted attics, went back to Warsaw. The few pretty American girls who bothered to come to such a stuffy little town stopped baffling Frenchmen by their bold naïveté, and left the tea shops and the cafés for Evanston, Illinois. The cool long-limbed Swedes smelled snow, and hurried back to their own ski slopes.

Now, instead of a dozen accents in the halls of the Faculté, you heard only one, and it was German. There were Lithuanians and Danes and Czechs, but German was the tongue.

The girls all looked much alike, thick and solemn. They walked silently about the streets, reading guidebooks, in flat broad shoes and a kind of uniform of badly tailored gray-brown suits.

The men, most of them, were young and pink-cheeked and oddly eager. They sat lonesomely in the cafés, and seldom spoke to one another, as if they had been told not to. The Dijonnais students, who were still fighting the war of '71, when the Boches had besieged the town, were politely rude to them, and they seemed to be scattered like timid sheep, longing for a leader. It was only at the University that they dared band together, and almost before the first class of the new semester, they elected a Prussian the president, as if to prove that there at least they were united and strong.

I had not much to do with the student body as such; my own life with Al was too absorbing and complete. But I couldn't help feeling surprised to learn that Klorr was our new leader.

He was quite unlike any of the other young Germans, who seemed to dislike and almost fear him, in spite of their votes. He was as tall as they, probably, but there was something about the set of his bones that made him seem slight and weak. He wore his brownish hair rather long and slicked back against his head, not in a fair brush; and he dressed in bags and tweed jacket like an Englishman, not in a stiff short coat that showed his hips, and narrow trousers, as his compatriots did.

He had a thin sneering face, too, all of a color with his pale slick hair, and it stuck forward on his neck, instead of being solid between his shoulders.

He was, I think, the most rat-like human I have ever seen, and at the same time he was tall, well set-up, intelligent looking . . . a contradictory person. I dismissed him from my thoughts, as someone I would not care to know, and most surely never would.

I noticed him, though, because he and a girl distracted me several times in class before I knew who she was. I was surprised to see him with her. She was one of the big pallid ones, and I'd have thought him the type who would marry her finally but spend his "student days" with someone small, light, exciting.

The two of them always seemed to be sitting right in front of me in classes, and always very close together, so that her thigh pressed hard against his and her large face almost touched him. They would whisper all through the lectures. It annoyed me. I found it hard enough to keep my mind on the professorial drone about the preposition "à" without having to sort it out from their moist Germanic hissings.

Usually they were reading parts of letters to each other, and usually Klorr sneered coldly at the girl, who seemed to be defending what they read.

Then at the end of class they would go silently out of the room, she carrying all his books as well as her own. Often she carried his thick topcoat, too.

I found myself interested enough in them to tell Al about them. They seemed such a strange pair to be so intimate, and I was very naïve then about the many visages of love.

One night at supper Madame Biarnet tore through her meal faster than ever, pushed her plate away and the dog Tango off her lap as if she had come to a great decision, and in her slowest, richest Burgundian accent asked us to make up our minds. At once, she said. There and then.

Her voice rose like a general's. Her long nose whitened. Her beautiful hard shrewd eyes, deep in wrinkles but young, looked at us with infinite enjoyment of the comedy she was playing.

"The time has arrived," she said harshly, and we wondered in a kind of stupor what joke she would tell, how soon she would burst into a great gust of laughter and release us from her teasing. We were used to her by now, but constantly fascinated, like a magician's petted nervous rabbits.

Monsieur Biarnet stirred fussily, and popped a vigor pill under his little waxed gray moustache. "Eugénie," he murmured. "Enough. Don't shout so, please! My nerves tonight . . ."

She slapped, absently, fondly, at his shoulder. "Make up your minds! You Americans are all dreamers! Are you going to stay or go?"

"Go where? Why? Do you want us to go, Madame?" We were stammering, just as she planned us to, and we must have looked quite flabbergasted at the thought that we might want to leave our snug small home at the top of the house.

She shrieked, delighted with her game, and then wiped her eyes with her napkin and said softly, almost affectionately, "Calm yourselves! It's about renting the rooms. We'll have a new guest tomorrow, and if you plan to stay she shall have the third floor room on the street, next to Jo's. And if you . . ."

"But of course we plan to stay . . . as long as you want us."

"That's the ticket, then," she said in pure gutter-French, with a malicious grin at her husband.

And as always, as if to prove to himself or someone that he at least was a man of the world, the *upper* world, he murmured in his most affected way, "Charming! Charming children!"

Madame whispered to us before noon dinner the next day that the new boarder was in the dining room. She was Czech, a ravishing beauty, daughter of a high official, someone completely sympathetic and destined to be my undying confidante.

Of course, it was Klorr's friend. Her name was Maritza Nankova, and she spoke when spoken to, in French somewhat better than mine was then. She was very shy for many days, but I could tell that she was lonely and envied me for being gay and happy and in love. I was almost completely uninterested in her.

She spent much of her time alone in her room when she was not at the Faculté. Now and then we would hear her solid shoes climbing the stairs late at night, and I would feel a little ashamed of my own fullness, and think I should go pay her a visit, talk with her about her country and her family and clothes . . . things girls are supposed to talk about together.

A few weeks after she came, there was a minor drama going on in the Biarnet ménage. We could only guess about it. Madame's voice was more hysterically high than ever, and her nose whiter in her red face; and quite often her husband and Jo did not eat at home, or sat icily silent through a meal. Finally one day Maritza was not there for lunch, and as if she had pulled a cork out of the situation when she went through the little door into the street, all three Biarnets started talking at once to us. We felt flattered, of course, and somewhat dazed. Even Jo waved his delicate hands excitedly, and shook back his silky hair with dainty fire.

Madame, they all told us, had been asked by La Nankova to

make a place at the table for her friend Klorr. "No, no, and again no," the two men thundered in their small ways.

"But he will pay well," Madame said. "Even filthy Boches must eat."

"Not here. Not with us. The food would choke us," they answered.

"But," she said, "La Nankova says he is very powerful, and important already in Germany . . . and what if someday he comes here the way they came in '71? *Then*," she went on triumphantly before they could interrupt, "then we will be glad to have a friend in him."

The enormity, the basically female realism of it, floored us all for a minute.

Then Monsieur, with a flattering little bow to me, and a slight twist of his moustache with two fingers to prove himself not only masculine but always the *boulevardier*, said, "It is bad enough, Eugénie, my dear, to have to see that well-behaved but clod-like peasant virgin twice a day, sitting in the same room with you and Madame Fischer. The addition of a yearning Prussian swain is more than I could bear."

Madame laughed delightedly. "Virgin, yes," she agreed shrilly. "Swain, definitely not. Klorr is much more interested in finding a good meal than exploring Maritza's possibilities. She has the appeal of a potato."

Jo flushed. "Papa is right," he said, and I thought that at last he had expressed himself, even so circumspectly, on a sexual matter. But he went on, "Mademoiselle Nankova is dull enough. No Boches, please, Belle-mère."

Madame looked gently at him. He usually called her Madame. It was as if anything more intimate to this coarsely vital woman who had taken his dead mother's place would betray him and his father too, and he was endlessly cruel to her, the way a young person can be.

She laughed again, then, and banged on the table. "I give up," she cried. "You are all against me . . . yes, you two smug American lovers too. No Boche. If we starve, we starve together. But," and she looked maliciously at her husband, "when Paul is away on business this Klorr can eat here. My stomach is not so delicate as some, and Klorr may not be bad-looking, even if he is a German."

So she won, after all. We celebrated the ambiguous victory with a little glass of *marc* all 'round. It was the nicest lunch Al and I had eaten with them, because we felt that we were no longer well-mannered paid-up boarders, but confidants of the family. We wished Maritza would stay away oftener, or always.

The cold winter dragged into Lent. Klorr came a few times to the dining room, always when Monsieur was away, and if Jo was caught there he ate almost nothing and excused himself. The German sensed it, I think. He was very charming to Madame, and was an entertaining talker, except for his lisp. He had a way of leaning across the table after a meal, rolling bread crumbs between his white knobby fingers, with his small strange eyes fixed almost hypnotically on his listener's.

He paid little attention to me, and none at all to Maritza, but seemed much attracted to Jo when he was there, and to Al. Al met him a few times in cafés, and told me Klorr talked mostly of the coming renaissance in Germany. Klorr said it would be based on a Uranic form of life.

I looked up the word Uranism. I *think* it was Uranism. It seemed to agree with what I had seen of Klorr, at least in his attitude toward Maritza. She never spoke at the table when he was there unless he addressed her by name, and then she flushed and seemed almost to tremble. It was a strange kind of love affair, I thought.

I grew more curious about her, and determined, tomorrow or tomorrow, to see more of her, go chat with her in her room. She never looked either happy or unhappy, except now and then after a meal, when she and the Madame would go into a kind of orgy of ghost stories.

Then Maritza's face would flush under her white skin, and her large dull eyes would be full of light and almost beautiful. She would talk rapidly in her up-and-down Czech accent, and laugh and clasp her big strong hands in front of her.

Madame loved it, and sometimes matched her, tale for tale, and sometimes let her go on alone, with her strange village stories of ghouls and charms and lost cats miraculously found, and of what it meant to sneeze three times . . . that sort of thing. Maritza's eyes would stare into the steamy air, and sometimes they almost frightened me with their mute superstitious mysticism. There was the same thing about them that I have never been able to accept in some Wagnerian music, a kind of religious lewdness, maybe.

One night Al and I came through the silent streets quite late, midnight or so. We had gone to a movie and then sat drinking *café-crème* and listening to the exhausted music at the Miroir, hating to go out into the raw cold Dijon air.

We saw that Maritza's two windows were brightly lighted, with the curtains not drawn. It was strange; always before, ever since she came, they had been dark when we unlocked the little door. We both spoke of it, and then went on tiptoe up the stairs, forgetting her for ourselves.

Much later, I opened our windows. There, across the deep silent courtyard, her inner window still shone, beside Jo's dark one. The curtains were not pulled.

It upset me a little. I stood watching for a minute, but I could see nothing. I got back into bed. I would surely go see her tomorrow, I thought . . . maybe ask her to have tea with me.

I was asleep when the knock came on the door. We both sat up sharply, like startled children; it was the first time anyone had ever come to our door at night. Al clambered out, and ran on his bare brown feet to open it, with his heart probably pounding like mine, from sleep and bewilderment.

It was Jo. He stood there in a mauve woolen bathrobe, carefully not looking toward me in the bed, and asked softly, "Is Madame here? I beg her pardon a thousand times, and Monsieur Fischer's

. . . but if Madame would perhaps come." He was stammering, speaking very softly with his eyes cast down.

"What's wrong?" Al asked bluntly, taking him by the arm. I don't know what he thought had happened.

"It's Mademoiselle la Nankova. She still has the light on in her room, and I can hear her. But I don't know whether she is laughing or crying. It is very soft. But it is late. I'm worried. I thought Madame Fischer, as a woman . . ."

"I'll come, Monsieur Jo," I said, and he bowed without looking at me. We heard his light steps down and up the zigzag stairs, and then the firm closing of his door on the landing across the courtyard.

Al looked upset. "Why not ask Madame Biarnet?" he said. "I don't like your being called this way. It's cold tonight. It's . . . it's an imposition."

"You're jealous," I said, while I put his warm bathrobe over my pajamas. "You'd like to go yourself."

"That pudding!" he said, and we both had to laugh, even while I hurried, and his eyes blinked at me with curiosity in them as well as sleep and crossness and love.

The light was on over the top zigzag of the wide stone staircase. I went quickly, wondering what was wrong with the girl. She seemed such a dull lump. Probably she was homesick, or had cramps . . . I knocked on her door, and while I listened I could hear a little rustling in Jo's room; he was listening too, close there behind the safety of his wall. There was no sound at all in Maritza's room. I knocked again. Finally a chair was pushed back, and I heard what I thought were her firm steps across the room.

But when the lock turned and the door opened, deliberately, it was Klorr who stood there, with a white napkin held to his mouth.

I don't know what I thought: I was not embarrassed for either of us, and for some reason not surprised. We stood looking at each other, and I could see that his eyes were not pale at all, as I had thought, but very dark above the napkin. He kept patting his lips.

In the room behind him I could hear Maritza breathing in long soft moaning breaths, monotonously.

I started to say why I had come, but he interrupted me in a smooth courtly flow . . . I was so kind to worry . . . just about to call me . . . our little Czech friend seemed upset . . . he had stopped for a few minutes in passing . . . undoubtedly a small indisposition that I, a sister creature, would comprehend . . . a thousand thanks, goodnight, goodnight. And he was off down the stairs, silent and unruffled as a rat, with the napkin in his hand.

I went reluctantly inside. The room was bright with light from an enormous bulb that hung, unshaded, over the middle of the big bed. I went quickly to the curtains, and covered all the windows, like a fussy old nursemaid or like a mother protecting her daughter's modesty, for Maritza was lying there in that light, naked except for a few crumbs and grapeskins on her belly.

When I had with my instinctive gesture made things more seemly, I looked full at her.

The bed was covered with a big white sheet, as if it were a smooth table, and she motionless in the middle, lying with her arms at her sides. I was surprised at how beautiful her body was, so white and clean, with high firm breasts and a clear triangle of golden hair, like an autumn leaf. There were no pillows on the bed, so that her head tilted back and I could see pulses beating hard in her throat. Her eyes were closed, and she kept on breathing in those low soft moans.

I leaned over her. "It's Madame Fischer, Maritza."

She did not answer or open her eyes, but at the sound of my voice she started to tremble, in long small shudders that went all over her, the way a dead snake does. I spoke again, and when I picked up one heavy arm it fell softly back. Still, I felt she knew everything that was going on.

I was not exactly puzzled . . . in fact, I seemed at the time to take the whole thing as a matter of course, almost . . . but for a minute I stood there, wondering what to do. Maritza's face was very hot, but the rest of her was cold, and shaking now with the long shuddering ripples, so I covered her with a coat from her armoire, after I had pushed the grapeskins and crumbs off her.

They were only on her belly. There were several crumbs down in her navel, and I blew at them, without thinking it funny at all. I put them all in my hand, and then onto a plate on the little table, before I realized how strange it was.

It was set up by the fireplace, with a linen tablecloth, and placed precisely on it were a plate of beautiful grapes with dark pink skins, an empty champagne bottle and a fine glass, and a little round cake with a piece out of it. It looked like the kind of table a butler arranges in the second act of an old-fashioned bedroom comedy, except that there was only one glass, one plate, one fork.

I knew Klorr had been supping there, while Maritza lay naked on the bed and moaned for him. And I knew that he had put the empty grapeskins on her unprotesting flesh without ever touching her.

My hands felt foul from them. I went to the armoire, to look for some alcohol or toilet water to rub on them, but I could see none in the neat bareness of the shelves.

I ran silently as I could to our rooms. Al was lying in bed, reading, and when he asked me mildly what was going on, I suddenly felt a strange kind of antagonism toward him, toward all men. It was as if Maritza had been ashamed in some way that only women could know about. It was as if I must protect her, because we were both females, fighting all the males.

"Nothing . . . it's all right," I said crossly. "She's got the jitters."

"Oh," Al said, and went on with his book.

I ran down the stairs with a bottle of eau de Cologne. I thought I would rub Maritza with it. I closed her door, and pulled the coat gently off her.

"It's Madame Fischer," I said, because her eyes were still closed.

I rubbed in long slow motions up her arms, and up her legs from her ankles, the way I remembered being massaged in a Swedish bath when I was younger. Gradually she stopped making the moan with every breath, and the unnatural shudders almost ceased. Her face was cooler, too.

"You are better, now, Maritza," I kept saying as I rubbed the toilet water into her fine white skin. "You are all right now."

It was like quieting an animal, and had the same rhythm about it, so that I don't know how long it was before I saw that the door had opened silently, and Klorr stood there watching me.

Maritza's eyes were still shut, but she felt something in my hands, although I did not feel it myself, and she began the long hard shuddering again.

Klorr was staring at me with jet-bead eyes, and hate seemed to crackle out of him in little flashes, like electricity in a cat's fur. I glared back at him. I must have looked fierce, because as I got up slowly and approached him, he backed away and out into the hall by Jo's door. He had the napkin in his hand, and he held it out to me. I closed the door into the girl's room.

"What do you want?" I asked, speaking very distinctly. I could hear my own voice, and impersonally I admired my accent. I am in a rage, a real rage, I thought, and rage is very good for the French accent.

Klorr smiled weakly at me, and wiped his lips again.

"I was just passing by," he said for the second time that night. "I . . . how is our little Czech friend? I appreciate your unusual interest in her. How is she, if I may be so bold as to enquire? Tell me, dear Madame . . . what is wrong with her?"

His smile was stronger now, and he was speaking smoothly, with his eyes staring scornfully, sneeringly at me.

Then I drew myself up. It sounds funny even to write about now, or think about, but I actually did draw myself up, until I seemed much taller than he. And very distinctly, in the most carefully enunciated and completely pompous French that has ever been spoken outside a national theatre, I said, "What is wrong with her? Mademoiselle Nankova, Monsieur Klorr, is suffering from an extreme sexual overexcitement!"

Those were my words, which sprang unsought for into my furious brain. Yes . . . they rolled out magnificently . . . *une sur-ex-ci-ta-tion se-xu-el-le* . . . syllable by mighty syllable, even to the final "le," like a quotation from Racine.

Klorr looked away. He bowed stiffly, and then as if he could not stand it any longer he threw the napkin at me and ran again down the stairs, as silent as a rat.

When I went back into the room, Maritza was curled up like a child in the middle of the bed, crying peacefully into her hands. She was rosy and warm, and I put the coat over her and turned out the light and went home. I felt terribly tired.

Al was asleep. He never asked me anything about it, and I never told him.

The next day Maritza was the same as always, shy and dull as if she did not know me, and in about a week she left, without saying goodbye to any of us. Madame said that she and Klorr, by a very odd coincidence, were going to be in Venice together for the Easter celebrations.

"Love is hair-raising," Madame said. "Imagine that great lump in a gondola."

"I for one am thankful," Monsieur said, rolling his eyes first toward the good God in heaven and then toward me. "Now we can resume our old chats, without having to wait for La Nankova to keep up with us, and without having to escape her questionable Prussian acquaintance. It will be excellent for practice, for perfecting the accent."

Jo looked at me, and before he lowered his soft eyes in their deep curling lashes, he smiled in an abashed way at me, and murmured, "But Madame's accent is already excellent at times, Papa."

And I burst out laughing, and could tell nobody why. Whenever I say those words in my mind, I must laugh now, in spite of the feminine shame I feel to think of that table laid in the bright room, and the strange ways of satisfying hunger.

The Measure
of My Powers

When the Rigagniers rented the house on the Rue du Petit-Potet from the Biarnets, they took us along with the stuffed deer's head and empty *Souvenirs de Verdun*. We stayed on in our little mustard-and-purple rooms, crammed by now with our own bookish castings, and we ate in the same stuffy spotted dining room. Our new friends were as extravagantly lavish as the others had been penny-pinching, and we tasted some of the headiest dishes of our lives there.

We were the first boarders the family had ever had, and I am sure that we ate and drank much more every month than we paid for. There was nothing to do about it; the family was on the brink of complete financial ruin, after twenty years of living on Madame's enormous but now vanished *dot*, and even if we had tried to eat one less slice of brandy-cake, one bowl less of hot creamy soup, the Rigagniers would have gone on, bilious and gay, buying fine legs of lamb and casks of wine and baskets of the most expensive vegetables.

Madame herself did the cooking, helped by a series of numb orphan slaveys, and even in the better days, when she had commanded her own small staff of servants, I think she probably kept one foot in the kitchen. She was the daughter of the finest *confiseur-pâtissier* in Alsace, a spoiled stuffed daughter who when her husband's penchant for provincial backstage beauties drained the last francs from her fabulous *dot* dropped all her elegant . . .

It is strange . . . or perhaps it is natural . . . that I cannot go on as I had planned.

I meant to write about what I learned, my gastronomic progression there with the Rigagniers . . . and even if I'd willed it otherwise there would have been some of that progression, close as I was to people who knew flavors as their American counterparts knew baseball batting averages, whether they were twelve like Doudouce or seventy-five like Papazi.

But now when I think of the hot quarrelsome laughing meals: the Sunday dinners in the formal *salle à manger* and the enormous suppers so soon afterwards, when Papazi produced his weekly triumph of a tart as big as a cartwheel, with all the apple slices lying back to belly to back in whorls and swoops; the countless birthdays and name days and saint days with their champagne and their truffled geese; the ordinary weekday suppers, "light" after the heavy meal at noon, when soufflés sighed voluptuously at the first prick, and cold meats and salads and chilled fruits in wine and cream waited for us . . . no, when I think of all that, it is the people I see. My mind is filled with wonderment at them as they were then, and with dread and a deep wish that they are now past hunger. They were so unthinking, so generous, so stupid.

Papazi and Mamazi, the grandparents, lived in another house, a lovely place with chestnut trees in the courtyard and thin-legged gold chairs in the darkened drawing room, but their hearts were still in Alsace in the fine rich days of wealth, when Papazi was known everywhere for his chocolates and his wedding cakes. Now he hob-nobbed like an exiled king with the better of the Dijon *confiseurs*, and listened to Beethoven concerts on his TSF, and every week or so baffled his grandchildren with a deft masterpiece for Sunday supper or for fun. He was a merry old man, in spite of his pomposities.

Mamazi was a small bewigged woman, still weeping for her son lost in the first war, and meekly waspish. She shook like an idling ocean liner from all the digitalis she took, and died a little while after I saw her last.

The two old people would come every Sunday to dinner, which was a long delicious almost overpowering meal, and then would stay for supper, which was also such a long delicious almost overpowering meal that Al and I finally took to sneaking away, as soon as we had partially recovered from the first one, and going to Crespin's for a few oysters, or to any place at all for a salad and a piece of bread.

Sometimes M. Rigagnier would see us, on his way home after an afternoon of café-gambling or other more active gambols, and then there would be red-eyed Monday questions from Madame. It was impossible to tell her that we simply could not eat for a few hours; she did not know people like that.

She herself was one of the most unreservedly sensual people I know of. She was not at all attractive physically. She neglected her person, mainly because she gave every ounce of her time and energy to feeding us. So she was bedraggled and shiny and often smelled. And, what is even more distasteful, she was needlessly ailing. Such a state is repulsive to me. She had really violent monthly headaches which were, even to my ill-trained eye, pure bilious attacks. For three or four days she would stagger from stove to table and back again, cooking and then eating with the same concentrated fervor as always, while her eyes were almost mad with pressure, and her face was gray.

She connected these *crises de nerfs névralgiques*, as she always called them, in some way with her unhappiness in marriage, and spent a good part of her time convincing her one daughter that taking the veil was much preferable. In spite of my exasperation with her, as I saw her eating with such steady gourmandise at her own rich soups and tarts and stuffings, I knew she suffered like hell and I longed to help her.

She was still a terrible snob, in spite of the cruel way her life had changed from its first spoiled lavish opulence, and would sweep and market all morning and then put on her one good black dress and go to a concert, where she sat in the stiff position taught her in school in Germany and listened to music which her poor tired ears could never hear. She saw to it that somehow her children went to the correct piano teachers and the best schools, not because she wanted them to be well educated but because she was proud in the face of her own steady social decline, and knew that she was better than any of the plump matrons who now occupied the position she had once taken as her right.

She was a stupid woman, and an aggravating one, and although I did not like her physically I grew to be deeply fond of her and even admiring of her. For years we wrote long and affectionate letters, and on the few times I returned to Dijon we fell into each other's arms . . . and then within a few minutes I would be upset and secretly angry at her dullness, her insane pretenses, and all her courage and her loyal blind love would be forgotten until I was away from her again.

When we were living with her, she often said that she would like to teach me what she knew about cooking. In many ways I was a fool not to accept her offer. But I knew that she would drive me crazy, shatter all my carefully educated reserve and self-control, so that I might scream at her or hit her with a spoon. Instead, I said that my university work took all of my time, and without her knowing it I learned much more from her, perhaps, than she could ever have told me. I learned about omelets and salads and roasts of meat, as well as sauces both natural and concocted and a few human foibles, both despicable and fine.

We used to talk a lot about marriage. I was interested in hers, because after almost twenty years it was so obviously a bad one. She admitted that herself, and in the insidious way of good women she managed beautifully to make the three children hate their father for her battered sake. She had been married, thanks to her dowry, to a promising young automobile inventor, and then spent the rest of her life watching him laugh and wink his way through all the money and a hundred careless jobs, until at last he was a garage mechanic and she was a penniless slave; and still she believed passionately that the provincial French system of marriage was the only successful one. I on the other hand argued as fervently for the American way of encouraging young people physically attracted to one another to marry in spite of a complete lack of parental and financial blessings.

Madame and I got divorces in the same year, and exchanged somewhat woe-begone letters on the subject. Hers were full of a kind of courage I shall probably never have, and were written by a mind perhaps ten or eleven years old.

After the divorce she left Dijon, where she had struggled so miserably against poverty and the town's pity, and went with Papazi and the two younger children nearer their dear Alsace. Then she was evacuated. . . .

Monsieur Rigagnier was a coarse kind-hearted man, who in this country would belong to the American Legion and any local clubs that had good times. In Dijon he lived mostly in the cafés, playing cards and talking about the happy war-days, when he'd been a captain and had a mistress who later became a famous movie star. He'd also won a few decorations, but they were not important to him compared with *la belle Arlette* or whatever her name was.

He drank a lot, especially if he knew that Madame had one of her headaches or there were an unusual lot of bills to be paid. He was always polite, and even gay, with us, but sometimes he used to snarl at the children. Papazi he feared and respected, and borrowed money from, as if the old man had supported him for so long that it was only logical to continue. Papazi was equally polite, and as soon as Dédé was twenty-one paid for a divorce. He despised his son-in-law.

The children did too, in that insidious way of young things . . .

never openly mocking, but always a little too meek, too indomitably servile.

Dédé was the oldest, a surly oafish boy, with thick outlines and small eyes like his father's. He openly hated the way his mother had to work, and was the only one of the family who ever seemed to resent our presence. His table manners were dreadful, and I resented him even more than he did me, probably.

He studied with a kind of dogged hopelessness for Saint-Cyr, and finally got in, the last name on the list. His mother wrote of his marriage . . . much beneath him, she managed to imply. And when France fell he was a captain in the *Pompiers de Paris*, and had a "pretty eight-room apartment near his garrison where Amélie awaits the first-born son," Madame wrote in her fine over-crossed lines of purple ink. So much for Dédé. He was a boor, in spite of his fine palate.

Plume was another thing entirely. He was the most like an elf of any person I have known, and also like a monkey, with the same bright inhuman gaze. He was about fourteen when we knew him. He refused to go to school, so in turn Papazi bribed every reputable candy-maker in Dijon to take him as an apprentice. He made all the workers laugh so hard they ruined the bonbons and the tarts, and the bosses shivered in their beds with worry over his next trick. Would Plume decorate the wedding cake of a maiden trying to hide her Semite origins with a Star of David made of rosebuds? Would he put oil instead of Cointreau in the little chocolate bottles for the Bishop's Christmas party?

Plume, in spite of Papazi's renown, was forced to conclude that he would like to be a piano-tuner, a watchmaker, a lawyer, and a dancing master. Nothing perturbed him, and he flitted like a gentle grinning little satyr through the offices and factories and streets of Dijon.

We used to see him sometimes coming out of the most expensive brothels, always with the same mischievous detachment in his small face, and some of the prostitutes told Al that he was a great favorite among them, so tender and courteous and charming. He was that way at home too, and we all loved him.

After we left he got a job with the automobile factory where his father had once been well known, and suddenly, perhaps because of the divorce, his fey attitude clarified and he became almost a wizard with engines. He went to Algiers. His mother wrote happily about him. He was invalided home once while I was in France, and I saw him for a minute, shaking with fever. He bent over my hand. I still felt as if he were fourteen, not in his twenties, and could hardly keep from smiling. I felt his kiss on my skin for a long time.

Then, in the first criminal hysteria of mobilization in France, he was snatched from the auto works where by now he was a prized technician, and put to digging trenches. Within a few days he died of pneumonia.

"When you watch the dirt being shoveled onto your son's coffin," his mother wrote to me in her precise flowing hand, "you have an almost uncontrollable desire to throw back your head and howl like a wounded beast."

And Doudouce? Her name was France, because she was born on the first Armistice Day. She was a serious little girl, short and round, with worry in her eyes, and her mother's sensual mouth. Even when we knew her, starting her teens, she worked heavily and earnestly at her lessons. She was already resolved never to marry, never to subject herself to the monthly headaches and the daily labor that she saw in her mother, and she had decided for herself that being a teacher was better than being a nun. We used to try to make her seem more like a little girl, but it was not until after we left, after the divorce, that Plume taught her gaiety. Doudouce kept on with her studying, but she danced too.

She passed her examinations. Then, to her mother's proud bewilderment, she went all alone to Paris, studied medicine, and became a roentgenologist. She was there when the city fell, and I wonder now whether Papazi's fanatical hatred of the Boches has upheld her, or whether the latent sensuality in her small round body has taught her that headaches are not always made by men, even German men.

I think often of her, and of Plume so quickly out of it, and of my poor stupid friend their mother, and the pouting Dédé. I remember with a kind of anguish the prodigal bounty of their table, and their childlike inability to conceive of anything but richness and warmth and sensory perfection for themselves and their friends. They were less able than ordinary people to withstand the rigors of physical hunger.

I think of them as I used to see them, the three children bending over the steaming stove, their eyes intent and beautiful, their ears listening reverently to Papazi as he waved a spoon and told them the history of the *sauce Soubise* or the carp dumplings he concocted, while Madame sat for a few stolen moments at the dining-room table, account books spread before her straining eyes but a little plate of *truffes au chocolat* beside her one free hand, or a small glass of *anisette* . . . I long impotently to feed those kind simpleminded friends of mine, if they still live.

Perhaps Papazi was luckiest. "You will be saddened, my dear," Madame wrote a few months before war started, "that our beloved Papazi is no more. His end was one you will appreciate, as the good God's special reward to such a devout and faithful servant of Epicurus.

"Lately my poor father has forgotten his many financial misfortunes, and our table has been worthy indeed of the greatest *confiseur-pâtissier* of Alsace, past, present, and future. Wednesday noon, in honor of Plume's new position at the factory, Papazi prepared with his own hands and very little help from me a repast such as we have not seen for years. We began, as a compliment to me, with my own recipe for *Potage Richelieu* (Bring 200 grammes of the finest butter to the bubble, add . . . but I shall write it on another sheet of paper, my dear . . .), and then had snails which Plume and Doudouce and I gathered ten days ago in the woods, just as in the old days . . . do you remember the many times we starved them in the courtyard, and you helped us wash the shells with Papazi's little brushes? . . . and after a small but delicious soufflé of Gruyère to refresh our palates, we ate a tongue with *sauce Philippe*, which recipe I shall also enclose in case you do not remember it.

"I do not wish to weary you, my very dear friend. Suffice it to say that at the end there was to be a *Diplomate au Kirsch d'Alsace*, made just as always with the marinated fruits. With that, having opened almost the last of our best bottles for the first part of the repast, I planned to serve coffee in the Algerian way to please Plume, rather than champagne as we used to do it in Dijon.

"But just before we reached that course, our dear Papazi . . . this is painful, as you will understand . . . our dear Papazi, who had been gay and young all day, suddenly stood up, emptied his glass, and then sat down again with a strange smile on his face. His stomach gave out a loud rumble, and he was gone from us."

Noble and Enough

1929–1931

We lived for almost three years in Dijon, which the Burgundians called without any quibble and with only half-hearted contradictions "the gastronomic capital of the world." We were lucky to know people there of almost every class, and to be within ourselves eager, interested, and above all husky-gutted. Most of our orgies were voluntary, but even so I doubt if more jaded livers than ours could have stood the thousand bilious blows we dealt them.

We went as often as we could afford it to all the restaurants in town, and along the Côte d'Or and even up into the Morvan, to the Lac de Settons, to Avallon . . . and down past Bresse. We ate terrines of pâté ten years old under their tight crusts of mildewed butter. We tied napkins under our chins and splashed in great odorous bowls of *Ecrevisses à la nage*. We addled our palates with snipes hung so long they fell from their hooks, to be roasted then on cushions of toast softened with the paste of their rotted innards and fine brandy. In village kitchens we ate hot leek soup with white wine and snippets of salt pork in it.

And in Dijon we went to Ribaudot's when we were flush, or perhaps the Chateaubriant, which we never grew to like much, except in the summer when we could eat dust and iced fruits on the sidewalk. At the end of Liberty Street was the Buffet de la Gare. It had a good old reputation, and was nice in the winter because of the enormous iron stove as well as the ancient waiters and the bowls of flowers from Nice that conductors on the PLM expresses would throw off every day, probably in memory of good food they had eaten there. The Buffet was especially proud of its *Tournedos Rossini*, which my husband liked very much, with its suave combination of fresh beef and almost putrescent pâté de foie gras.

Back up the main street, across from the Chateaubriant, was the Grande Taverne, which tried hard to bring a snappy big-business Parisian atmosphere to Dijon, and failed completely. Its electric lights were all masked in slabs of cheap frosted glass cut on the diagonal . . . *l'art moderne*, the proprietor said proudly . . . and signs on the mirrors recommended regional specialties with a kind of condescending fervor. But the Dijonnais who had been reading *Le Temps* and *L'Intran* under its lights since gas was first installed continued to go there . . . and the chef would always push aside his "Burgundian delicacies" long enough to make me a rum omelet, with three harsh scars of burnt sugar across its plump top where he laid the poker on to make an F for me.

Then there was Crespin's, the simplest and one of the best places in the world. It was on one of the oldest streets, between the markets and the church I liked the best, and in the winters an old oysterman stood outside always by his fish, stamping his feet like a horse and blowing on his huge bloody mottled hands. He was the best one I have ever seen for opening those devilish twisted shells, but still there was always a fresh cut somewhere on his grotesque stubs of fingers.

He had baskets of dark brown woven twigs, with the oysters lying impotently on seaweed within . . . Portugaises, Marennes, Vertes of different qualities, so fresh that their delicate flanges drew back at your breath upon them. Inside the little restaurant you could eat them with lemon and brown buttered bread, as in Paris, or with a plain crust of the white bread of Dijon.

Then there were snails, the best in the world, green and spitting in their little delicate coffins, each in its own hollow on the metal plates. After you pulled out the snail, and blew upon it cautiously and ate it, you tipped up the shell for every drop inside, and then with bread you polished the hollow it had lain in, not to miss any of the herby butter.

Crespin's always had *tripes à la mode de Caen*, too, in little casseroles in which it could keep indefinitely, and salad and a piece or two of cheese. And that was all . . . another proof of my firm belief that if a restaurant will be honest about a few things, it can outlive any rival with a long pretentious menu.

There was another place almost as simple, down on the Place d'Armes near Ribaudot's, but plain in the same self-contained deliberate way. It was called the Pré aux Clercs, and my husband liked to go there because it made very good grilled rare steaks with watercress, which at that time were beginning to be in great vogue in the big cities among the younger generation . . . *"les sportifs"* . . . but were dismissed with impatient disgust by older gourmands raised in the intricate traditions of fine sauces and culinary disguise.

And of course there were places like the stand out in the park that made wonderful sandwiches of crisp rolls with loops and dollops of sweet home-cured ham in them . . . and the houses along the canal that sold hot minnows, cooked whole and piled unblinking in a bowl . . . and little cafés that because their proprietors liked hot cheese cakes made hot cheese cakes once a week.

And everywhere, in every village pub or great temple of gastronomy, there were the proper wines, whether they came out of a spigot into a thick tumbler or slipped from a cradled cobwebbed bottle into the bottoms of glasses that rang thinly in the faintest stir of air. We grew to know, but always humbly, what wines of Burgundy and which years were regal, and how to suit the vintage to the hour. (Much of what I learned then I've forgotten. I feel it is a pity, but perhaps like any fish I shall remember how to swim if I am thrown back in the water before it is too late.)

Much of the time we were learning and tasting all these things, we were living with the Biarnets or the Rigagniers, so that some of our tutelage was of course involuntary. With them most of it, thank God, was good as well.

Of course I, as the wife of an almost-faculty-member, had to go to tea with my almost-colleagues much too often; I was young and felt earnestly that afternoons spent in the upstairs salon of Michelin's eating almost unlimited pastries would help my husband's career. And once we had to go to a formal luncheon at the Rector's.

He was to French pedagogues what a combination of Nicholas Murray Butler and Robert Hutchins might be in this country, and Al and I were invited mainly because a visiting New England scholar had to be entertained. Like most ambassadors sent for one reason or another from America, he did not speak the language of the country he was to win to whatever cause he represented, and since I had gradually erased the firm impression among the faculty wives that all Yankee women either got tight in public on strange cocktails or spat in the drawing room, I was seated next to him.

He was a nice man, head of the English Department in a famous university. He had the same apparently instinctive naïveté of Wendell Willkie, which of course always wins people, especially when it is accompanied by slightly rumpled hair and a wide grin.

The luncheon was the most impressive private meal I have ever gone to. (Thank God, I add. I sometimes feel that I am almost miraculously fortunate, to have lived this long and never sat through one of the "state banquets" I have read about.) The Rector was noted for his table, but this time his chef had been helped by Ribaudot, and several of the *restaurateur's* best men were in the dining room with the butler and regular footman.

There were ranks of wine glasses, and the butler murmured the name and year of each wine as he poured it. Each one was beautiful.

All the ladies, including the hostess, wore hats, and some of them gloves rolled up around their wrists, and I felt slightly hysterical and almost like something out of Count Boni de Castellane's visits to Newport in the 1880s.

One of the courses was whole *écrevisses* in a rich sauce, served of course with the correct silver pliers, claw-crackers, gouges, and forceps.

The guest of honor was being very diplomatic, bending his white top-knot first to the hostess and then to me, but when he saw the hard big coral fish lying in their Lucullan baths, he leaned against my shoulder and most unacademically he muttered, "Help, for God's sake, sister! What do I do now?"

I knew, because I had struggled before with the same somewhat overrated delicacy, and I had no patience with manmade tools in such emergencies. It would have been tactless for me to remind him that he could watch his hostess, so I winked at him and said, "Watch me."

I picked up a shrimp between my left thumb and forefinger, cracked both its claws with the silver crackers, ate what meat I could with the little fork, and then dunked the rest out of the sauce with a crust of bread. The visiting scholar sighed happily, and set to.

And that is the way everybody at the long oppressively polite table ate the rest of the course, and from then on things went fairly amicably and faculty feuds were forgotten or ignored, and at the end Madame la Recteur embraced me and made a date for tea.

(The whole incident sounds a little too charmingly barbaric. . . "these delightful American savages" . . . but I still do not believe that a host should serve anything that cannot be eaten with ease and finesse by all his guests who are reasonably able-bodied. In the case of *écrevisses* it is different of course when they are served with the claws cracked and the tails split. But in France it was felt, I think, that such sissy preparation ruined much of the flavor . . . and I have yet to see the most adept gourmet succeed in eating even one such crustacean with the prescribed tools. Cuffs rolled back, napkin under chin, an inevitable splash or two and more than that number of loud sucking noises: that is the routine at Prunier's, at the Rector's and at the Café de l'Escargot d'Or down on the edge of any lake in shrimp season.)

Of course, there was the Foire Gastronomique every autumn,

in Dijon: we went to the long tents and drank quite a lot of *vin mousseux*, but we were not important enough to be invited to any of the official banquets and could only read the fantastic menus in the paper. Prices went up for the visitors, most of whom were wine dealers, and gossip said that all the restaurants put an extra lot of seasonings in their sauces so that even mediocre wines would taste superlative. We liked Dijon better in its normal state of mass-gourmandise.

Probably the most orgiastic eating we did while we lived there was with the Club Alpin. Monsieur Biarnet proposed us for membership soon after he had decided for himself, over the dinner table in his stuffy little dining room, that we were amusing and moderately civilized. It was supposed to be an honor, as well as making it possible for the club to get better rates on its feasts by having a larger number of members, and certainly it was a fine although somewhat wearing experience for us.

We heard good French from the lawyers and retired army officers and fuddy-duddy architects like our friend Biarnet who belonged, for one reason or another but mostly gastronomic. We saw castles and convents and wine *caves* that were seldom bared to public eyes. We walked and crawled and slithered and puffed over all that corner of France, in the cold March rains, the winy gold-leafed days of autumn, April's first tantalizing softness.

We all had to wear properly stiff heavy boots, and on almost every one of the bi-monthly promenades we managed to find a small safe grotto or gully to explore, so that the Alpine part of our club's name would not be too much of a joke, even in the heart of smooth-rolling Burgundy. Our rooms in Dijon were in one of the most perfect and beautiful fourteenth-century townhouses in Europe, and we often listened solemnly to lectures there about the places we would visit in the future.

The real reason, though, for submitting to these often boring duties was that every time we spent half a day plugging doggedly across muddy fields and shivering in bat-filled slimy ruins, we spent an equal amount of time sitting warmly, winily, in the best local restaurant, eating specialties of the village or the region more ardently than ever peak was scaled or Gothic arch gazed on.

The schedule was always the same: a brisk walk from the station and the little train that had brought us from Dijon, four or five hours of eating and drinking, and then the long promenade, the climbing, the viewing of monuments and fallen temples. Al and I were probably the youngest in the club by some thirty years, but more than once pure bravado was all that kept us from tumbling right into the nearest ditch in a digestive coma. The colonels and counsellors slapped their aged chests enthusiastically as the air struck them after the long hours in the restaurants, and they surged like a flock of young colts out into the country. We trotted mazily after them, two thin little American shadows convinced for a time at least that they were cousins of Gargantua.

The meals went on for hours, in spite of the length of the walk planned for later, and as a matter of pure research, based of course on our interest in folkways as well as culture, we arranged to taste not only the most noted dishes of the cook of the house, but also the Widow LeBlanc's way of pickling venison, and Monsieur le Curé's favorite recipe for little whole trout marinated in white wine and served chilled with green sour grapes.

The chef and his family would come in to enjoy our enjoyment, and then Widow LeBlanc and the Curé and the Curé's cook, and all of us would compare, with well-selected examples, the best local and district wines for each course. We always paid due homage to the ordinaries first, and then gradually lifted ourselves toward the heights of local pride, the crowned bottles known to every connoisseur alive, but never treated more respectfully than in their own birthplaces.

Sometimes the mayor or the lord of the château, knowing the Club Alpin of Dijon for what it really was, would send with his compliments a few bottles of such wines as I can only dream of now, wines unlabeled, never tired by travels, inviolate from the prying palates of commercial tasters. Then the gabble would die down, and Monsieur le Curé would bend his head over his goblet as if he were praying, and finally one or two of the old warhorses would murmur reverently, with eyes focused far inwards, "*Epatant . . . é-pa-tant!*"

The club secretary always tried to arrange our sorties so that after we had studied a regional cuisine with the thoroughness it deserved, and had made solemn notes both physical and spiritual on the vintages that flourished there, or there, or there, we could devote ourselves with equally undivided zeal to the promenade itself.

More often than not, though, we would quite by accident find that along with the château in a little village some two hours' walk past dinner, there was also a tiny pastry shop where a certain ancient dame made sour-cream *fantaisies* the like of none other in all France.

"My God," Monsieur Vaillant, the retired advocate, would cry, halfway through our tour of a private country house where one of Maintenon's exiled lovers had spent twenty leisurely years painting Chinese pagodas on the wainscoting. "My God and double-*zut*! This is infamous! Here we are within ten minutes' delightful promenade from one of the great, the *great* pastry-makers of all time! She is modest, yes. She is content with a small fame. She made her *fantaisies* for my dear mother's First Communion. They came in a wooden trunk, packed in layers of silk-paper and dead leaves to survive the trip.

"Stop the tour!" Monsieur Vaillant would snort, his face flushed with inspiration, and a dawning appetite in his rheumy old eyes. And he would send a boy ahead, to warn the old witch to start up her fire and bestir her bones.

And then after we had looked dutifully at the rest of the wall-paintings, and some of the more erudite had identified classical symbolism in the obscure little scenes, and some of the more lecherous had identified with equal pleasure a few neo-classical positions among the slant-eyed nymphs and mandarins, we would head for the pastry shop. Even Al and I would forget our surfeit, whipped by the clean air and Monsieur Vaillant's jubilant memoirs into a fresh hunger.

Sure enough, the toothless village heroine's sour-cream *fantaisies*, light, delicate, fried in pure butter to a color clearer than gold, paler than Josephine Baker but as vital, would be the most delicious pastry in all of France, and Monsieur Vaillant the proudest member of our club.

We'd drink hot wine . . . "Nothing better against these November winds," we agreed with Vaillant valiantly . . . and then climb up perhaps only three of the four hills planned on by the optimistic secretary, before we caught the stuffy train back to Dijon. We'd smoke and talk and doze, in that intimacy peculiar to a third-class French "local" on Sunday night, and never once did we regret in any way, digestive or moral, the day's licentious prodigality of tastes and sensuous pleasures.

Once a year, on Ascension Day, the club left all such energetic ideas of rising above the earth-level strictly to the church, and held its annual banquet without benefit of sortie, promenade, or appreciation of any well-preserved ruins other than the fellow members.

The only year I went to the Ascension Day banquet we dined for six hours at the Hôtel de la Poste in Beaune. That was long before the old place had its face lifted, and we ate in the dark odorous room where generations of coachmen and carriage drivers and chauffeurs had nourished themselves as well as their masters did "up front."

There was a long table for us, and an even longer one for the wines. Piles of the year's last grapes made the air tingle with a kind of decadent promise, but there were no flowers to interrupt our senses.

We toasted many things, and at first the guests and some of the old judges and officers busied themselves being important. But gradually, over the measured progress of the courses and the impressive changing beauty of the wines, snobberies and even politics dwindled in our hearts, and the wit and the laughing awareness that is France made all of us alive.

The Measure
of My Powers

1931

When I went back to Dijon, after the summer spent with my family, it was plain that the time had come for Al and me to live by ourselves. For two years we had eaten all our meals with good, interesting, even affectionate people, and lived in their house. We had learned much from them and accepted a thousand courtesies. Now, suddenly, they were intolerable, they and their sad quarrels and their gay generosities, they and their fine feathery omelets and their shared meats and vintages. We loved them, and we fled them like the black pox.

Even after so long in an army town, I still could not always tell a *"gros numéro"* from a reputable house, and managed to interrupt several business transactions and even exchange a few embarrassed salutations with unbuttoned University friends before I found the little apartment we were to live in.

It was in a "low quarter," everyone assured us with horror. The tram ran past it, and it looked down on a little square that once had held the guillotine and now, under the shade of thick plantains, housed two or three *pissoirs* and an occasional wandering side-show, with small shops all around.

Indeed, the quarter was so low that several Dijonnais who had been friendly with us stopped seeing us altogether. What had been an amusing social pastime in the fairly dull town life, coming to tea with us in the Rue du Petit-Potet safely surrounded as we were there by mayors and bishops and the smell of thirteenth-century cellars, became an impossibility when it meant walking through streets that were obviously inhabited by nothing but artisans and laborers. We basked in the new freedom, and absorbed sounds and vapors never met in a politer life.

Our apartment was two floors above a pastry shop, Au Fin Gourmet, and was very clean and airy, with a nice smell. The smell was what made me decide to take it, after days of backing confusedly out of brothels and looking at rooms dark and noisome and as lewdly suggestive as the old crones who showed them to me.

We signed several official certificates, bending over peach tarts and a row of soggy *babas* to reach the ink bottle. The proprietor looked at our signatures, and asked, "Married?"

"Yes," Al said, raising one eyebrow almost invisibly in a way that meant, in those days at least, that in spite of his politely innocent manner his words carried a tremendous reprimand or correction or general social commentary. "Yes. You see we have the same name, and I have marked us as Monsieur and Madame."

"Well," the man said, "it is less than nothing to me, you understand. But the police must be satisfied." He looked amicably at us, wiped his hands again on his sugary apron, and marked out Madame and my profession as student. In place of it he wrote, "Monsieur Fisher, and woman."

His wife, a snappish-looking small woman with pink eyebrows and tight mouth, gave us our keys and warned us again that the chambers were now in perfect condition and were expected to remain that way, and we went up the stairs to our own private home for the first time in our lives.

There was a big room with a shiny but uneven tiled floor and two wide windows looking down on the dusty little square. The bed, half-in-half-out a little alcove, did not keep everything from looking spacious and pleasant, especially when we pushed the round table into the corner and put books on the fake mantelpiece under the wavy old mirror. There was a kind of cupboard, which Madame the owner had called "*la chambre noire*"; we got some candles for it, and turned one of our trunk tops into a washstand, and it was very matter-of-fact in spite of its melodramatic name.

Outside our front door, on the landing, was a little faucet, where we got water for washing and cooking. It was a chore to carry it, and even more of one to empty the pail from the Black Chamber and the dish water and what I washed vegetables in, but it was something so new that I did not much mind it. There was a fountain in the square, of course, and I soon learned to take my lettuces and such down there and let the spout run over them, like the other women in the quarter.

The kitchen was astonishing to me, because I had never lived in a place like New York, where people cook on stoves hidden in their bureau drawers, I've heard. It was perhaps five feet long, perhaps three wide, and I had to keep the door open into the other room when I stood at the two burner gas-plate. There was a little tin oven, the kind to be set on top of a stove, and a kind of box with two shelves in it, for storage and instead of a table.

And there was the window, one whole wall, which opened wide and looked down into the green odorous square, and out over the twisted chimney pots to the skies of the Côte d'Or. It was a wonderful window, one of the best I can remember, and what I saw and thought and felt as I stood in it with my hands on the food for us, those months, will always be a good part of me.

Of course, we celebrated, the first night in the new place, and dined well and late at Ribaudot's, so that in the morning it was fun to lie in our niched bed and listen to the new noises.

They made a pattern we soon knew: the workers in their hard shoes, then the luckier ones with bicycles, and all the bells ringing; the shop-shutters being unhooked and folded back by sleepy apprentices; a great beating of pillows and mattresses, so that now and then brown feathers floated past our windows; and always the clanging of the little trams going up into the center of things.

That first morning there was something more, something we were to hear every Wednesday and Saturday, a kind of whispering pattering rush of women's feet, all pointed one way. I should have listened harder and learned.

When we finally got up, and went to the little café on the corner for our first breakfast, we saw that the soft rushing came from hundreds of women, all hurrying silently, all dressed in black and carrying black strings or pushing little carts and empty baby buggies. And while we were sitting there in the sun, two easy-going foreigners, some of the women started coming back against the stream, and I knew that they came from the big market, *les Halles*.

Their bags and carts were heavy now, so that the hands that held and pushed them were puffed and red. I saw the crooked curls of green beans and squashes, the bruised outer leaves of lettuces, stiff yellow chicken-legs . . . and I saw that the women were tired but full of a kind of peace, too. I had no black-string bag, no old perambulator. But I had a husband who enjoyed the dark necessity of eating, as I did myself. And I had a little stove. . . .

I stood up. It was almost noon, and too late now to go to the market. I planned innocently to pick up enough food at local stores to last until the next regular day, and headed for a store I'd often passed, where pans hung in rows in the window, and on the sidewalk clay casseroles and pots lay piled.

The first week I tried to feed us was almost too difficult. I learned a hundred things, all the hard way: how to keep butter without ice, how to have good salads every day when they could only be bought twice a week and there was no place to keep them cool (no place to keep them at all, really), how to buy milk and eggs and cheeses and when and where. I learned that *les Halles* were literally the only place to get fresh vegetables and that two heads of cauliflower and a kilo of potatoes and some endives weighed about forty pounds after I'd spent half an hour walking to market and an hour there and missed three crowded trams home again.

I learned that you bought meat and hard cheese and such by the kilo, but that butter and grated cheese, no matter how much you wanted, always were measured in grams. I learned that the stall-keepers in the market were tough loud-mouthed people who loved to mock you and collect a little crowd, and that they were very friendly and kind too, if you did not mind their teasing.

I learned always to take my own supply of old newspapers for wrapping things, and my own bowls and cans for cream and milk and such. I learned, with the tiredest feet of my life, that feeding people in a town like Dijon meant walking endless cobbled miles from one little shop to another . . . butter here, sausage there, bananas someplace again, and rice and sugar and coffee in still another place.

It was the longest, most discouraging, most exciting and satisfying week I could remember, and I look back on it now with an envy that is no less real for being nostalgic. I don't think I could or would ever do it again; I'm too old. But then, in the town I loved and with the man I loved, it was fine.

We ate well, too. It was the first real day-to-day meal-after-meal cooking I'd ever done, and was only a little less complicated than performing an appendectomy on a life-raft, but after I got used to hauling water and putting together three courses on a table the size of a bandana and lighting the portable oven without blowing myself clear into the living room instead of only halfway, it was fun.

We bought four plates and four forks, instead of two, so that we could entertain! Several of the people we knew found it impossible to condone our new address even with the words "whimsical" and "utterly mad," and very conveniently arranged to meet us in restaurants when they wanted to see us. The faithful ones who picked their way through the crowded streets and up our immaculately clean tenement steps were few, and they were welcome.

I wanted to invite the Rigagniers, but even if we could have asked them to bring their own plates and forks, I did not think the little stove would be able to cook anything they would honestly or even politely call a meal. And by then I was already beginning to have theories about what and how I would serve in my home.

I was beginning to believe, timidly I admit, that no matter how much I respected my friends' gastronomic prejudices, I had at least an equal right to indulge my own in my own kitchen. (I am no longer timid, but not always adamant, when it is a question of religion or old age or illness.)

I was beginning to believe that it is foolish and perhaps pretentious and often boring, as well as damnably expensive, to make a meal of six or eight courses just because the guests who are to eat it have always been used to that many. Let them try eating two or three things, I said, so plentiful and so interesting and so well cooked that they will be satisfied. And if they aren't satisfied, let them stay away from our table, and our leisurely comfortable friendship at that table.

I talked like that, and it worried Al a little, because he had been raised in a minister's family and taught that the most courteous way to treat guests was to make them feel as if they were in their own homes. I, to his well-controlled embarrassment, was beginning to feel quite sure that one of the best things I could do for nine tenths of the people I knew was to give them something that would make them forget Home and all it stood for, for a few blessed moments at least.

I still believe this, and have found that it makes cooking for people exciting and amusing for me, and often astonishingly stimulating for them. My meals shake them from their routines, not only of meat-potatoes-gravy, but of thought, of behavior. Occasionally I am fond enough of a person to realize that any such spiritual upset brought about by my serving an exotic or eccentric dish would do more harm than good, and I bow. It is usually women past middle age who thus confound me, and I have to be very fond of them indeed. They are few fortunately, and in spite of my solicitude I still think sometimes I am betraying them and myself too.

Perhaps it is not too late for them, I think; perhaps next time they come I will blast their safe tidy little lives with a big tureen of hot borscht and some garlic-toast and salad, instead of the "fruit cocktail," fish, meat, vegetable, salad, dessert, and coffee they tuck daintily away seven times a week and expect me to provide for them.

Perhaps they *should* feel this safe sand blow away so that their heads are uncovered for a time, so that they will have to taste not only the solid honesty of my red borscht, but the new flavor of the changing world. But when they come, they are so polite, so dazed, so genteelly dead already. . . .

The people who came oftenest to our room above the Fin Gourmet were Norah, on her free Thursday afternoons away from the convent, and the American student Lawrence, who was like our brother. They were both simple people, and reassuring. For Norah I would get a pitcher of milk and a pot of honey. I'd put them with the pat of sweet butter on the table, and a big square block of the plain kind of Dijon gingerbread that was called *pavé de santé*. There would be late grapes and pears in a big bowl.

Norah and I would sit by the open window, listening to the street sounds and playing Bach and Debussy and Josephine Baker on the tinny portable phonograph. The food was full of enchantment to my sister, after her gray meals in the convent, and she ate with the slow voluptuous concentration of a *dévouée*.

Lawrence was as satisfactory. He came for real meals, of course, and always brought a bottle of red wine, cheap but good. There would be candles on the table, because the one light-bulb in the room was far in the opposite corner, by the bed.

We would have a big salad always, and something I had made in one of the clay casseroles. I invented with gusto, and after the first days of experimenting with stoves, pots, and the markets, I turned out some fine odorous dishes that were a far cry, thank God, from the Hindu eggs that tortured my little sister Anne, the first time I ever let my imagination conquer over the printed recipe.

Our long stay with the Rigagniers, where Lawrence still lived, had given all of us a lust for simplicity after Madame's heady sauces. As I remember, the thing we all liked best, with the salad and Lawrence's wine, was a casserole of cauliflower, and bread and fruit afterwards. I made it so often that it became as natural as sneezing to me, and I was put off the track completely when I got back to America and found how different it was . . . the manner of doing it, the flavor, everything.

There in Dijon, the cauliflowers were small and very succulent, grown in that ancient soil. I separated the flowerlets and dropped them in boiling water for just a few minutes. Then I drained them and put them in a wide shallow casserole, and covered them with heavy cream and a thick sprinkling of freshly grated Gruyère, the nice rubbery kind that didn't come from Switzerland at all, but from the Jura. It was called *râpé* in the market, and was grated while you watched, in a soft cloudy pile, onto your piece of paper.

I put some fresh pepper over the top, and in a way I can't remember now the little tin oven heated the whole thing and melted the cheese and browned it. As soon as that had happened we ate it.

The cream and cheese had come together into a perfect sauce, and the little flowers were tender and fresh. We cleaned our plates with bits of crisp bread crust and drank the wine, and Al and Lawrence planned to write books about Aristotle and Robinson Jeffers and probably themselves, and I planned a few things, too.

And as I say, once back in California, after so many of those casseroles, I found I could never make one. The vegetable was watery, and there was no cream thick enough or unpasteurized and fresh. The cheese was dry and oily, not soft and light. I had to make a sauce with flour in it. I could concoct a good dish, still . . . but it was never so *innocent*, so simple . . . and then where was the crisp bread, where the honest wine? And where were our young uncomplicated hungers, too?

Quite often Jean Matruchot would come at noon.

He never went anywhere at night, and of course at the Lycée and the University where he taught there were a hundred stories about his licentious nocturnals. The truth was, I think, that the state of his poor popping eyes, which made it almost impossible for him to read large print in daylight, turned nights into a complete black-ness which his pride would never let him confess. He was a mis-anthrope, and like most such men had fifty friends who would have been glad of a chance to walk with him along the dim crooked streets; but instead, he sat alone in his hideously furnished "bach-elor suite" and went about only in daylight.

He ate his meals in the *pensionnaires'* room at Ribaudot's, and when he came to us for lunch he was like a man breathing after being almost too long without air.

"No rich dark-brown gaudy sauces," he would mutter, bend-ing over his plate and sniffing what he could hardly see. "No an-cient meats mummified with spices, exhumed and made to walk again like zombies! My God, no dead birds, rotting from their bones, and hiding under a crust five men have spent their lives learning how to put together so my guts will fall apart!

"Madame," Jean would say, rising gallantly and spilling all the red wine in our glasses, which he did not see, and putting his nap-kin carefully on top of the salad, which was two feet away and therefore invisible to him, "chère Madame, a true victim of gas-tronomy, a fugitive from the world-famed Three Pheasants, a starved soul released temporarily from the purgatory of la Cuisine Bourguignonne, salutes you!"

Jean would bow, I would thank him, Al and I would whisk the more obvious damage from the table, and we would sit back to a somewhat heavy but enjoyable noon dinner.

Jean liked potatoes, so there would be a casserole of them fixed in the cauliflower routine, and quite often a watercress salad and steaks broiled somehow on the top of the stove. Then we would eat some good cheese . . . the Brie from the shop across the square was wonderful in that autumn weather, with the hot days, and the chilly nights to keep it from ripening too fast . . . and drink some more wine.

He had been an interpreter for the Americans in the last war, and on his good days he would tell us fantastic stories about the peace-ful occupation of Beaune and all the homesick generals who called him Johnny. On his middling days he would tease me masterfully, like a fat Voltaire, for my class translations of "Gilpin's Ride." And on his bad days he would mutter such cynicisms as we had never heard, in French as rich and ripe as the cheese he loved, about the world and his honest hatred of it.

He was a strange passionately cold man, the kind who wants to be disliked and has true friends like us to refute all his intellectual desires. I think often of him, and of the hunger he showed for our food, and of the half-blind way his eyes would watch our faces, as if behind all the smug youthful foolishness he saw something he was looking for.

He was very different from Miss Lyse. She came often to eat with us, too, and I don't think she ever looked once at us. If she did, we were simply a part of all the sixty or so years of people who had fed her. She was charming to us; she sang for her supper, as life had taught her to, and she ate with the same ferocious voracity of any little bird while she kept us entertained.

She was about eighty then, I think, with a small pyramid of a body, and a fine proud little head with dark eyes and an ivory skin inherited from her Portuguese father. She had lived in Dijon since she was a girl, teaching English to the upper families. She still knew some conversation, all of it in simple words for the children she was used to talking to, but it was plain the French was more comfortable for her. She spoke it with a rank British accent, which she had promised her Devonshire mother never to abandon, and in spite of all the decades she had spent in the nurseries and drawing rooms of Burgundy, she sounded like a schoolgirl on a month's holiday from London, except for her volubility.

For years now, since her tyrannical dam breathed one last command and folded her hands in the death-grip over her cut jet locket, Miss Lyse had been cadging meals. She did it charmingly, amusingly.

She knew everybody, and all of the provincial gossip. She went to all the weddings of her former pupils, and then the christenings and the weddings of their children . . . and when the season was slack, and they remembered, they sent baskets of wine and cakes and butter to her attic room, as if in apology for the lack of festivals.

She was a character, everyone in Dijon said. She had followed the Bishop up the bloody steps of Saint Jacques, during the great troubles between Church and State, and had been stoned for it. Sadi Carnot had lain dying in her arms, assassinated. She had been a child in India where her father was ambassador and she knew how to charm snakes. That was the way the Dijonnais felt about her.

Myself, I was more than interested; there was something so indomitable about the set of her head and the fine flash of her old, old eyes. But it was the hunger that held me.

I don't know how she ate so much at one time. It was the result of years of practice, surely, years of not knowing just when another good meal would come her way. She was like a squirrel, with hidden pouches for the future. Norah and Lawrence and Jean Matruchot were as spindly ghosts compared with her, and meals big enough for six of us melted to a few crumbs almost before I had the time to serve them. Her manners were good, and she talked constantly in her funny mixture of nursery-English and London-French, and yet the lunch would be liquidated in the time Al and I usually spent on a salad or a tart.

I tried sometimes to see if I could stump her; I would make a bowl of two whole kilos of Belgian endive, cut into chunks and mixed with marinated green beans and sweet red peppers and chives. There would be a big casserole of fish and mushrooms and such in cream. I'd buy rich tarts at Michelin's.

Halfway through the meal Al and I would lie back in our chairs, listening and watching in a kind of daze. Miss Lyse was like something in a Disney film . . . nibble bite chew nibble nibble . . . through everything on the table, until it would not have surprised us at all to have her start conversationally, daintily, with a flick of her bright dark eyes and a quirk of her white head, on the plates themselves and then the books, right down the mantelpiece,

Shakespeare, Confucius, *Claudine à l'Ecole . . . les Croix de Bois,
The Methodist Faun . . .* nibble nibble crunch.

"That was so delicious, my dear," she would say at the end, wiping her mouth nicely and getting up with a brisk bob. "You are most kind to an old lady. And now I must thank you and be off. The Countess Malinet de Rinche is in from the country and I am having tea with her. This was *such* a nice little lunch together! Shall we say for the same day next week? Then I can tell you all about the dear Countess! Her sons! *Mon Dieu!*"

And Miss Lyse would give me a dry sweet-smelling peck on both cheeks and be out of the door before we could even get to our feet.

Would she really have tea with the unknown Countess What's-her-name, whose sons were less interesting than dead sea-fruit to us? Would she eat again until we next saw her? Did she really have *sous* enough for bread? We never knew.

It worried me, and I resolved to buy nine caramel tarts, instead of six, for the "little lunch" we knew she would not forget to take with us in exactly a week. . . .

I had one letter from her after the invasion. It was vigorous and amusing, although by then she must have been almost a hundred years old. She had been evacuated to a wretched little village near Clermont-Ferrand, and she had organized all the children into a band, to be ready to greet the Tommies in their own tongue when they came marching in. She said nothing about herself . . . but I have a belief that as long as there was life in that proud-headed little body, she would find crumbs.

The Measure
of My Powers

1931–1932

I

One night about ten o'clock, perhaps a week after Al was awarded
his doctorate at the Faculté, we stopped on our way home from a
dinner party and stood looking at each other for a minute in the
cold street.

Then, without a word, we headed for the station. We bought
two tickets for Strasbourg on the midnight train, *that* midnight,
not the one a week away when we had planned to go.

Most of our things were ready to be shipped. We arranged with
the station master to have them brought from our apartment in a
day or two. Then we ran down the back streets to our flat, routed
out the saw-faced cake-maker who lived just below us in his libel-
lously named shop, Au Fin Gourmet, and arranged in five minutes
all such questions of refunds, taxes, rental papers as he would have
preferred to spend five hours on. We threw what wasn't already
packed into suitcases.

We left the door open on our dear little apartment without one
backward glance of regret or even gratitude, and when we were finally sitting in the Buffet de la Gare, drinking a last coffee with a

porter who had become our friend in the past years, we breathed again.

We were fleeing. We were refugees from the far-famed Burgundian cuisine. We were sneaking away from a round of dinner parties that, we both felt calmly sure, would kill us before another week was over.

Ever since Al's masterly and amusing public oral defense of his thesis, which drew almost as big a crowd in the Faculté amphitheatre as had the last visit from a footloose Balkan regent, we had been deluged with invitations. Most of them were from lawyers, viscounts, and even professors who, in spite of the obvious cordiality of the Faculté Dean and the Rector toward us, had peered suspiciously at us over the tops of their newspapers and waited until now to bestow the accolade of their social recognition.

For almost two and a half years they had watched us, and observed to their cynical amazement that we were breaking every precedent established by former American students: we stayed; we didn't get drunk; Al actually worked hard enough to be awarded a degree, and I actually let other men alone, in spite of wearing the same color lipstick as the upper-bracket broads. And now we were guaranteed safe. Al had earned a right to wear a little round bonnet edged with rabbit fur and I, fortunate among all women, could now look forward to being the wife of a full professor some day, instead of an instructor.

"They really seem charming," people whispered about us in the discreetest drawing rooms of Dijon. "Lunch? A small dinner?"

Suddenly we were like catnip, after all those blessed months of being stinkweed. The closed doors swung open, and we found ourselves drowning in a sea of Burgundy's proudest vintages, Rheims' sparkle, Cognac's fire. Snails, pâtés, *quenelles de brochet*; always a great chilled fish *in toto* on a platter; venison and pheasants in a dozen rich brown odorous baths; intricate ices and well-laced beaten creams . . . and all of them served to the weighty tune of polite conversation, part condescending and part awed: it was too much for us.

The unsuspected strain of getting ready for the doctorate and then this well-meant deluge of hospitable curiosity made us feel that "we must press lettuce leaves upon our brows," or die.

And that is why we were hiding in the Buffet, that cold November night. We suddenly felt rested, knowing the train was almost there for us. We would send telegrams . . . I would write letters. . . .

Our friend the porter piled us into the compartment. We shook hands. The train shivered for a minute, and then started slowly to pull northward.

We heard a shout outside.

The porter was running along beside our window, and with him was Paul de Torcy, little hunchbacked Paul who adored Al, Paul who was rich and spent all his money publishing volumes of dreadfully poor poems for bankrupt provincial welshers. Paul loved Al more than any of them, and showed him his most private room, hung with black velvet and with . . . yes, it is true . . . with a skull on the carved oak desk. Paul wore a flowing tie. Paul hated me. Paul's drunken father had thrown him down the château steps when he was little.

And there he was running desperately along the platform, his great head with its sunken temples rolled back against his hump. How had he learned that we were fleeing? What suspicions hissed behind his wild pleading eyes?

He was weeping, glaring up at Al. And without wanting to, God knows, we began to laugh, there in the hastening train, in our own safety and warmth. We stood in the window looking down at Paul and *laughing*, because his eyes, so enormous and hopeless, looked like the eyes of a planked turbot we had been served so few hours before at dinner.

The turbot lay regally on its linen couch, bedecked with citrons and fresh herbs. Paul, more alive, ran crazily along the gray platform, unadorned. But their eyes, their great deep glassy eyes, were the same eyes, wild and full of a mute adoration and a terrible humility.

We kept on laughing, in a kind of sickness. And as the porter grabbed Paul's arm to stop his running, Al raised his fingers in a queer gesture that was half kiss, half salute.

II

It was early morning when we got to Strasbourg. By then we were numb with weariness. We went across the big square in front of the station to a hotel, and it wasn't until almost eighteen hours later that we woke up enough to realize that we were in the biggest bed either of us had ever seen. It must have been ten feet across, and it was clean and very comfortable. We felt fine.

Our watches had stopped, and when we telephoned to the clerk we found that it was long after midnight. He sent us up some cold sausages and rolls and beer, good Walsheim beer. We ate every crumb, and licked the foam from the stein-rims, and then slept again for several hours. When we awoke the second time we felt even finer. Al had his precious doctorate, and we were in love, and Strasbourg lay before us.

We bathed and dressed, and went out into the icy streets. There were already ranks of little fir trees in the Place Kléber, and gingerbread stands readied for Christmas, as there had been the year before when we went through on our way to Nürnberg. And we remembered our way to the great rosy-faced cathedral, and to the Kamarzellhaus that crouched beside it.

The Kamarzellhaus was almost objectionably quaint, but downstairs there was a cozy little taproom, and upstairs in the small restaurant the food was always better than good when we went there.

The first time, on our way to Germany, we had sat downstairs while our meal was being made. There were big soft leather chairs, and on the dark table was a bowl of the first potato chips I ever saw in Europe, not the uniformly thin uniformly golden ones that come out of waxed bags here at home, but light and dark, thick and paper-thin, fried in real butter and then salted casually with the *gros sal* served in the country with the *pot-au-feu*.

They were so good that I ate them with the kind of slow sensuous concentration that pregnant women are supposed to feel for chocolate-cake-at-three-in-the-morning. I suppose I should be ashamed to admit that I drank two or three glasses of red port in the same strange private orgy of enjoyment. It seems impossible, but the fact remains that it was one of the keenest gastronomic moments of my life.

And of course by the time the waiter called us upstairs, Al's carefully chosen dinner was more than wasted on me. I felt very sorry about that. He forgave me, and we went back, that next time in Strasbourg, and ate it over again.

There were several other restaurants of some note in the town, but there was the same kind of confusion in them that we felt everywhere; they were neither French nor German, and certainly there was no proof that the autonomy so fiercely wished for by many of the Alsatians could succeed in their kitchens. Almost every little pub advertised its own *choucroute garnie*, of course, and sometimes it was good indeed, and sometimes it was a sad and soggy mess, a dingy pile of sauerkraut no longer sour, gray aged potatoes, and *wursten* wrinkled as autumn leaves but less delectable.

There was one tavern run by the Walsheimbier concern, where Al and Norah and I used to go on Sunday afternoons after our long cold walks along the Rhine and into the little woods.

Norah was in a convent in the town then, after Christmas. It was plain she was a North-type woman, even in her fourteenth winter: she bloomed like a beautiful young pine tree in the cold air of Strasbourg, and there was a kind of leashed vitality about her that I have never seen so plainly since. She had to be back inside the convent gate by six, so we would end our walks as soon as the sun began to set, at three-thirty or even three, and head by bus or tram-car, the quickest way, toward the Walsheim tavern.

It was very German, noisy warm *good* German, filled with large families who had spent their Sundays much as we had and were hungry in the same tingling robust way. We would sit with other people, usually, who smiled and greeted us and then went on with their own lives, and we would order large beers and whichever of the two specialties we had decided on during the walk: Walsheim-platten, which were plates covered with a dozen or so small but sturdy open-faced sandwiches, or bread-and-cheese.

Cheese there meant one kind, the soft ripe Münster, like Lim-burger or our Liederkranz or a strong Brie. It was always served with a pile of chopped onion and one of caraway seeds, and the whole combination was what my father would describe as "fruity."

I have often wondered what olfactory effect Norah had on the nice little girls in her dormitory, most of whom had spent Sunday either on their knees or in the chaste company of visiting cousins. We had things so well timed that just as the Sister at the gate put her key in the lock Norah, like a large happy uniformed bat straight from the mouth of a purely Protestant hell, would shoot past and into the convent, trailing an almost visible cloud of beer and cheese and good humor behind her. She would turn once and wink at us, and then murmur, "*Merci, ma soeur,*" and bow her head in its neat convent hat with a kind of regal docility as she disappeared until the next Sunday.

Perhaps it was wrong to take such a young girl into a public tav-ern with us, and let her drink beer, but it did not seem so. Physi-cally she was bigger and stronger than either Al or I . . . and in other ways I like to think that the walks and then the honest smells and tastes and sounds of the pub left something good in her heart, as they did in mine.

The other place in town where Al and I went most often was called Philippe's. It was a big extravagant *brasserie* exactly like the best ones in Paris, and it was supposed to be financed and directed by the French government, as part of the propaganda to keep Al-sace away from the Germans. Certainly it was run with an almost frantic lavishness. The service was perfect, and everything from a glass of beer to a ten-course dinner with the finest wines was not only the best but the cheapest, probably, in all that part of France.

We went there most often with a man named Franz, who was

ostensibly the manager of the government tobacco factory in Strasbourg, but was really a secret agent. He told us that Philippe's cost the taxpayers thousands of francs a day, and I could see how. I have never eaten better oysters than there. They came by plane every morning from the coast. And *moules marinières* . . . the memory of them makes me sigh. And of course pâtés of Strasbourg, in aspics, in crusts, in mousses. . . . And the wines in carafe were the finest I have ever tasted. Franz said the government went so far as to buy bottled vintages and then empty them into the cheap open pitchers, to make the Alsatians learn to know something besides beer and the Rhine wines imported at low prices by the Germans.

Yes, we went often to Philippe's, by ourselves or with Franz and his strange little protégé, the Annamite prince, whose political education was also a part of Franz's peculiar duties, as well as an obviously amorous pleasure. There was something exciting about the whole place, and very wrong, like a beautiful young woman with a cancer.

III

Al and I lived for two or three months in the top of a house out by the Orangerie, but it did not work.

We had a queer little kitchen which every morning had an icicle on the one water faucet, and a dingy little living room with one round window in it about the size of a Thanksgiving pie, and then at the other end of a long hall a small bedroom. There was no way of bathing, so that in spite of bi-weekly treks to the municipal bath-house I felt an inevitable dirtiness creep over me.

There was a little black tiled stove in the living room which held about a pint of coke at a time and had to be stoked at least once every half-hour to stay even lukewarm.

We were almost three miles from markets. Al was good about bringing things home, and when I was too cold to cope with trams I would walk up to the café at the corner and telephone for groceries. But still it was discouraging to have to put on my fur coat and gloves to cook a meal in the little kitchen, where steam would stiffen into ice as soon as it hit the sloping uninsulated ceiling.

I tried to write . . . I think then I had decided, with mistaken smugness, that I could turn out a much better shilling-shocker than many already in print . . . but my hands and head were too cold.

I used to go across into the Orangerie when I felt too cold to sit still, and watch what animals had thick enough fur to wander outside their cages. I'd stand and stand, waiting for some sign of life from the rumpled creatures on the other side of the bars, but even the guinea pigs were too stiff to carry out their usual haphazard copulations. The storks, symbol of Alsace, would stare bleakly at me and occasionally drop a languid feather into the frozen filth, and I would turn back to my home, stumbling a little in my haste to get there before the fire went out again.

Some time every early morning, a pair of very old beggars hobbled cursing and singing past the house. I began to wait for them. Several times I looked at them, while I stood shuddering in the bedroom window. The man had a peg-leg, and the woman, as far as I could ever see in the moonlight on the snow, no face at all. They were always drunk, and sometimes they would stop and caress each other and sometimes the old man would knock his partner down a dozen times before they disappeared toward the end of the street.

I stopped watching them, but I began to know when they were coming long before I heard the tap-tap of his leg on the ice, and finally I knew, in spite of all my good sense, that one night he would come in through the locked gate, through the door, up the stairs, through our own solid door, into the room, tap-tap-tap. . . .

Then Al decided to make a tamale pie. I had never tasted one, which was his excuse, but he may have felt about it rather as I had about the potato chips at the Kamarzellhaus. He spent days preparing it, and buying the proper casserole, the best Greek olives, a chili powder sent down from a grocery in Paris, cornmeal found finally at an obscure "health food store."

At last everything was assembled. He stayed home from the University, where he was doing some work, and thanks to his enthusiasm and probably his actual physical presence, the apartment was almost warm. I was glad I had not spoken of my foolish fears. We made a little salad of bland Belgian endive, a good complement to the spices of Al's masterpiece, and drank a firm-bodied red wine, and the tamale pie was very good indeed.

It was probably one of the best that has ever been made, anywhere in the world where anyone would bother to make one, and I hope it was the only one I shall ever eat.

Of course it was not the concoction itself that broke my spiritual back. I know that well. But a little while after I finished eating it (I should say well within the four-hour period of a more or less normal digestion), I began to cry. It was the first time Al had even seen a tear in either of my eyes. Now there were thousands. They fell down my cheeks without a sound or a sigh from me, and my nose did not even turn red. I simply sat wordless, held in a kind of stupefaction, too limp to put a handkerchief to my drenched cheeks. I was humiliated, but without the energy to hide myself.

Al watched me for a time, and asked like any normal male, "What have I done?" Then, for he was practical as well as erudite, he stoked the fire, put a glass of brandy within reach of my numb hand, and left for the University.

I sat in the gradually chilling room, thinking of my whole past the way a drowning man is supposed to, and it seemed part of the present, part of the gray cold and the beggar woman without a face and the moulting birds frozen to their own filth in the Orangerie. I know now I was in the throes of some small glandular crisis, a sublimated bilious attack, a flick from the whip of melancholia, but then it was terrifying . . . nameless. . . .

When it was time for Al to come home I drank the brandy, which stopped the steady flowing of my large soft tears, and made myself as pretty as I could. I felt desperately ashamed, and full of bewilderment.

We went to Philippe's for supper, and everything was fine until we started homeward. Then tears began to slip down my face again, and all my bones turned sick and limp. I could only roll my eyes dazedly at my poor husband, and shake my head.

He was wonderful. He took me to the warmest hotel-room in all the town, full of firelight and plump white pillows and red-damask featherbeds with ruffles. He ran a bath for me in a huge white tub with bronze spigots shaped like spitting swanheads. And while I made myself feel really clean for the first time in weeks, he went all the way back to our apartment on the tram and got some nightclothes for us.

And the next day we moved to the Pension Elisa, without any words of question or reproach, then or ever.

The Elisa was much too expensive, and we stayed there in a cozy careless hibernation for the many weeks before we went south. It was near the University, and I saw much more of Al.

For a time I was languid, like a convalescent, and at night listened willy-nilly for the tapping of the beggar's wooden leg. In daylight I lay on a chaise-longue behind the white linen billows of curtain in our alcove and listened to the homesick Polish consul in the next room play on his concertina, and watched the bridge across the canal. I got to know many Strausbourgeois, and just when, each day, to look for the school children, the fat furred rich women with their matching dachshunds on studded leashes, the pale clerks, the mincing prostitutes.

Gradually I began to work again. It was very poor stuff I wrote, but healthy. I went to the Cathedral a lot, and the museums, and felt warm all the time, and Al and I had fun together, in the taverns and the streets and in the dark dining room of the Elisa, where we ate even darker meals of roasted wild-boar meat and such. There were always purées, as I remember, as if the fifty-odd *pensionnaires* had no teeth: peas, lentils, potatoes, chestnuts, rubbed to a suave paste and decorated unfailingly with gouts of a sauce which never varied its fairly potent flavor nor its rich blackish shade.

Soon I forgot the awful way tears had rolled from my eyes, as if I were not human. By now all I can say about that evil day, really, is that I am content with utter illogicality to dislike the thought of eating a tamale pie again.

Sea Change

1932

The next time we put to sea, in 1932, was not so much later, about a year . . . but I was more than a year older. I don't know why; I simply matured in a spurt, so that suddenly I knew a lot about myself and what I wanted and what I had to do. It made me soberer, and I was much less shy.

It was hard to leave Europe. But I knew that even if we stayed, our young days there were gone. The first insouciant spell was broken, and not by the act of buying tickets, as Al seemed to believe. Nor could it ever be recaptured; that would be monstrous, like a man turned child again but still caught in his worn big body.

We ate lunch before the boat sailed at a restaurant on the Old Port in Marseille. Al and I had often been there before, and Norah, who was unusually acute about flavors, almost like a French child, was excited at the prospect of one final orgy of real *bouillabaisse*. We almost didn't get it, though.

It was the first time I had ever been turned away from a restaurant, and it left me strangely shaken; we walked in the door and a waiter came hurrying toward us through the crowded room and before we knew it we were out on the street again . . . shoo, shoo, as if we were impudent chickens on a lawn.

Then the proprietor rushed out. He recognized Al and me. He

screamed at the officious waiter. We all laughed and laughed . . .
the waiter had seen my accordion, which Al carried under his arm
because we couldn't find a safe parking place for it before the boat
sailed, and had thought we were hungry street-singers planning to
cadge a meal.

We bowed and grinned and blushed, and there Norah and Al
and I were, sitting at the best table on the balcony, looking down
on the Old Port in the full spring sunlight, drinking several different kinds of the proprietor's private stock of wines and trying not
to wonder how we could bear to leave this land.

The *bouillabaisse* sent up its own potent saffrony steam. We
mopped and dunked at its juices, and sucked a hundred strange
dead creatures from their shells. We toasted many things, and
often, but ourselves most of all.

And then it was time to go. I played the proprietor and several
waiters my best tune, still feeling, through the good wine and
food, a sense of shock that I or anyone else in the world could be
turned away from a door. We all had a final drink, in a *marc du Midi*
that would jar Jupiter, and then we left France.

The ship was a small Italian freighter, carrying about fifteen passengers. She was called the *Feltre*, I think, and was lightly loaded
with wines and oils for sale, a small famous sailing boat being taken
to America to race, and an enormous quantity of food for the crew,
since Mussolini would not allow any but Italian products to be
eaten by his men on the three months' voyage.

(The ship's cargo was also suspected, by the Marseille police, of
including two desperate men who had killed bank clerks and taken
a sum of money that increased from twenty-five hundred to a
quarter of a million francs while the holds were searched and the
captain fumed. Finally, after everything including my poor accordion had been undone, unbuttoned, and unlocked, the police went
crankily away, and we could creep past all the docks . . . the smallest, silentest start on a sea voyage I have ever made.)

We stopped at several Spanish ports, big ones like Barcelona or
simply a pier thrust weakly into the water, covered with square

gleaming tins of olive oil. Once there was a great slick of oil to meet us, and the crew cursed the idle Spanish stevedores who stood smiling and smoking and refused to load any of the tins. They were splitting in the sun, so that the greenish oil dripped from every crack in the pier.

It was sabotage, the captain told us: things were in a bad way in Spain . . . the Communists, of course . . . there would be revolution soon.

We wallowed for two days in the slick swell. A few dozen cans were found whose solder had not melted, and we loaded them and left, with the fine rich smell of the lost oil following us for hours over the water.

In Malaga we sat under a tree by a café and drank dutifully of the thick brown wine, and then after a decent interval switched gladly to watered *Anis Mono* . . . a savage combination, but I think it offended no one.

I decided I wanted to live near Malaga. On deck, drinking weak Italian beer, we watched the tawny hills slip by, and it was like California between Balboa and San Diego, and I loved it.

Then, days later, when we moved slowly past the Canaries, I decided, almost, that I wanted to live there. What would it be like to live on an island, such a small intensely islandic island? No. . . .

It would be something like living for so many somnolent weeks on a small ship, as we did. There would be unrecognized emotions, and perhaps sudden flarings of strong action, and tears and then quiet again among the inhabitants. It takes detachment to live in a place where the physical boundaries are visible in every direction. And for me there is too little of life to spend most of it forcing myself into detachment from it.

The captain was a young fat man with impersonal eyes which should have been full of light. I felt that he resented and disliked passengers and his life as a kind of wet nurse to them, and I could not blame him. But even without us, I don't believe he was a sea captain, the way a Dutchman or a Swede or perhaps even an Italian can be. He seemed as far from his ship as from us, which gave me an uncomfortable sense of insecurity.

He was perhaps less cool with other people; there were at least two bursts of jealous tears somewhere in the Caribbean, I remember, because he talked in his cabin with the two strong-chinned American girls returning from a year in Florence instead of with young Mrs. Feinmann, who had run away with an Italian and was being brought back to her forgiving husband by her mother. ("Isn't it just like something on the radio?" both women asked me with romantic and proud relish a few hours out of Marseille, when they told me for the first of perhaps forty times about the flight, the pursuit, the capture.)

Al and Norah and I, because of our natures, kept sea changes to ourselves, and lived in a small proud world. Our cabins on the upper of the two tiny decks opened into a kind of salon, and we ate there with a family of four Swiss people as quiet as we.

My little fingers and toes went to sleep, of course, and for a few days outside of Gibraltar I was more frightened than I had been in all the months Norah was my charge; the two of us, for the only times in our lives, had cruel earaches, so that we moved and spoke as if we were made of glass. There was no nurse on board, which is against international law, I believe. The captain had medicines in his cabin, but I felt something ridiculous in our going there, two tall fair women, asking that fat impersonal man for pills.

"Drink a lot of water and keep warm," I said firmly to Norah, my mind trembling around words like mastoid, and my head pierced with hot wires.

And in about four days we suddenly were free again. I wonder about that . . . whether it was a germ . . . certainly we did not dream it, nor I the repressed panic I felt about Norah and all the water between her and help.

The other changes were less violent, less tangible.

I don't know about Al; he looked at the water, and talked with the man who sailed the racing boat for an American millionaire, and with a big Italian wrestler from San Francisco. He made notes on tiny papers in his almost invisible writing. He was very good to look at, when we got down into the real warmth and he could wear white cotton clothes. But inside . . . I don't know at all.

It is almost the same with Norah. She read a lot of French novels I had brought for myself (and I in turn read *Monte Cristo* in eight volumes and religious tracts borrowed from the Swiss). One time I heard her talking in her cabin, and I went to see why. She was standing in the middle of the little white room, looking at the beetles that roamed the walls and ceiling as they did everywhere, and saying, "I won't stand it another minute. I simply refuse to stand it!"

She was crying, and stiff with anger at the black bugs. I felt very sorry for her, but I said, "You are twelve days from Gibraltar and about twenty from the next port, Norah," and went back to my own cabin.

She was all right by lunchtime, but for two or three days she had a quiet almost exhausted look about her. It is hard to recognize inevitabilities with grace, and probably she will never quite recover from the shock of hearing me say what she was trying not to admit. She was very young for such a thing.

And I was by myself most of the time, knitting and reading and cautiously poking into my own mind. I had found out several things about my relationship to my family, and to other men than Al, and while the ship rolled slowly forward across all the waves, I discussed them, usually alone but sometimes with him.

I don't think he really heard me, knowing perhaps that I was talking to myself. And perhaps he too was talking silently. That seemed natural, there on the quiet little ship. Nothing was real except what happened in my mind. (Would that be true on an island, too?) The outside things were shadowy, the pleasant daily rhythm of meals and greetings and gossip, and even earache and the occasional obtruding passions of other voyagers.

There was of course another kind of life going on, among the crew, but they seldom came near us. They were quiet for Italians, and not gay. Our cabin boy was a pale blond boy named Luigi, who shook with embarrassment when we spoke to him, and had a very strong smell. I cannot remember the waiter, except that he was nice. When it got too hot to eat the veal and pork we had every noon, he worried, especially about Norah, and brought small strange salads to her. That was against orders, because by then there was just enough lettuce left for the Captain's Dinner, some four weeks away.

The cheeses and the bread were delicious, and there was always wine on the table. Sometimes it tasted strange after the red and white Burgundies we had grown to know. It was more like the wines of the Midi, not the ones that were exported for gourmets, but the local kinds, fuller, coarser, heavier. I liked it. The waiter would bring me a little ice, and I would drink it with everything: the heady slices of salami, the cheeses, the fruit.

When we began to touch at ports in Central America we had wonderful papayas, cold and smooth as butter, and green-skinned oranges as big as melons, and bananas. There were avocados too, good with the fine crusty bread. And the dark yellow wines, the bluish red ones, were just what I wanted with these things, simple and straightforward in all the lush heat of the coastal waters.

We were really hard-up, and what money we had was carefully apportioned: one beer a day, one vermouth before dinner, tips at San Pedro, "incidentals." Al did not favor the wines. His mind's palate still echoed to the firm notes of a Chambertin '19, and he could ill adjust himself to lesser vintages. So Norah and I gave him our beers, not suffering much from such watery losses.

Once, on her birthday, we drank champagne. It was sweet and warm, and little gnats swarmed over the glasses in the steaming dark. Outside we could hear natives splashing in the stockade built in the bay to keep out sharks. The ship was silent. The captain lifted his glass shyly to us, and we all sighed, wishing that we could like one another.

I was even stupider then than I sometimes admitted; now it seems plain to me that poor Al did not stay aboard because bad pork surged in his bowels. He had a deep and violent and really fearful hatred of insects . . . bugs . . . things that sucked and bit. Probably he lay wanly in his bunk because of them, of knowing that where we would go the earth teemed with them, and every tree was heavy with them. Probably . . . I hate now to think of my dull misunderstanding . . . probably he was sickened to think of my coming back from those dreamy trips ashore, covered with invisible pests. But he said nothing, and I went with Norah and the others into the jungle villages.

Once I looked at a man in one of them, and stood fixed, a moth on a pin; he was very brown, in old tattered pants like a movie beachcomber's, and he had blue eyes and six fine strong toes on each foot. I do not know how I saw two such startling facts at once, but I did.

And when I stopped looking at him, I turned mazedly to speak to Norah, and could not because an old woman so leprous that only the bare white bones of her hand rested on Norah's arm, stood clutching at her. I turned hot with horror, and then shrugged . . . it was all part of the dream, and rushing for antiseptics and scaring people and shocking them would do no good. I gave the old woman some money, and as she moved off into the shadows, like a rotten apple rolling, I said nothing. What use?

I put my hand just where the leper's had lain, and we too went into the shadows.

Once, I remember, we sat for hours in a cool bar with a dirt floor, drinking milk from coconuts which the boss pulled up from a deep covered well in the center of the room. He would get down on his knees as he saw us tipping the shells back further, and haul up the nuts in a kind of seine, cold and dripping. He could poke the eyes out with his thumb. We drank in a kind of frenzy. The milk was like balm after the coarse wines and the sea air. We felt a little sick for a few hours, but it was good to sit there so quietly with the earth under our feet.

Another time everybody on ship went to a palmy courtyard for a dinner. It was inside a hotel, a small dirty place without any doors, where the toilet was a hole in one corner of a room with several hammocks in it and several sleeping men in the hammocks.

We walked through a few little streets where every house was open, with a handsome Sears-Roebuck bed under a lithograph of the Sacred Heart, like the whores' rooms in Cristobal, and then hammocks swung for the real family life.

We started to eat, in a patio filled with vines and parrots and our long table, before the light left. A tiny gray-bearded man in white cotton trousers and a pink silk polo-shirt served us, helped by two children only a little taller than he.

We ate and ate. I can't remember much of it except avocados in several different manners. There was meat, though, probably found at great cost and, for me at least, impossible either to chew or swallow. There were dozens of little dishes of sweet cooked fruits and flat tidbits which could have been bats' ears or sliced melon-rind. The man, his large eyes devoutly veiled, slid them in front of us, hour after hour.

Occasionally came a dish of chicken boiled with peppers and chocolate . . . something like that, as loud as a trumpet call in all the sweetness.

We sat eating, big pale strangers, and the patio grew dark. By the time we had drunk coffee and finished our beer and paid, the night was black. Under a streetlight three prisoners stumbled past us. Their irons rang against the occasional pavements, and sucked at the mudholes. And outside the village, before we came to the dock, fireflies taunted us in the forest, like mischievous candles, the biggest in the world.

The Captain's Dinner was strange, too. We were off the coast of Lower California. The water was so calm that we could hear flying fish slap against it. We ate at a long table out on deck, under an awning between us and the enormous stars.

The captain looked well in his white uniform, and smiled almost warmly at us all, probably thanking God that most of us would leave him in a few days. The waiters were excited, the way the Filipino boys used to be at boarding-school when there was a

Christmas party, and the table looked like something from a Renaissance painting.

There were galantines and aspics down the center, with ripe grapes brought from Italy and stranger fruits from all the ports we'd touched, and crowning everything two stuffed pheasants in their dulled but still dashing feathers. There were wine glasses on stems, and little printed menus, proof that this masterpiece of a meal was known about in Rome, long since.

We ate and drank and heard our own suddenly friendly voices over the dark waters, and forgot that Mrs. Feinmann was in her cabin because the captain wouldn't put the Italian wrestler in irons for "making a pass at her," and that Thoreau's grand-niece was very pale from the hemorrhage that had engulfed her earlier in the day. The waiters glided deftly, perhaps dreaming that they served at Biffi's instead of on this fifth-rate freighter, and we drank Asti Spumanti, undated but delightful.

And finally, while we clapped, the chef stood before us, bowing in the light from the narrow stairs. He wore his high bonnet and whites, and a long-tailed morning coat, and looked like a drawing by Ludwig Bemelmans, with oblique sadness in his pasty outlines.

There was a silence after our applause. He turned nervously toward the light, and breathed not at all. We heard shufflings and bumps. Then, up through the twisting white closeness of the stairway, borne on the backs and arms of three awe-struck kitchen boys, rose something almost too strange to talk about.

The chef stood back, bowing, discreetly wiping the sweat from his white face. The captain applauded. We all clapped, and even cheered. The three boys set the thing on a special table.

It was a replica, about as long as a man's coffin, of the cathedral at Milano. It was made in white and pink sugar. There was a light inside, of course, and it glowed there on the deck of the little ship, trembling in every flying buttress with the Mexican ground swell, pure and ridiculous; and something about it shamed me.

It was a little dusty. It had undoubtedly been mended, after mighty storms, in the dim galleys of a hundred ships, better but never worse than this. It was like a flag flying for the chef, a bulwark all in spun sugar against the breath of corruption. It was his masterpiece, made years ago in some famous kitchen, and he showed it to us now with dignity . . .

Sea Change

1935

I

About three and a half years later, I think, in 1935 or 1936, I went back to France with Chexbres and his mother. The whole thing seems so remote now that I cannot say what was sea change and what had already happened on land. I know that I had been in love with Chexbres for three years or so.

I was keeping quiet about it; I liked him, and I liked his first wife who had recently married again, and I was profoundly attached to Al. Even while I hurried to New York for such an odd jaunt, with Al's apparently hearty approval, I was making plans for the next years with him, the rest of my life with him.

I was full of resolutions never to be caught in the whirlpool of being a "faculty wife," and was planning to adopt several children, raise goats, not feed more than twenty hungry students a week with my exciting stews and broths; that is to say, I was a typical young faculty wife. A few more years, and I'd have been wearing brown-satin afternoon dresses and wearily eating marshmallow salads at committee luncheons with the best of them.

Instead, I stepped aboard the *Hansa*, one ice-heavy February midnight.

The *Hansa* was a tidy, plump little ship. There was something

comfortable about her, and at the same time subtly coarse and vulgar, like a motherly barmaid married to a duke in an English novel.

Several things happened to me aboard her that I have often
wanted to write about, but I never have and perhaps never will because I feel very strongly about prejudicing people. These things
were about Germans, not the kind good Germans who cared for
us, but evil men and women. Before the war I did not want to rouse
distrust, and have the good judged by the evil ones . . . and in wartime there is enough hatred, both real and imaginary, without my
adding to it.

There was indeed too much ugliness on that pretty little ship. It
was all a part of what is happening now in the world, and has always happened, and always will happen while men stunt their
souls.

Fortunately it did not touch many people then. Chexbres'
mother did not know about it, nor would she have recognized it if
it had reared and hissed at her, so excited was she to be once more
pointed toward the Paris of fifty years before, when she studied in
Chaplin's *atelier* and her homesick father, wordless and bewildered, fished with the other old men along the quais.

Yet, it is better, I think, to forget the bad things on that ship.
There were many good ones, and funny too . . . like the concert-
grand piano in the Ladies' Salon, painted a rich creamy pink (with
mother-of-pearl keys), so that it looked like a monstrous raspberry
in the pistachio mousse décor. Or like my attitude toward life during the first two days of the voyage, when I spent much of the time
beating my breast and being Good, Noble, and High-minded.

Then came a small storm. I found myself standing alone in the
cold moonlight, with spray everywhere and my black cape whipping, and my face probably looking a little sick but covering, I am
sure, wild and unspeakable thoughts. Suddenly I seemed so ridiculous, so melodramatically Mid-Victorian about my Hopeless
Passion, that I blushed with embarrassment, straightened my hair,
and went down to the bar.

Chexbres was there, of course. We celebrated, with the first of ten thousand completely enjoyable drinks: I, my release from my own private soap-opera, and he, my God-sent recovery from what was to him an inexplicable case of frigid and sour-pussed ill humor. Everything was all right after that, for as many more years as he was on the earth, and I lived secure and blessed for those years too, through many terrors.

Sometimes at night, after the Grand Concert or the Dancing had finished and Chexbres' mother had gone to bed, we sat in the bar, watching and drinking and talking. But the men there did not drink well, or at least not according to our tastes. They liked Turkish Blood, which was English ale and red vintage Burgundy mixed together . . . an insulting thing to do to good wine, I felt. They drank champagne, too, but doggedly and often laced with brandy or even whiskey.

The favorite cocktail was called an Ohio. It was drunk at any time of the day or night, from double-sized champagne glasses which must have held ten or twelve ounces of the mixture, and were rimmed heavily with sugar.

I knew the formula, from watching the barman make so many, but I forget everything now except that it was coarse, stupid, and fantastic, like the men who drank it. There were two or three cherries in each glass, and several kinds of alcohol: brandy, gin, cordials. Champagne was used as a filler.

I never tasted one, but the barman, who spent what spare time he had in practicing elaborate scroll-writing under the top of the bar, told me they were very sweet. He said I wouldn't like them.

I didn't like the way they made people act, certainly, and after one nightcap in the bar I was always glad to go to my cabin.

It was clean and cosy, with light shining on the cherry-satin feather-puff and the gleaming sheets, and I could lock the door against evil, which for the first time had touched me, there on that little ship in my twenty-seventh year. At first I thought it was part of the sea change, to see what one man did, and how the purser quailed before a name famous in the Reich, and how my maid wept, knowing why I must lock my door. Now I think it was all part of the sickness and terror of the *Hansa's* homeland.

There was always a little silver tray in my cabin at night: thin sandwiches of rare beef, a pepper mill, a tiny bottle of cold champagne. (Chexbres said his sandwiches were bigger, and his tipple was stout . . . for his mother there was hot chocolate in a thermos, with little cakes which in spite of her disinterest in them were always gone by morning.)

I would bathe elaborately, calmly, and then lie safe under the feathers, moving with the water all around me, flat so that when the ship rolled I could feel my guts shift delicately against my spine. I would sip, and nibble, and read somnolently of other more tepid dramas than my own, mystery stories as mild as pap beside what was happening on that ship. . . .

The days, which began for me with a twelve-o'clock beer in the bar with Chexbres, were like a gluttonous dream. I was not hungry, really, nor was anyone else on the *Hansa*, as far as I could see, but the passengers ate systematically, steadily, thoughtfully, through all the waking hours. I myself was interested in this German way of keeping them occupied, and I went to most of the ship's meals except breakfast. But I felt that most of the other people were eating almost as if the whipped cream and pressed ducks and pâtés de foie gras would be stored somewhere in their spiritual stomachs, to stay them soon, too soon, in a dreadful time of hunger.

There was a small restaurant, a pleasant room with wide windows and birds in cages, where we lunched. Each day the meal was copied from a different country, always in a heavy German accent, of course. The strangest was probably the one called Mexican, which started with what might be called enchiladas, and then went philosophically back to stuffed Munich goose. The Swedish and even the Italian were really good, in an incredibly heavy-handed way.

It was like playing a game, to order the North German Lloyd equivalents of every national apéritif and wine and punch and beer. The aquavit was fine, the only possible introduction to the almost endless meal that followed. And the vodka was fine too, when we ate almost enough caviar at the Russian lunch.

Most of the thirty or so passengers in the little room, though, drank three Ohios before each meal. They were real swells, and they always came in to their tables a few seconds after the enormous glasses full of cherries and liquors had been lined up in a row before each place. They stood up and lifted their glasses to the picture of Hitler at one end of the room with the first drink. By the end of the third, their monocles were falling out, but it didn't matter.

I know it seems strange now that Chexbres and his mother and I sat there in our own private enjoyment, under such a picture with such fat starving souls. So it was, though.

And the last night, or perhaps the one before, we went to a Forest Feast or some such thing. The picture was still there, but almost hidden by real pine boughs everywhere, with cabin boys hidden behind them whistling like birds, and a delightful smell in the air. The meal was long and amazing, with things like *truites au bleu* and wild boar . . . wild things that did not taste as if they had made countless trips in tanks and freezing units. Whenever the hidden but occasionally giggling boys had to rest their whistles, a phonograph played "Tales from the Vienna Woods" and such.

And at the end of this solemn banquet, so elaborately planned and carefully performed, we were given wooden pistols and baskets of little white cotton balls. It was so funny, so weighty and well-meaning, that Chexbres' mother laughed like a girl and popped one bullet straight at a small dour professor who always ate alone, never speaking or smiling. He stood up, bowed, and left the room.

It was a good idea; the party was over, and Chexbres, and his mother, still smiling delightedly at herself, and I in a dress I had never dared wear when I chaperoned dances at Al's college, drank quite a lot of champagne, all by ourselves in the room with the pink piano.

II

Coming back to America, a few months later, the ship was almost the same as the *Hansa*.

There was a pink piano. There was a Forest Festival, with hidden birds and toy guns and extravagant rich dishes. The captain was small and fat instead of lean and dourly tall, and was quite candid about liking to get drunk in the bar every night. There was evil, too.

Chexbres' mother was tired from so many weeks of trying to recapture what she remembered from fifty years before, and I think even she heard at last the undervoice of decadence and hysteria that was there among the Germans. Chexbres was like a cat, always watching, sharpening his claws.

By this time I felt no fear, nor even much disgust. I watched a beautiful girl fall into pieces in the seven days. I heard her cry out for love of me, and saw ten famous brewers on a Good Will tour to Milwaukee pour champagne between her breasts, and the next day take out their monocles and pose with steins for newsreels, with the Statue of Liberty for a background. I read English thrillers under my cherry-satin feather-puff, and drank quietly and perhaps more thoroughly than ever before with Chexbres, and ate of the familiar crazy "lunches" in a copy of the other restaurant on the *Hansa*.

But for the first time at sea my little fingers were hardly numb, except at the tips. I knew why. It was because I was so occupied with sorting my thoughts and making my plans that even the tides had not been able to affect me. I was almost *in absentia*, like a woman concentrating on bearing a child.

The world I had thought to go back to was gone. I knew it, and wondered how I could make Al know too, and help build another one.

Sea Change

1936

The next ship was a delightful one, a little Dutch passenger-freighter. Al and I boarded her at San Pedro, in 1936.

She stopped at fewer Central American ports than the *Feltre* had, but at the English end of the voyage we spent days in Liverpool and Southampton and London, and in Glasgow, where the stevedores seemed almost toothless, and ate like wolves at gray doughy meat-pastries wrapped in old newspaper. In Liverpool we sat in a bar-parlor by a fire, and I ate winkles off a pin.

The captain was a fine man. All his family for centuries had either taught or sailed, and he was a combination, so that he loved to give little lectures, always over a glass of Katz-gin and to an audience of one, about stars and ships and winds. He was a very brave man, too, and only a while ago I read of how he had taken a crippled ship into port, after a bombing. I hope to know his like again, or better yet, know him.

His ship was like a well-loved animal or woman, sensitive and intelligently grateful, the realest ship I ever knew.

There were several young Merchant Marine officers on board, getting their training. They ate in a different mess, and we seldom saw them. They were shy, polite, with pink cheeks, and looked longingly at me and two English girls from under their pale lashes.

The captain was firm with all three sets of us, passengers, crew, trainees: no mixing.

Al went a few times to the chief engineer's cabin; we exchanged paperbound thrillers with him. And occasionally we had a drink before dinner with him, the captain, the swarthy first mate, and the timid young doctor, who ate at a table together in our dining room.

There was one passenger, a sweet-faced old lady, who was something of a tosspot in her genteel way. She was newly widowed, a typical relic of that type of prosperous American business man who "protects" his little wife to the point of imbecility. Now, at sixty-seven or more, she was feeling the first titillations of freedom, which she naturally interpreted as grief.

She believed she was making a sad pilgrimage on the last ship she and her dear husband had sailed in, to keep his image fresh in what was left of her mind after fifty years with him, but as a matter of fact she blossomed like a weak but pretty old apple tree between San Pedro and the mouth of the Thames. She was spoiled and foolish and boring, but there was something truly heartening in her . . . one more proof that it takes a lot to kill the human spirit.

She loved to drink, on doctors' orders of course, and would sit for hours absorbing whiskey-and-soda and Al's talk. He was wonderful with her; he would start with palmistry, and without her knowing it end with *Das Kapital*.

The only thing she could not forgive either the captain or us was that we refused to play bridge with her. We compromised with cribbage, rummy, and cocktail parties, at which the few passengers who could or would drink anything sat in a stiff circle, their chairs buttoned to the oilcloth floor, while the old lady stood in the center like the dauntless DAR she was, and the whiskey in her glass tipped to the roll of the ship but never spilled. She was happy, convinced that her social poise and bravery in the face of personal grief was bringing some light into our lives. She was generous, and we drank well and ate the special canapés the chef always fixed for such chaste orgies.

They were, for the most part, hot meat croquettes, which someone had told him should be nibbled daintily from toothpicks at the cocktail hour. His were three or four inches long, and so heavy that the little wooden sticks bent like paper under them. They were hot as hell, and the outer crispness covered what was almost a soup inside . . . but we ate them somehow, knowing that Kris watched every bite we took, to report it to the proud chef.

Kris was the steward. He took care of our drinks, our wants on deck and in the big room with the piano, and our behavior. He was the crankiest man I have ever met. He was dreadfully bent with arthritis, so that until we grew used to him it was active pain for us as well as him to order a bottle of beer and have him shuffle along the deck with it.

He loathed the sea, and every time he got to Rotterdam he signed off, said goodbye to the captain, and took his earnings. Then he got soaking drunk, and signed on again, wherever the captain was. The two men had been together since the captain's first voyage, when Kris was already snarling, stiffening, almost middle-aged. The captain told us he had been thinking for several years that every voyage would be the last for Kris . . . the sea was bad for his pain.

For two weeks or so I was scared of him, as I always am of bad-tempered people. Then I got used to him, and finally I found myself liking him.

I think he felt a little the same way: first I was an annoyance, then I was simply neutral, and by the time we smelled Ireland he began to have a grumpy respect for me, so that he would pour my beer without a cuff, knowing I liked it that way, or gruffly mutter to me to watch off portside if I wanted to see a pretty ship in half an hour or so.

In the mornings he was in the greatest pain, and it was agony to watch him stand by his tray at eleven, handing hot soup to the passengers, with his fingers like twisted, knotty rope. When the days grew hot we had a sickly purplish kind of ice in the midmornings, too thin for sherbet but almost too stiff to drink. It was in water glasses, and it was sweet and oily. I don't know whether it was Dutch, or merely an inspiration of the chef's, like the dainty cocktail canapés. I never said anything about it, but whenever we had it Kris would bring me a glass especially full, and look at me from his small old eyes, almost grinning. I would thank him, and then grin too. It was his way of teasing me, to let me know he liked me.

I used to stay on deck, in my chair, very late at night when it was hot. Sometimes I would see him, far forward, prowling restlessly in bare feet. We never spoke . . . but the next day the captain would ask me carefully how I had slept, and I knew Kris had talked to him, just as he did if ever the English girls exchanged even a faint smile with any of the training men.

I don't remember much about the food, except that it was very different from the almost lavish cuisine of the other freighter we knew, the Italian one. It was dull, good, heavy food, but there were many vegetables and salads all the way to England. The coffee was fine, and this time we could afford to drink Dutch beer when we wanted it, and quite a lot of delicate Rhine wine.

The baker had a fight with the chef soon after we left port, and the barber took over all the pastry making . . . or so we heard. We had cake twice a day, in many different shapes but always the same. It was almost like cold omelet, as if it were made of hundreds of egg yolks stirred with a lot of sugar and a little flour and then baked. It was usually in thin solid pieces, like small bricks, elaborately topped with glacéed fruits and always served with flavored whipped cream.

We often had a thick green soup, in the colder seas, filled with cabbage and potatoes and leeks and always with slices of link-sausage floating in it.

And there was one unattractive but delicious thing, a kind of sludge of different vegetables flavored with ham, which the waiter called Udgie-pudgie. I finally saw on a menu that it was Hodgepodge. The captain said the crew loved it, and it was indeed good, in a simple crude way that might offend or bore sophisticated palates.

There were about twenty passengers. Aside from the awakening old widow, and the two giggling English girls who spent most of the time trying to get past Kris to the training quarters, I remember little about them. Three or four, or maybe more, were taking the long quiet voyage after serious illnesses, so that when they came to the dining room at all they were barricaded behind bottles of tonic, peptic powders, and laxatives.

One was an old schoolteacher, returning to Scotland on her pension. She was seasick constantly, and came on deck only once in all the five weeks, like a gaunt gray-faced bean-pole, with the elaborate and youthful clothes she had spent all her money on slapping wryly against her poor weak shanks.

The young doctor worried about her, and timidly asked me to see if when I was in her cabin she would not forget her queasiness long enough to swallow a little gruel or tea. She would struggle into a ridiculous shell-pink satin negligee puffy with cheap maribou . . . she had always wanted one, she told me, and *wouldn't* it just impress her relatives in Glasgow! . . . and we would talk and drink broth secretly reinforced with brandy and vitamins by the worried doctor. And then she would dash weakly for the bathroom, and I would try not to listen, and feel very queasy myself in sympathy.

It was useless. I told the doctor and the captain that perhaps the trip to Scotland, which she had saved and planned for during almost fifty years, was really the end of her life, and that now she was actually on her way she was trying to die rather than arrive there. They looked at me doubtfully, worriedly. The sea does strange things, they said.

When we got to Glasgow she was still alive. She looked like an ancient molting flamingo, standing on the dock with all her dour cousins. They hired a taxi, and as it drove off she looked back longingly at the little Dutch ship, and us waving. . . .

Define This Word

1936

I

That early spring I met a young servant in northern Burgundy who was almost fanatical about food, like a medieval woman possessed by the devil. Her obsession engulfed even my appreciation of the dishes she served, until I grew uncomfortable.

It was the off season at the old mill which a Parisian chef had bought and turned into one of France's most famous restaurants, and my mad waitress was the only servant. In spite of that she was neatly uniformed, and showed no surprise at my unannounced arrival and my hot dusty walking clothes.

She smiled discreetly at me, said, "Oh, but certainly!" when I asked if I could lunch there, and led me without more words to a dark bedroom bulging with First Empire furniture, and a new white bathroom.

When I went into the dining room it was empty of humans . . . a cheerful ugly room still showing traces of the petit-bourgeois parlor it had been. There were aspidistras on the mantel; several small white tables were laid with those imitation "peasant-ware" plates that one sees in Paris china stores, and very good crystal glasses; a cat folded under some ferns by the window ledge hardly looked at me; and the air was softly hurried with the sound of high waters from the stream outside.

I waited for the maid to come back. I knew I should eat well and slowly, and suddenly the idea of dry sherry, unknown in all the village bistros of the last few days, stung my throat smoothly. I tried not to think of it; it would be impossible to realize. Dubonnet would do. But not as well. I longed for sherry.

The little maid came into the silent room. I looked at her stocky young body, and her butter-colored hair, and noticed her odd pale voluptuous mouth before I said, "Mademoiselle, I shall drink an apéritif. Have you by any chance—"

"Let me suggest," she interrupted firmly, "our special dry sherry. It is chosen in Spain for Monsieur Paul."

And before I could agree she was gone, discreet and smooth.

She's a funny one, I thought, and waited in a pleasant warm tiredness for the wine.

It was good. I smiled approval at her, and she lowered her eyes, and then looked searchingly at me again. I realized suddenly that in this land of trained nonchalant waiters I was to be served by a small waitress who took her duties seriously. I felt much amused, and matched her solemn searching gaze.

"Today, Madame, you may eat shoulder of lamb in the English style, with baked potatoes, green beans, and a sweet."

My heart sank. I felt dismal, and hot and weary, and still grateful for the sherry.

But she was almost grinning at me, her lips curved triumphantly, and her eyes less palely blue.

"Oh, in *that* case a trout, of course—a *truite au bleu* as only Monsieur Paul can prepare it!"

She glanced hurriedly at my face, and hastened on. "With the trout, one or two young potatoes—oh, very delicately boiled," she added before I could protest, "very light."

I felt better. I agreed. "Perhaps a leaf or two of salad after the fish," I suggested. She almost snapped at me. "Of course, of course! And naturally our hors d'oeuvres to commence." She started away.

"No!" I called, feeling that I must assert myself now or be forever lost. "No!"

She turned back, and spoke to me very gently. "But Madame has never tasted our hors d'oeuvres. I am sure that Madame will be pleased. They are our specialty, made by Monsieur Paul himself. I am sure," and she looked reproachfully at me, her mouth tender and sad, "I am sure that Madame would be very much pleased."

I smiled weakly at her, and she left. A little cloud of hurt gentleness seemed to hang in the air where she had last stood.

I comforted myself with sherry, feeling increasing irritation with my own feeble self. Hell! I loathed hors d'oeuvres! I conjured disgusting visions of square glass plates of oily fish, of soggy vegetables glued together with cheap mayonnaise, or rank radishes and tasteless butter. No, Monsieur Paul or not, sad young pale-faced waitress or not, I hated hors d'oeuvres.

I glanced victoriously across the room at the cat, whose eyes seemed closed.

II

Several minutes passed. I was really very hungry.

The door banged open, and my girl came in again, less discreet this time. She hurried toward me.

"Madame, the wine! Before Monsieur Paul can go on—" Her eyes watched my face, which I perversely kept rather glum.

"I think," I said ponderously, daring her to interrupt me, "I think that today, since I am in Burgundy and about to eat a trout," and here I hoped she noticed that I did not mention hors d'oeuvres, "I think I shall drink a bottle of Chablis 1929—*not* Chablis Village 1929."

For a second her whole face blazed with joy, and then subsided into a trained mask. I knew that I had chosen well, had somehow satisfied her in a secret and incomprehensible way. She nodded politely and scuttled off, only for another second glancing impatiently at me as I called after her, "Well cooled, please, but not iced."

I'm a fool, I thought, to order a whole bottle. I'm a fool, here all alone and with more miles to walk before I reach Avallon and my fresh clothes and a bed. Then I smiled at myself and leaned back in my solid wide-seated chair, looking obliquely at the prints of Gibson girls, English tavern scenes, and hideous countrysides that hung on the papered walls. The room was warm; I could hear my companion cat purring under the ferns.

The girl rushed in, with flat baking dishes piled up her arms on napkins, like the plates of a Japanese juggler. She slid them off neatly in two rows on the table, where they lay steaming up at me, darkly and infinitely appetizing.

"*Mon Dieu!* All for me?" I peered at her. She nodded, her discretion quite gone now and a look of ecstatic worry on her pale face and eyes and lips.

There were at least eight dishes. I felt almost embarrassed, and sat for a minute looking weakly at the fork and spoon in my hand.

"Perhaps Madame would care to start with the pickled herring? It is not like any other. Monsieur Paul prepares it himself, in his own vinegar and wines. It is very good."

I dug out two or three brown filets from the dish, and tasted. They were truly unlike any others, truly the best I had ever eaten, mild, pungent, meaty as fresh nuts.

I realized the maid had stopped breathing, and looked up at her. She was watching me, or rather a gastronomic X-ray of the herring inside me, with a hypnotized glaze in her eyes.

"Madame is pleased?" she whispered softly.

I said I was. She sighed, and pushed a sizzling plate of broiled endive toward me, and disappeared.

I had put a few dull green lentils on my plate, lentils scattered with minced fresh herbs and probably marinated in tarragon vinegar and walnut oil, when she came into the dining room again with the bottle of Chablis in a wine basket.

"Madame should be eating the little baked onions while they are hot," she remarked over her shoulder as she held the bottle in a napkin and uncorked it. I obeyed meekly, and while I watched her I ate several more than I had meant to. They were delicious, simmered first in strong meat broth, I think, and then drained and broiled with olive oil and new-ground pepper.

I was fascinated by her method of uncorking a vintage wine. Instead of the Burgundian procedure of infinite and often exaggerated precautions against touching or tipping or jarring the bottle, she handled it quite nonchalantly, and seemed to be careful only to keep her hands from the cool bottle itself, holding it sometimes by the basket and sometimes in a napkin. The cork was very tight, and I thought for a minute that she would break it. So did she; her face grew tense, and did not loosen until she had slowly worked out the cork and wiped the lip. Then she poured an inch of wine in a glass, turned her back to me like a priest taking Communion, and drank it down. Finally some was poured for me, and she stood with the bottle in her hand and her full lips drooping until I nodded a satisfied yes. Then she pushed another of the plates toward me, and almost rushed from the room.

I ate slowly, knowing that I should not be as hungry as I ought to be for the trout, but knowing too that I had never tasted such delicate savory morsels. Some were hot, some cold. The wine was light and cool. The room, warm and agreeably empty under the rushing sound of the stream, became smaller as I grew used to it.

My girl hurried in again, with another row of plates up one arm, and a large bucket dragging at the other. She slid the plates deftly on to the table, and drew a deep breath as she let the bucket down against the table leg.

"Your trout, Madame," she said excitedly. I looked down at the gleam of the fish curving through its limited water. "But first a good slice of Monsieur Paul's pâté. Oh yes, oh yes, you will be very sorry if you miss this. It is rich, but appetizing, and not at all too heavy. Just this one morsel!"

And willy-nilly I accepted the large gouge she dug from a terrine. I prayed for ten normal appetites and thought with amused nostalgia of my usual lunch of cold milk and fruit as I broke off a crust of bread and patted it smooth with the paste. Then I forgot everything but the exciting faint decadent flavor in my mouth.

I beamed up at the girl. She nodded, but from habit asked if I was satisfied. I beamed again, and asked, simply to please her, "Is there not a faint hint of *marc*, or perhaps cognac?"

"*Marc*, Madame!" And she awarded me the proud look of a teacher whose pupil has showed unexpected intelligence. "Monsieur Paul, after he has taken equal parts of goose breast and the finest pork, and broken a certain number of egg yolks into them, and ground them *very*, very fine, cooks all with seasoning for some three hours. *But*," she pushed her face nearer, and looked with ferocious gloating at the pâté inside me, her eyes like X-rays, "he never stops stirring it! Figure to yourself the work of it—stir, stir, never stopping!

"Then he grinds in a suspicion of nutmeg, and then adds, very thoroughly, a glass of *marc* for each hundred grams of pâté. And is Madame not pleased?"

Again I agreed, rather timidly, that Madame was much pleased, that Madame had never, indeed, tasted such an unctuous and exciting pâté. The girl wet her lips delicately, and then started as if she had been pin-stuck.

"But the trout! My God, the trout!" She grabbed the bucket, and her voice grew higher and more rushed.

"Here is the trout, Madame. You are to eat it *au bleu*, and you should never do so if you had not seen it alive. For if the trout were dead when it was plunged into the *court bouillon* it would not turn blue. So, naturally, it must be living."

I knew all this, more or less, but I was fascinated by her absorption in the momentary problem. I felt quite ignorant, and asked her with sincerity, "What about the trout? Do you take out its guts before or after?"

"Oh, the trout!" She sounded scornful. "Any trout is glad, truly glad, to be prepared by Monsieur Paul. His little gills are pinched, with one flash of the knife he is empty, and then he curls in agony in the *bouillon* and all is over. And it is the curl you must judge, Madame. A false *truite au bleu* cannot curl."

She panted triumph at me, and hurried out with the bucket.

III

She *is* a funny one, I thought, and for not more than two or three minutes I drank wine and mused over her. Then she darted in, with the trout correctly blue and agonizingly curled on a platter, and on her crooked arm a plate of tiny boiled potatoes and a bowl.

When I had been served and had cut off her anxious breathings with an assurance that the fish was the best I had ever tasted, she peered again at me and at the sauce in the bowl. I obediently put some of it on the potatoes: no fool I, to ruin *truite au bleu* with a hot concoction! There was more silence.

"Ah!" she sighed at last. "I knew Madame would feel thus! Is it not the most beautiful sauce in the world with the flesh of a trout?"

I nodded incredulous agreement.

"Would you like to know how it is done?"

I remembered all the legends of chefs who guarded favorite recipes with their very lives, and murmured yes.

She wore the exalted look of a believer describing a miracle at Lourdes as she told me, in a rush, how Monsieur Paul threw chopped chives into hot sweet butter and then poured the butter off, how he added another nut of butter and a tablespoonful of thick cream for each person, stirred the mixture for a few minutes over a slow fire, and then rushed it to the table.

"So simple?" I asked softly, watching her lighted eyes and the tender lustful lines of her strange mouth.

"So simple, Madame! But," she shrugged, "you know, with a master—"

I was relieved to see her go; such avid interest in my eating wore on me. I felt released when the door closed behind her, free for a minute or so from her victimization. What would she have done, I wondered, if I had been ignorant or unconscious of any fine flavors?

She was right, though, about Monsieur Paul. Only a master could live in this isolated mill and preserve his gastronomic dignity through loneliness and the sure financial loss of unused butter and addled eggs. Of course, there was the stream for his fish, and I knew his pâtés would grow even more edible with age; but how could he manage to have a thing like roasted lamb ready for any chance patron? Was the consuming interest of his one maid enough fuel for his flame?

I tasted the last sweet nugget of trout, the one nearest the blued tail, and poked somnolently at the minute white billiard balls that had been eyes. Fate could not harm me, I remembered winily, for I had indeed dined today, and dined well. Now for a leaf of crisp salad, and I'd be on my way.

The girl slid into the room. She asked me again, in a respectful but gossipy manner, how I had liked this and that and the other things, and then talked on as she mixed dressing for the endive.

"And now," she announced, after I had eaten one green sprig and dutifully pronounced it excellent, "now Madame is going to taste Monsieur Paul's special terrine, one that is not even on the summer menu, when a hundred covers are laid here daily and we have a headwaiter and a wine waiter, and cabinet ministers telegraph for tables! Madame will be pleased."

And heedless of my low moans of the walk still before me, of my appreciation and my unhappily human and limited capacity, she cut a thick heady slice from the terrine of meat and stood over me while I ate it, telling me with almost hysterical pleasure of the wild ducks, the spices, the wines that went into it. Even surfeit could not make me deny that it was a rare dish. I ate it all, knowing my luck, and wishing only that I had red wine to drink with it.

I was beginning, though, to feel almost frightened, realizing myself an accidental victim of these stranded gourmets, Monsieur Paul and his handmaiden. I began to feel that they were using me for a safety valve, much as a thwarted woman relieves herself with tantrums or a fit of weeping. I was serving a purpose, and perhaps a noble one, but I resented it in a way approaching panic.

I protested only to myself when one of Monsieur Paul's special cheeses was cut for me, and ate it doggedly, like a slave. When the girl said that Monsieur Paul himself was preparing a special filter of coffee for me, I smiled servile acceptance; wine and the weight of food and my own character could not force me to argue with maniacs. When, before the coffee came, Monsieur Paul presented me, through his idolater, with the most beautiful apple tart I had ever seen, I allowed it to be cut and served to me. Not a wince or a murmur showed the waitress my distressed fearfulness. With a stuffed careful smile on my face, and a clear nightmare in my head of trussed wanderers prepared for his altar by this hermit-priest of gastronomy, I listened to the girl's passionate plea for fresh pastry dough.

"You cannot, you *cannot*, Madame, serve old pastry!" She seemed ready to beat her breast as she leaned across the table. "Look at that delicate crust! You may feel that you have eaten too much." (I nodded idiotic agreement.) "But this pastry is like feathers—it is like snow. It is in fact good for you, a digestive! And why?" She glared sternly at me. "Because Monsieur Paul did not even open the flour bin until he saw you coming! He could not, he *could* not have baked you one of his special apple tarts with old dough!"

She laughed, tossing her head and curling her mouth voluptuously.

IV

Somehow I managed to refuse a second slice, but I trembled under her surmise that I was ready for my special filter.

The wine and the fortitude had fled me, and I drank the hot coffee as a suffering man gulps ether, deeply and gratefully.

I remember, then, chatting with surprising glibness, and sending to Monsieur Paul flowery compliments, all of them sincere and well won, and I remember feeling only amusement when a vast glass of *marc* appeared before me and then gradually disappeared, like the light in the warm room full of water-sounds. I felt surprise to be alive still, and suddenly very grateful to the wild-lipped waitress, as if her presence had sustained me through duress. We discussed food and wine. I wondered bemusedly why I had been frightened.

The *marc* was gone. I went into the crowded bedroom for my jacket. She met me in the darkening hall when I came out, and I paid my bill, a large one. I started to thank her, but she took my hand, drew me into the dining room, and without words poured more spirits into my glass. I drank to Monsieur Paul while she watched me intently, her pale eyes bulging in the dimness and her lips pressed inward as if she too tasted the hot, aged *marc*.

The cat rose from his ferny bed, and walked contemptuously out of the room.

Suddenly the girl began to laugh, in a soft shy breathless way, and came close to me.

"Permit me!" she said, and I thought she was going to kiss me. But instead she pinned a tiny bunch of snowdrops and dark bruised cyclamens against my stiff jacket, very quickly and deftly, and then ran from the room with her head down.

I waited for a minute. No sounds came from anywhere in the old mill, but the endless rushing of the full stream seemed to strengthen, like the timid blare of an orchestra under a falling curtain.

She's a *funny* one, I thought. I touched the cool blossoms on my coat and went out, like a ghost from ruins, across the courtyard toward the dim road to Avallon.

The Measure
of My Powers

1936–1939

I

Un pâquis, the French dictionary says, is a grazing ground or pasture. But when we bought our home in Switzerland, and found that it had been called Le Pâquis for several centuries by all the country people near it, we knew that it meant much more than "pasture" to them. The word had a tenderness to it, like the diminutive given to a child or a pretty girl, like the difference between *lambkin* and *lamb*.

One reason our Pâquis had this special meaning was that it was almost the only piece of land in all the abrupt terraced steeps of the wine coast between Lausanne and Vevey that did not have grapes on it.

Instead, it was a sloping green meadow, held high in the air above the Lac Léman by stone walls. A brook ran through it under pollarded willows, and old trees of pears and plums and apples bent away from the pushings of the lake winds. The ancient soil was covered with a dazzling coat always, low and filled with violets and primulas and crocuses in the spring, waist-high with such flowers in summer as I have only seen like shadows in real gardens.

They would be delicate in the beginning of the year . . . blue hepaticas along the icy brook, and all the tender yellow things. And then as the summer came and the time for harvesting, the colors grew more intense, more violent, until finally the wild asters bloomed, *les vendangeuses*, the flowers that meant all the village girls must go into the vineyards again to cut the grapes.

Three times every summer the man across the road reaped our hay, while we could not bear to look . . . and then in a week or so the flowers were back again, pushing and growing and covering all the short grass with a new loveliness, while the fruits ripened and the little brook ran busily.

There was a fountain, too, near the road by the stone house. It had been there for longer than even the Federal maps showed, and people walking up the long pull from lake level knew it as well as they knew their mothers, and stopped always to drink and rest their backs from the pointed woven baskets they wore. Even after we came, and planted more trees and added rooms to the house, they continued to stop at the fountain, and that made us feel better than almost anything else.

And all those things . . . the fresh spouting water, the little brook under the willows, the old rich bending trees, the grass so full of life there on the terraced wine-slopes laced by a thousand tiny vineyards . . . they were why when the peasants said Le Pâquis they meant The Dear Little Meadow, or The Sweet Cool Resting Place, or something like that but more so.

II

We started a garden before the ground thawed, while the Italian masons burned their fingers on the cold stones for the new part of the house. We had to make all the beds in small terraces; hard work in the beginning, but wonderful to work in later, when the paths were set and the little patches lay almost waist-high waiting to be cared for. As soon as we could we planted, while we kept on building walls and cultivating the rich loam, and by the time my father and mother came to see us, at our apartment down on the Market Square in Vevey because the house was not yet ready, the peas were ripe, and the evenings were softly warm.

We would go up the hills from town after the workingmen had left, and spread our supper cloth on a table under the terrace apple tree, among all the last rubble of the building. As fast as Father and Chexbres could pick the peas, Mother and I would shell them, and then on a little fire of shavings I'd cook them perhaps four or five minutes in a heavy casserole, swirling them in butter and their own steam. We'd eat them with little cold pullets cooked for us in Vevey, and good bread and the thin white wine of the coast that lay about us.

The evening breeze would freshen across the long sweep of the lake, and as the Savoy Alps blackened above the water, and it turned to flat pewter over the edge of the terrace, the first summer lights of Evian far down toward Geneva winked red at us. It was always hard to leave. We'd put our things silently into the baskets, and then drive with the top of the car lowered along the narrow walled roads of the Corniche, until we came to a village where we could sit again on a terrace and drink bitter coffee in the darkness.

Chexbres was a fine gardener; he read books and liked to experiment with new ways of doing things, but besides all that he had the feeling of growth and fertility and the seasons in his bones and his flesh. I learned all the time from him, and we worked together two summers in Le Pâquis.

The peasants of our village, and all the vineyardists, thought we were crazy not to leave such work for hired gardeners, gardeners who *knew*. They used to lean over the walls watching us, occasionally calling suggestions, and it embarrassed us when oftener than not we did things as they had never before been done there in that district, and got much better results for less effort in less space. That seemed almost like cheating, when we were newcomers and foreigners too . . . but why should we put in fifty tomato plants with elaborate stakes, as our neighbors told us to do, when we could get as much fruit from ten plants put in the way we thought best? Chexbres studied the winds, the soil, the way the rains came, and he knew more about how to grow things than the peasants could have learned in a thousand years, in spite of their cruel toiling. He felt truly apologetic about it.

Our garden grew and grew, and we went almost every day up the hill to the sanatorium for poor children with the back of our little green Fiat filled with fresh things to eat.

I canned often, too. We had three cellars, and I filled one of them with beautiful gleaming jars for the winter. It was simple enough to do it in little bits instead of in great harried rushes as my grandmother used to, and when I went down into the coolness and saw all the things sitting there so richly quiet on the shelves, I had a special feeling of contentment. It was a reassurance of safety against hunger, very primitive and satisfying.

I canned tomatoes and beans and vegetable juices, and many kinds of pickles and catsups more for the fun than because we wanted them, and plums and peaches and all the fruits. I made a few jams, for company, and several big jars of brandied things. I was lucky; nothing spoiled, everything was good.

When we left, before the war came, it was hard to give up all the bottles of liqueurs and *eaux-de-vie*, not yet ripe enough to taste, harder than anything except the bottles in the wine cellar, some still resting from their trips from Burgundy, and all our own wine made from the little yellow grapes of our vineyard for the two years past. . . .

In spite of the full shelves in the cellar, though, and our trips up the hill for the children and the baskets we took to friends in Vevey whenever we could stop gardening long enough to go down there, things grew too fast for us. It was the oldest soil either of us had ever touched, and it seemed almost bursting with life, just as it was alive with insects and little creatures and a hundred kinds of worms waiting to eat what grew in it. We ran a kind of race with it, exciting and exhausting.

One time Chexbres put down his hoe and said loudly, "By God, I'll not be dictated to! I'll show you who's boss!" He was talking to the earth, and like a dutiful wife I followed him up past the violently fertile terraces to the house, and listened while he telephoned to the Casino at Evian and reserved a table in the main dining room and ordered an astonishing meal and the wines for it.

I despaired somewhat in dressing: my nails were rough and stained, and I was too thin and much too brown for the dress I wanted to wear, and high heels felt strange on my feet.

But by the time we had driven over the Haute Corniche to Lausanne, right into the setting sun, and had sat at a little deck table on the way to Evian, wrapped in the kind of sleepy silence that those lake-boats always had for us, I felt more beautiful than possible, and knew that Chexbres in his white dinner coat and his white top-knot was that way too. The maître d'hôtel and the barman and the sommelier agreed, when we got to the Casino, and it was a decadent delightful night.

But when we drove into Le Pâquis in the first shy sunlight, we shed our city clothes and bathed and put on dungarees again, and hurried down into the garden. We had been away too long.

We grew beautiful salads, a dozen different kinds, and several herbs. There were shallots and onion and garlic, and I braided them into long silky ropes, and hung them over the rafters in the attic. In one of the cellars we stored cabbages and apples and tomatoes and other things on slatted shelves, or in bins. And all the time we ate what we were growing.

The local cuisine was heavy, a wintery diet influenced by the many German-Swiss who lived near by. I talked more with the Italian-Swiss, and learned ways of cooking vegetables in their own juices, with sweet butter or thick olive oil to encourage them a little: tomatoes and onions and sweet peppers and eggplants, and all the summer things. And Chexbres could fry tomatoes the way his family cook Madie did, in Delaware, so that the slices were dark brown and crisp all through, and yet delicate and tender. Sometimes we made corn oysters. We'd sit right by the stove, and lift the shaggy little cakes from the hot butter to our plates, and float them down with beer chilled in the fountain.

(The corn we brought from America, and except for young cow-corn eaten by a few hardy peasants near Zurich, it was the only such thing for humans in all Switzerland, I think. The passing country people watched it curiously, and so did we, because it behaved as if it knew itself to be in alien lands, helpless before strange winds and stranger weather, and sent out a dozen crazy tassels for every ear, to be sure of survival. The next year it was less hysterical, and several neighbors planted it from our seed, and ate it from our recipes.)

III

The part of the house we added to the little stone building was, I suppose, quite impractical for anyone but us. It disturbed and shocked the architect and all the contractors for floor and plumbing and such, because it was designed so that we, the owners of the place, could be its cooks and servants. That was not becoming to our station. We got what we wanted, though, and the kitchen and pantry were part of the living room . . . up and down a few steps, around a corner or two . . . so that music and talk and fine smells moved at liberty from one part to another.

It was fun to invite Swiss people there for meals; they were baffled and titillated. Once in the winter, I remember, some oddly mixed expatriates and French-Swiss friends came from Montreux. They knew us only in restaurants and as dancing partners and such until then, because we were too content alone at Le Pâquis to invite many others there, and they were frankly curious about the house and the way we lived, so different from anything they knew.

Because it was winter and the dormant garden gave us leisure, Chexbres and I had made everything ready long before they came. After conventional canapés . . . for the conventional people we knew our guests to be, so that they would not be alarmed at the start . . . we planned to let them serve themselves in the kitchen from a large pot of really masterful stew, and a big salad, and a basket of crisp rolls made up in the village that afternoon. Then there was to be a chilled bowl of pears baked in a way I'd evolved, with honey and kirsch, and served with sour cream.

In the kitchen there was only the casserole on top of the stove, while the salad chilled in the cellar with the dessert, and the rolls waited warmly in a napkined basket out of sight. Plates and silver tools looked like part of a pattern on the old dresser. The ventilator whirred almost silently, and in the wide deep windows my ferns moved a little. There were pictures on the walls, and cookbooks mixed with pewter plates on the open shelves, and it was indeed a deceptive place to be called a kitchen in the average vocabulary.

When the people came they exclaimed as everyone did at the first sight of the big living room, with the windows looking over the terrace and the far lake into another land. Then, almost frightened by the distance of their vision, they came down near the fireplace, and comforted themselves with its warmth and the reassurance of the drinks waiting for them on the long oak table.

In many polite ways they began to ask about the house: was it true we had no servants living with us, and only part-time help from the village? But how . . . but what . . . ?

They began to look alarmed, thinking of the long cold drive from Montreux to this strange place without a dining room, without a cook and a maid or two. And when they wandered up the stairs into what they could only guess to be a kind of stage-kitchen, and they saw no signs and smelled no smells of supper, their faces were long and dismal under all the politeness.

Chexbres and I let them suffer until we thought the alcoholic intake was fairly well adjusted to their twelve or fifteen rather jaded bodies. Then, with the smug skill of two magicians, we flicked away the empty glasses and the tired canapés, and slid the salad and the rolls into place on the old dresser. He gave the *ragoût* a few odorous stirs while I saw that little tables in the living room were clear of ashtrays and such . . . and the puzzled hungry people, almost tittering with relief and excitement, flocked like children into the kitchen for their suppers.

They ate and ate, and talked as they had not dared talk for too many years, and laughed a great deal.

There was an old Swiss judge, important as God to himself and his small community, who drank a special little toast to his fat wife, and said without any importance at all in his suddenly human voice, "Anneli, my dear, I had forgotten I could have such an agreeable evening with you in the room." She lifted her glass to his with great dignity, knowing what he meant after so many years of provincial respectability.

Monsieur Kugner, who owned the kind of small luxurious hotel in Montreux that always had at least two Eastern princes in it, and a handful of the kind of pre-war munitions magnates who traveled with personal chefs as well as valets and chauffeurs and secretaries, tucked his napkin under his chin and murmured, "*Ça alors! Formidable!*"

Several times during the evening he took Chexbres or me aside, and asked who our cook was. He refused, quite candidly and politely, to believe that I had made the stew, just as he refused to accept my recipe for it; he was convinced that in our pride we were hiding a famous chef somewhere in the cellars. It was a little embarrassing, but funny, to think of our being able to afford a hidden cook at all, and then to be accused of guarding him so jealously that we even faked recipes for him.

The stew itself was good, but the reason it seemed so *formidable* to poor Kugner was because for most of the years of his life he had been eating in luxury hotels. He was so sated by their uniform excellence, and by the obsequious waiters, the silver-covered dishes, the smooth linen, that when he could eat an honest stew from an old soup plate with a spoon, he thought it was ambrosial.

He thought, "Why not hire the chef who made this, and let him serve it to me whenever I command it? There is undoubtedly some special secret about it, because I who have not been really hungry for forty years am now going to that ridiculous sham-kitchen for a third plateful. Therefore I could charge a great deal . . . have it made on order for my favored guests. . . ."

If Monsieur Kugner had not felt so well, in the warmth and talk and pleasantness that evening, he would have been more than haughty at our stubborn selfish way of lying to him! As it was, he laughed and even sang a little, very pink at first above his pointed beard and then forgetting his dignity entirely to buzz out five long verses of a Romanche ballad he assured us was unprintable. When someone suggested writing an open letter to one American who was too ill to come, he slapped the table as he had probably not done since he was an apprentice at the Paris Ritz, and was the first to sign the long piece of paper I mailed the next morning to our bedridden compatriot (who, Chexbres and I knew all the time, was indeed in bed, but not alone and certainly not in need of hot bottles, liniments, or our sympathies to keep him warm).

"Dear Mr. Courtney," Kugner wrote, in the English we had decided would be most cheering to a sick Texan. "We are sitting so comfortable by a beautiful American cheminée fire, by Lager beer, thinking of you and take a big mouth full. L. Kugner."

"Dear Friend" . . . "My dear old chap" . . . "Hello" . . . the other notes were none too interesting, until the last one, written by a fading Danish countess, a fabulous flirt in the days when Montreux was a giddy little town full of gamblers and royalty. She had stayed on after all the others left, because her husband was there in a private insane asylum. She always had lovers, attracted by her enormous income and her great reputation for wifely devotion. And she was a gay charming creature, as well.

"Dearest Court," she wrote, "If you believe or not . . . we give a damn, but we thought more on you as you probably believe. Every think we took . . . thinking on poor old Court . . . enjoying the food, so sorry that Court can't taste. It is rested two inches below the heart a pear with kirsch, so take my love. Eva."

Yes, the suppers by the American *cheminée* were nice, now and then, but in the summer it was really better. When the terrace was too cool or breezy we set a long table in the living room in front of the open French windows, and if the lake seemed too wide, the Alps too high, we could look into the great mirror opposite and make them more remote, less questioning of us.

In the summer there were always a lot of people; Vevey was on the road to almost any place in Europe, and Le Pâquis was such a *pleasant* little stop, everybody said. Sometimes Chexbres and I wanted to run away . . . but we were proud of where we lived, and like many hospitable people we were somewhat smug about being so. Sometimes there were complications, political, national, religious, even racial, but in general we managed to segregate the more violent prejudices. Only once did Chexbres have to take three men who were on their way to join the Spanish Loyalists to Cully for filets of perch while I served supper at Le Pâquis to several charming but rabid Fascists from Rome, one of them a priest and all of them convinced that Communists were their personal as well as national enemies.

And once we were sitting on the terrace drinking sherry before a rather elaborate dinner, all of us dressed in our best bibs in honor of an old English lady who had arrived trailing chiffon, diamonds, and monkey fur, when down the path from the road came the clanking of a cowbell, and behind it the great hulk of a Princeton halfback.

He had walked and hitchhiked that day from the French Alps, and he was burned magenta-red and wore nothing but shoes, slacks, and the cowbell around his neck. There was nothing in the house big enough to cover his shoulders except a blue and white striped milking jacket from Fribourg, the kind with silver buttons and embroidered edelweis and little puffed short sleeves. We stuffed Princeton into it somehow, after a quick shower, and sat him next to the dowager at dinner.

At first she was frankly scared of him, and looked at him sideways. The two people down from the village to serve dinner were timid too, and held dishes precariously on the very ends of their hands when they got near the boy. Chexbres and I despaired.

But Princeton was such a kind simple person, and the dowager was in her own way so much simpler even than he, that halfway through the second course she was beaming at him and shrieking to all of us, as if he could not understand her, "But *listen* to him! He's *amazing*! Poor poor lad . . . he's *hungry*!"

He was indeed, and thanks to his unannounced arrival there was less leeway than I'd planned on, so that when he said to me, in a slow benevolent drawl that could not possibly offend, "The trouble with this piece of meat, ma'am, is that it's too small," I felt only gratitude to have the old Englishwoman plop the rest of her course onto his plate.

It was probably the most unconventional thing she had ever done in her life, and her son looked at me as if he had just seen one of the family Romneys thumb its nose.

I nodded solemnly to him. He needed reassurance: the night was young, and before it was over he was going to sit calmly by while his mother, in one of the most abrupt and vivid little love affairs I've ever watched, put a big white daisy behind Princeton's ear and watched him do the Lambeth Walk for her, and then patted his enormous red arm in its silly little puffed sleeve when he said solemnly to all of us, "Gee, I *like* this old lady!" We did too.

Once, that same year, we had a queer dreamlike dinner, and a sad one too, in a muted wordless way.

My brother David was there, resting after a summer course at the University of Dijon which he had managed somehow to follow from the fairly distant beaches of Cannes and Monte Carlo. His fatigue was understandable, but it melted like mist in the sun when he learned that his favorite prom-date was in Geneva, and from then on he spent most of his time catching and riding on trains to see her. Finally, in order to see something of him before summer ended and his boat sailed for America, I suggested that he invite her to Le Pâquis for a day.

He seemed pleased, in a casual way. Perhaps inside he was nervous, wary, as I would have been at his age to bring a stranger before the eyes of my family, but it did not show. Le Pâquis was full then . . . Chexbres' sister Anne, my sister Norah, three or four friends . . . and all of us loved David and were curious in our various ways about any girl who was more attractive to him than our combined company. She was the first woman any of us had seen him with, in the real male-female way, and suddenly he seemed even younger than he was, and terribly vulnerable. We tried to keep from watching, from listening for false tones, from protecting with our older tact and knowledge and jealousy.

The girl was a very pretty pale limp one. She was about seventeen, I suppose, and world-weary the way children that age are often caricatured or satirized as being. It comes from a great shyness, and I knew it, and tried not to feel any mockery or amusement or pure exasperation at her manners.

She drooped everywhere, her eyelids, her little pink mouth, her slender shoulders. She murmured occasionally in an exhausted way, but never anything more than Yes or No, and never turned her head or even her eyes toward anyone else who talked. That was disconcerting; we all talked a lot that summer, and sometimes quite well.

She smoked one cigaret from another, and whenever it was time for a new one she did not reach for it or even ask for it, but instead let her smooth white arm drop slowly along the chair or the table toward David. Then she would let her fingers uncurl one by one, and he would watch like a hypnotized hen, so that there was almost a balloon above his head, funny-paper style, with the words in it, "Her tiny hand is like a flower, like an unfolding lily bud . . ." It was ghastly.

She came after lunch, and by teatime we were all of us so nervous, waiting for that precocious sensual thing to happen again, that we did not dare look at one another. We felt hysterical, and deeply embarrassed in a queer personal way that was mixed up with loyalty to David. And there was nothing to do about it: he was a hopelessly gone gosling; his nimble tongue was tied; his quick flashing mind was full of smoke.

In desperation we all went up back of the vineyards to a little bowling alley in a mountain meadow. The late summer sun slanted across the piney slopes, and the air was full of fragrance, and the click of the ancient hand-turned balls made an easy music. A big farm woman brought us tea and bread, and pots of wild green honey. It was one of the most idyllic moments I have ever known, very sharp, like a Breughel painting.

But the little blonde girl did not make a part of any of it. The game was too much for her, and the food was boring. She drooped wearily against the long crude table beside the alley, and whenever David seemed for a minute to forget her, she let her hand fall slowly toward him, let her soft pink fingers uncurl. It was wordless, and it was like the crack of a whip. He would drop anything . . . his bread and honey, the pins he was setting up, and come dazedly to watch her lift the fresh cigaret to her mouth and wait for him to light it.

Back at Le Pâquis we all bathed and dressed. By that time we were meeting one another secretively in rooms and hallways, whispering like conspirators. "Isn't it awful?" we'd hiss despairingly. "But we *mustn't* let David know. Poor David! We mustn't let him see what we think!"

We felt that we were betraying him, in a way, to be so consummately bored and annoyed by the girl he seemed to worship; we felt we must protect him from our own betrayal.

We all met as usual on the terrace for sherry. David's girl never drank sherry, he interpreted for us when she languidly shook her head at the glass Chexbres gave her. Apparently there was nothing in our cellar, which was a fairly interesting one at that time, that appealed to her, and we felt definite relief when she dragged herself to her feet, took David's arm, and broke all our habits of pre-dinner behavior by leading him off toward the orchard. She looked like a delicate drifting moonbeam in her long skirt, with her gold hair blowing long about her throat . . . and I felt as if her lily-hand on David's arm weighed five thousand pounds.

We could at least talk with the two of them gone; her weary murmurs and her dead drooping face stopped our mouths . . . from anything, that is, except words we would not say because we loved David. We sat happily with our sherry, and chattered in an easy peaceful way, while we watched the lake darken far below us.

Once from the garden we heard the girl say clearly, in the clipped flat drawl that was a badge of her expensive school, "*Who* did you say these people are, darling? I suppose I'll have to send a thank-you note. . . ."

"*Well!*" Chexbres' sister sounded crosser than I thought possible, and Norah remarked casually to me, "She can talk, after all. Maybe you'd better write out your name, with Hostess after it . . . pin it on your shoulder . . . it would be a pity to have her keep all that on her mind."

It seemed very funny, suddenly, and we had a little more sherry and let ourselves simmer in a kind of irritated merriment.

I was proud of the dinner. I had spent a lot of thought on it, because even before I saw the girl I felt an exaggerated loyalty to David, a kind of pity for the ordeal he might possibly be going through to bring her there to Le Pâquis before our curious inspection.

First we drank a delicate broth made of chicken stock and white wine and fresh tomato juice, the three iced and mixed together just before we sat down. Then there were little hot cheese tarts, made in Vevey that afternoon. With them we drank a three-year-old Faverges from the vineyard across the road, a high thin white wine like all those of the coast we lived on. Then there was a tray of cold roast pigeons lying on a bed of herbs from our garden, and a big earthen tureen of all the small summer vegetables we could find, cooked whole and separately and then tossed together with sweet butter. There was bread, fresh and crusty.

And we drank one of our best wines, a Corton 1929 sent from the Château for a present the year before. It was beautiful with the strong simple food. We all raised our glasses before the first sip, and then for a few seconds we could but stay silent, with its taste under our tongues. I looked down the long table through the candlelight and saw Chexbres, and all was well with me.

The little blonde girl smiled patiently at him now and then, but even he, charmer of all women, could not rouse her to more than an occasional murmur of response to his calculated nonsense. She smoked all during the meal, which none of us was doing, and once when she let her pretty arm fall toward Chexbres and the fingers unfold commandingly, I saw him pick up the cigaret box and offer it to her, so that she had to lift her hand again and choose one for herself, and I knew that he was deeply angry with her, in spite of his wisdom and his tolerance.

The rest of us were disjointing our little brown birds and eating them in our fingers, as is only proper on a summer night among friends in a friendly room. But the girl cut one little piece off one side of the breast, one little piece off the other, and then pushed the plump carcass almost fretfully away. She picked a few late-summer peas from the vegetables on her plate, and ate a little bread, and then asked Chexbres for coffee.

I saw him disappear into the pantry, where François, the village gravedigger and our self-appointed chaperon-houseman, was standing guard over hot plates and such for us, and in a few minutes she had a cup, made with a little filter because the big pot was still at work on what we planned to drink later. Chexbres raised his wine reassuringly to me, and I looked at David, to see whether his girl's supine disdain of all our ways, and of me as her hostess, and of most of the rules of so-called polite behavior, had hurt him.

But he seemed oblivious of any lack in the perfection of his own young world, content to leave his love to Chexbres' attentions while he bent adoringly toward Chexbres' sister. She too was tiny, and golden-haired . . . but she had the gem-like vigor of a humming bird about her, and her mind flashed in the same otherworldly light, so that I felt proud whenever I saw her with David, because of his good fortune.

All of us were recovering, too, from the first numbing effect of the girl. We found it easier to talk, to brush past her stony lethargy. The wines lay lightly in us, and sent fine vapors high into our palates and our brains, so that our conversation was perhaps almost as delightful as it seemed then. We ate fruits that had lain all day on ice in their blended juices and Tokay, and little crisp *gaufrettes* baked in the village by François' witch-like mother. The candles flickered, and cast the same transient lovely shadows on our faces as what we said did on my mind while I listened.

I saw the girl look, with her eyes almost open this time, at David as he bent away from her toward the other little blonde woman, the one so vital, so different. Then, as if she had a plan, she smiled faintly before she lowered the heavy lids over her beautiful flat blue eyes, and let her arm fall slowly again toward Chexbres. Again he offered her the whole box of cigarets, so that she had to pick up one herself. "Stuffy Old Uncle," I thought with amusement, "Peppery Old Colonel. . . ."

We were talking about swimming then, and drinking coffee at the table because it was too pleasant to leave, even for the terrace. Suddenly the girl spoke. Except for once in the garden, it was the first time any of us had heard her real voice, and we turned to watch her, almost shocked.

"Oh, yes," she was saying in a high deliberate way to Chexbres, "I adore swimming." Then she turned to look full at David, and I knew that in some way she was going to give back the hurt he had dealt her with his casual forgetfulness. "Didn't I tell you . . . don't you remember my letters from San Sebastian, darling? Don't you?"

David lowered his head and drank what was left in his coffee cup nervously. He looked terribly young, and she, with her head tipped back and her small mouth smiling strangely, was as old as an old mountain. She laughed softly.

"It was marvelous," she said to all of us, while we sat looking at her and listening in a kind of dreamlike dumbness. "We used to flock to the beach, simply flock, every afternoon, because the more of us there were, the more chance there was of an escape."

David pushed back his chair. He knew what was coming, I suppose, and didn't want to hear it. But she went on lightly, chattily, as if we were intimates. "*You* know . . . refugees trying to swim past the border into France, pretending they were summer people.

It was simply breath-taking! The guards always spotted them, because they couldn't help swimming too hard."

She laughed again, and lowered her eyes.

"And what then?" Chexbres' sister spoke gently, with the impersonal sternness of a doctor taking the last clips from a healing wound.

The girl leaned across David, who still sat with his head bent, and answered her, "Why, then there was always shooting. It was exciting. We'd dash for shore, of course, and there'd be the man, trying to escape, swimming all alone. It was easy for the guards then. They never missed. It was all right, though . . . the tide always carried the bodies farther along toward Bordeaux, where they'd wanted to go anyway."

There was nothing to say, but the silence did not seem clumsy. I felt that if I tried to start another kind of talk it would be cruel to my brother. I did not look at him but, perhaps mistakenly, I suffered for him as I would have suffered for myself if I had been eighteen or so and in love the way he was.

François came in with more coffee. Then David stood up.

"I'm sorry," he said to me, and when I looked at last at his face, it was smooth and meaningless, the way I can make mine too. "I'm afraid we'll have to go, if we make the last train."

I knew he was lying, because there was time to catch at least three more, but I thought he was right, and I felt better when Chexbres said, "Why don't you take the car? I don't need it until tomorrow noon. That would give you plenty of time to get back in the morning."

"I'll be coming back tonight," David said noncommittally. "I'd like to take it. Thanks."

And he made his manners and the little girl got her things from upstairs and they were gone.

We still sat around the table. The candles were low. We heard François tiptoe along the terrace, leaving. Chexbres and Norah went down to the cellars and brought back a very old bottle of Armagnac, and we sat for a long time with our elbows on the table and glasses in our cupped hands, gradually coming to life again, gradually recovering from the shyness we had felt when David walked with such dignity from the room, and from the helplessness we'd felt, too, knowing that in some way we, with our love, had made the little blonde girl do what she did to him.

That was perhaps the strangest meal we ever ate at Le Pâquis, Chexbres and I, with other people. But there was another time that was strange, too, in a different way.

It was at Easter. A young American was staying with us, on a vacation from Oxford. He was very easy to have in the house; every morning he piled twenty or thirty books around him, in the corner by the fire, and sat there like a somnolent young bull or stallion, storing up strength in ways of his own. Now and then, wordlessly, he would climb out of the big chair and over the books and get himself some bottles of beer from the cellar. A few times a day someone would bring food to him, sandwiches and such. Then at night he ate with us, and sang and drank and talked enormously.

He was stimulating, and we knew that he would be almost as important by now as he already is, but one night we ran away from him.

We all ate dinner together, and talked for a time, and then Chexbres and I sneaked away, blushing probably through our lies. He did not care; he was playing all the Russian records we had, and we made sure before we deserted him that there was firewood, and that the wine was ample.

I hurried to my room. That afternoon I'd found a big sheet of drawing paper on my desk, heavy with scrolls and banners and phoenixes: I was invited to Chexbres' studio at midnight, for an Easter supper. I made myself look as beautiful as I could, and then as a non-existent clock chimed twelve I went on tiptoe up the stairs to the attics where Chexbres lived, carrying a nest I'd made of grasses, with some painted eggs in it. They were very pretty, and I knew they'd please him.

Inside the studio there were many candles, and the upper part where the big bed and the armoires and such things were had meadow flowers everywhere. We stayed in the lower part.

He had hung all my favorite pictures, and there was a present for me on the low table, the prettiest Easter present I have ever seen. It was a big tin of Beluga caviar, in the center of a huge pale-yellow plate, the kind sold in the market on saints' days in Vevey, and all around the tin and then the edge of the plate were apple blossoms. I think apple blossoms are perhaps the loveliest flowers in the world, because of their clarity and the mysterious way they spring so delicately from the sturdy darkness of the carved stems, with the tender little green leaves close around them. At least they were the loveliest that night, in the candlelight, in the odd-shaped room so full of things important to me.

Chexbres was dressed as I was, very specially, and we whispered as if our friend two thick stone floors below us might at any moment suspect our skulduggery and march furiously up the stairs, and pound on the door to shame us.

There was a bottle of smooth potent gin, unlike any I'd ever tasted. We drank it in glasses Chexbres had bought for then, shaped like crystal eggs almost, and with the caviar it was astonishingly good. We sat whispering and laughing and piling the pungent little black seeds on dry toasted bread, and every swallow of the liquor was as hot and soft as the candle flames around us.

Then, after we had eaten almost all of the caviar and drunk most of the gin, and talked as Chexbres and I always talked, more and better than we ever talked with anyone else, I stood up, thanked him very politely for the beautiful surprise, and walked toward the door to the stairs.

For a minute he was too startled to do anything. Then he leaped to his feet, and got there in front of me.

"You are leaving now?" His voice was as polite as mine had been.

"Yes," I said. "Goodnight, and thank you."

"Goodnight," he said calmly, and I knew as I went silently down the stairs to my own room that he was watching me with incredulity.

I felt amazed myself; but suddenly there in the softly lighted studio with the two of us in our best clothes and the formal secret invitation still in my mind, I'd seemed to become a timid young girl watching her behavior in the apartment of a man of the world. I was unchaperoned, shy, flooded with a sense of propriety that had nothing to do with my real years, my real life with Chexbres. That is why I stood up and walked so primly past the upper part of the room, the part with the big bed and the clothes presses and such intimacies. That is why I said goodnight with such politeness to the only man in the world I knew. And that is why, long after I had lain me down in my small austere room, I heard from upstairs the sound of Chexbres' long gusts of laughter.

In the morning it was all right, except that by then both of us had recovered from the shock of my gauche flight, so that whenever we looked at each other we would grin and then laugh. We probably puzzled our young Oxonian, but no more than I had puzzled the two of us the night before . . . and as long as Chexbres lived the sight of caviar, of tender virginal apple blossoms, made us feel helpless with amusement.

Once I Dreamed

1938

Chexbres had awakened me, but I lay in bed watching the sky full of fast clouds. I heard him call to me, "Here is a fine cat, probably from the farm across the road—a lovely cat. It looks hungry."

That is nice, I thought: we need a cat.

In a few minutes I got up, and was somewhere in a bigger dressing room than my real one, washing my teeth, when I heard a scuffling in the wardrobe. It too was bigger than my real one. I knew that the strange cat had got in there under my clothes.

I heard a soft gentle laugh from the door—François the houseman stood watching.

Then, just behind the cat, Chexbres too came out from between the long silk dresses, looking proud.

The cat, which did not frighten me, was a young lioness, with the big bones of any kitten, and the cinnamon-and-coffee coat of a puma we once saw in Zurich.

"Look, Mary! She's caught a mouse!"

At that the great cat began to caper, and held up her paw; and caught on one of the long claws was a tiny bright-blue field mouse.

She came to my side, and laid the mouse on one of my bare feet while she curled herself, crouching, around my legs. I looked down at her beautiful rippled brownness. I felt tender and loving, as I knew she did, and I understood the gentility of her hunger.

She drew the little blue mouse onto her tongue, and crunched delicately once, and on my foot was a cool feeling from a spot of soft cerulean blood.

I Remember
Three Restaurants

1936–1939

I remember three restaurants in Switzerland with a special clearness: one on the lake near Lausanne, another behind it in the high hills toward Berne, and the last on the road to Lucerne, in German-speaking country.

When we went back, in June of 1939, to pack our furniture and bolt the shutters, we drove toward Lucerne one day. Children were selling the first early Alpine roses along the roads . . . tight ugly posies, the same color as the mottled purple of the little girls' cheeks.

At Malters, one of the few villages of that part of the country not almost overpoweringly quaint and pretty, we stopped at the Gasthaus zum Kreuz. We wondered if Frau Weber would remember us, and if her neurasthenic daughter Anneli would be yearning still to be a chambermaid in London, and if . . . most important . . . if there would be trout swimming in the little tank of icy water that stood in the dining room.

Frau Weber, looking more than ever like a virile Queen Victoria, did indeed remember us, discreetly at first, and then with floods of questions and handshakings and general delight. Anneli was there, fat, pale, still yearning, but this time for Croydon, where she hoped to exchange her Cockney accent for a more refined one. And the trout darted behind glass in the bubbling water.

We stayed there for many hours, eating and drinking and remembering incredulously that once we had almost driven past the Kreuz without stopping.

That was several years ago, when we were roaming about the country with my parents. The chauffeur was sleepy after a night spent in a hotel filled with unusually pretty kitchen maids, and he lost the way. We went confusedly along roads that led where we did not want to go at all; and we all got very hungry and perhaps a little too polite.

Finally we said to stop at the first *gasthaus*, no matter what it looked like. We could certainly count on beer and cheese, at the least.

Pierre stifled a yawn, and his neck got a little pinker; and in perhaps a minute we had come to an impressive stop in front of one of the least attractive buildings of German Switzerland, in the tight village of Malters.

The place had a sharp peaked roof and many little windows; but there were no flowers on the wooden ledges, and a smell of blood came from the sausage shop on the ground floor. Dark stairs led up from the street through a forbidding hallway.

We wanted to go on. It was late, though; and we were hungry and cramped and full of latent snarls. I told Pierre to see what the place looked like.

He yawned again, painfully, and went with false briskness up the dour, dark stairs. Soon he was back, beaming, no longer sleepy. We crawled out, not caring how many pretty girls he had found if there was something in their kitchen for us, too.

Soon life looked better. Frau Weber herself had led us solicitously to ancient but sparkling toilets, and we had washed in a porcelain bowl enameled with swans and lavender chrysanthemums, and were all met again in a little piney honey-colored room full of family photographs. There was a long table with chairs primly about it, and cupboards and a beautiful rococo couch. We felt happy, and toasted one another with small glasses of a strange, potent bitters.

"Whatever you have," we said to Frau Weber, and sat back complacently waiting for some sausage from her shop and maybe a salad. We watched the trout swimming in a tank by one of the windows, and thought them an odd, enormous decoration.

Anneli came in. She was pretty, in a discontented way; and we knew Pierre would have a pleasant lunch. We talked to her about England, which she apparently loved as some women love men or some men the bottle. She set the table, and then came back with a net and a platter. She swooped up a trout, held it by the tail, and before we could close our ears or even wince, had cracked its skull smartly on the sideboard.

My mother lay back farther on the couch and gulped wanly at her bitters; and Father muttered with a kind of sick admiration, "That's the way! By George, that's the way!" as Anneli whacked the brains loose in some ten trout.

She smiled and said, "You 'aven't long to wite naow," and hurried from the room.

By then we were eating slices of various strange sausages, surprisingly light, and drinking cold, thin white wine of the country. Nothing else much mattered.

Frau Weber and her daughter came in carrying a long shallow copper pan between them. They set it down carefully; and Anneli stood back puffing while the older woman lifted the lid, her white hair bristling upward in a regal pompadour, and her face flushed and dewy.

The trout lay staring up at us, their eyes hard and yet somehow benevolent. Our heads drew nearer to the pan, willy-nilly, pulled by one of the finest smells we had ever met. We sniffed and murmured. Frau Weber beamed. She scolded at the girl, who ran from the room for little white potatoes and a great bowl of hot buttered peas from the garden. The mother served the fish herself, and then disappeared proudly.

It was, of course, the most delicious dish that we had ever eaten. We knew that we were hungry, and that even if it had been bad it would have been good . . . but we knew, too, that nevertheless it was one of the subtlest, rarest things that had ever come our way. It was incredibly delicate, as fresh as clover.

We talked about it later, and Frau Weber told us of it willingly, but in such a vague way that all I can remember now is hot unsalted butter, herbs left in for a few seconds, cream, a shallot flicked over, the fish laid in, the cover put on. I can almost see it, smell it, taste it; but I know that I could never copy it, nor could anyone alive, probably.

Finally we were eating large, fragrant strawberries and drinking quite a lot more wine. It amused Anneli that we wanted our coffee in the tall porcelain goblets we saw in the cupboard. But it is the trout that really mattered. They were more important than getting to Lucerne, or than the pride of Frau Weber, or than the girl Anneli, frustrated and yearning. They were, we felt, important like a *grisaille* window or the coming of spring.

And we went back many times to the Kreuz, and the trout were always that way . . . important.

The second restaurant I remember now was near our old home, in Châtel St. Denis, where the Army used to send its ski-learners to use the fine, easy slopes all around. It was called the Hôtel des XIII Cantons.

We knew Mademoiselle Berthe there. She was tall; she had a thin, spirited face; and her dark hair was rolled in odd corkscrews behind each ear, in the disappearing fashion of her village. She had hips that were wide and firm, hung low on her legs; and her feet, on which she always wore exotic beach sandals, were very long and flat. She flapped about on them, and was the best waitress that I have ever known, in Europe or America.

The upstairs room held perhaps fifty people on market days and times like Easter; yet Berthe was always alone and always unruffled. Sometimes in winter, when Army officers were there, teasing and flirting and barking, she got more taciturn than usual. But no matter what kind of people she served, she was always skillful and the most impersonal woman I have ever watched.

She never made mistakes; and no matter how many people were tapping their empty glasses and calling, she would always see that plates were hot and platters properly bubbling above her innumerable alcohol lamps before she left one table for another. She sped about, flat-footed, heavy-hipped, unruffled, waiting for the day when her mother would die and she could renounce the dining room for the glories of the kitchen.

In the meantime, Madame reigned on the other side of the wide stairs which led to the square pine dining room, with its mirrors and white linen curtains and window ledges heavy with hideous, meaty begonias.

Madame Mossu was famous for her trout, her frogs' legs, and especially her shrimps. I have eaten them all many times. Some sticklers for gastronomic etiquette have criticized what she called *truites meunières* because the fish were always curled like *truites au bleu*. Once I asked Berthe why that was. She shrugged and said, "What of it? A trout dead not a minute curls with agony in hot butter. One can flatten him, I admit it. But Maman prefers to let him be as comfortable as possible." There was nothing more to be said.

The season for shrimps is short, and Madame Mossu paid well for all the boys and old men could find in their hundred icy streams. But there were never enough; so diplomats from Geneva and Bernese politicians and horny shepherds on their annual gastronomic bender in Châtel would make appointments in advance for cold shrimps in their shells, or in a *court bouillon* or a *bisque*.

There was a general who always had to unbutton his tunic, and at the bottom of the table a lieutenant with a gleam in his eye that meant, by God, some day he too would be a general. Once, on All Saints' Day, there were three peasants in full black-linen smocks, and two sat smiling quietly while the third stood up and sang a little mountain song. None of us listened, and yet we all heard; and probably we all remember his serious, still face flushed with feast-day drinking, and the way he sat down after the song, and wiped his lips and put a piece of trout between them with complete un-self-consciousness. Then, besides all the diplomats and such, there were *pensionnaires*; a tall, beautiful girl dressed like a Paris manne-quin, who played cards every night with the butcher and young Mossu, and then went away without a word; the lame pharmacist, who had widowed himself four times by his own vitality; a dried, mean, sad old woman who might have been the librarian if there had been a library.

One night a little woman with a black wig came in. She went straight to the long table usually reserved for the military and seated herself. Then a strange party of domestics sat down facing her. One was a woman who looked as though she took dictation daily from 10 until 2. Her hair was like mud, and she was probably a "companion." One was a flirtatious man with a mouth too sen-sitive; two others were poor, beaten-down maids with mean eyes and stringy skins; and last was a young, healthy, arrogant chauf-feur. Berthe scuttled with her usual dexterity around this motley table. First of all, as if she well knew what to do, she brought one glass and a large dusty bottle of the finest Cognac to the old woman, who poured it out hastily for herself, all her dirty dia-monds a-tremble. Then Berthe brought cheap wine for the others, who did not speak, but drank thirstily without looking at their mistress.

An enormous platter of twisted trout Berthe carried in next and put down before the old woman, who drained her glass for the fifth or sixth time and started shoveling fish on to the plates the others held out to her. While we all tried not to watch, the poor souls slashed and poked at the fish until each plate held its neat pile, with bones tidily put on a side dish. The clatter stopped.

Old Wig lifted her glass again, and tossed the brandy down. The servants stood up; and she looked at each plate with its heap of the best trout in Switzerland, boneless and delicate. She nodded fi-nally; and the companion, the weak-mouthed secretary, the two maids, the chauffeur picked up their plates obediently and went out the door and down the stone stairs.

Berthe's long face was expressionless, but her little ear-curls vibrated gently.

"Curiosity grips my bowels . . . excuse me," my husband said. In a few minutes he was back, full of news: the five servants, solemnly, as though they were serving some obscene Mass, had filed out into the little square before the Soldiers' Monument, and had stopped by three immense and antiquated limousines. In each car were three or four tiny feeble Mexican dogs, the shuddering hairless kind, yapping almost silently at the windows. The humans fed them, and then stood in the cold thin air for a minute, silent.

They came back to the dining room and ate well. The secretary flirted dispassionately with the companion and the less dreary of the maids, and the chauffeur stared arrogantly about. Old Wig ate little; but as the evening went on and the brandy warmed her, she smiled occasionally, and spoke to Berthe once about how cold she had been for the thirty years since she left Guatemala.

She makes me think of Monsieur Kuhn's sister, in the last of the three Swiss restaurants I remember so well.

Monsieur Kuhn ran the Hôtel de Ville et du Raisin at Cully, near Lausanne on the lake. He was quiet, with sad eyes and a long face. The only things in the world he cared about were fishing for perch and cooking his haul.

The inn itself was strange and secretive, like its keeper, with cold, high halls, dank air, and an enormous kitchen which never showed anything like a live fire or a sign of bustle. There was a gaunt dining room, always empty, and the café where we sat, a long, queer room with a big stove in the middle, local wine advertisements on the murky walls, and a paper rose in the vase that topped the elaborate coffee machine.

From that dead kitchen into that bleak, smoky room Monsieur Kuhn would send his wonderful filets. He ripped them from the live, stunned fish, as they were ordered. The filets were perhaps three inches long, always with a little crisp point of the tail left on.

Monsieur Kuhn would creep shyly into the dining room, after we had come to his café for a year or more, and bow and shake hands and smile painfully when we thanked him. His long, lined face was always sad and remote and we felt that we were wrong to distract him.

His sister and his wife were different, and grew to like us almost too much. At first we thought they were blood sisters: they both looked so virginal that we could not believe that one of them was married to Monsieur Kuhn, even though he himself looked quite beyond such bothers as co-habitation. It took us some time to learn that the taller of the two women was his wife.

She was very thin, and something about her was out of a drawing, out of an El Greco. Her eyes were bigger than human eyes, and slipped upwards and sideways; and her mouth was pale and beautiful. She was shadowy . . . a bad liver probably . . . but mysterious-looking. She wore black always, and her long hands picked up sizzling platters as if they were distasteful leaves from a tree. She had a light voice; and there was something good and fine about her, so that I always warmed to her.

Her husband's sister Mitzi was quite different. She was short; and although she had a thin face, she looked puffy, with a white, thick skin, the kind that would bend a hypodermic needle. She wore her mole-colored hair in an elaborate girlish mass of curls, and her hands were small and pretty. She, too, dressed in black; but her sweaters had gold threads in them, and her skirts were broadcloth.

Madame Kuhn adored her more plainly than is often seen, and saved all the easy work for her, and did all the ugly jobs herself.

One time we took Michel to the Raisin. He was the kind of short, virile, foxlike Frenchman who seems to have been born in a beret, the kind who is equally ready to shoot a wild boar, make love, or say something which seems witty until you think about it. He was unconscious of Mademoiselle Kuhn.

She, on the other hand, was completely upset by him. She sidled and cooed, and put down our plate of bread as such a thing had never been put down before, and smiled again.

We finished our celestial filets, and drank more wine. Madame

Kuhn hovered in the cold darkness near the kitchen, agonizing with her great dark eyes for the poor tortured sister. We paid the bill, cruel and wrapped in our own lives.

As we got into the car, Mademoiselle ran out with a knot of the first wild narcissuses, and thrust them loosely into Michel's hand.

"Some are for you, Madame," she cried, but she looked only at him, and his neat aristocratic bones and the power in his flesh. Then she ran back into the cold glare of the doorway and stood close against the stone, saying, "Oh, you are adorable, adorable . . ." in her bad Swiss-French.

Michel suddenly broke into a sweat, and wiped the flowers across his forehead. "*Mon Dieu!*" he cried.

We drove away as fast as we could, leaving the poor soul there against the stone, with Madame watching her through the colored-glass door, and the smell of the little filets all around.

But when we went back, that June of 1939, things were changed. Madame stood with a plate of bread in her long hands, and tears ran down her face. Mitzi was in a clinic. "Ah, she is not the same. My little dear will never be so sweet, so innocent again," the woman said. And her eyes, as dead and haunted as something from a Spanish portrait, stared at the wine posters on the murky walls. "Nothing is the same. Nothing will ever be the same."

She walked toward the cold, dank kitchen, truly grief-stricken; and we, sitting there in the café, felt lonely and afraid. The filets, though, were the same as always; and when Monsieur Kuhn came from the kitchen and smiled proudly at us, we forgot his foolish sister and why we were there at all, and remembered only that some dishes and some humans live forever—remembered it thankfully, as I do now.

Sea Change

1937–1939

I

And the eighth and ninth, the tenth, eleventh, twelfth trips? What have they to do with me, the gastronomical me? What sea changes were there, to make me richer, stranger? I grew older with each one, like every other wanderer. My hungers altered: I knew better what and how to eat, just as I knew better how I loved other people, and even why.

I came back alone to America, to tell my family that I was going to get a divorce from Al. Chexbres said, "Why not write it?" I had no answer; I felt I must do it myself, a kind of castigation for hurting good people.

The first three days aboard the large Dutch ship were rough, but not enough to make me feel as I did. I was prostrated . . . not seasick the way the stewardess wanted me to be, but flattened, boneless, with despair at having gone away from Chexbres. It was the strongest physical reaction I had ever felt, and I was frightened and dazed.

I lay shivering in my berth, but my mind was full of feverish plans, which I knew were unreasonable even while I worked on them: I would fake a contagious disease, one so awful the captain would turn back rather than approach New York . . . that sort of thing. I think now that my instincts were right. I should have turned back, not in the middle of the Atlantic as my brain was trying to make me do, but certainly as soon as I reached port. Something inside me stronger than my stubbornness was punishing me for leaving Chexbres, when there was to be so little time for us together.

It was a bitter period I spent there, alone in my neat chintz-curtained cabin. And when I finally got up and looked at the rest of the ship, and at the people on it, I found myself plunged into an atmosphere so much more tortured than mine that it was almost as sickening as my private woe had been.

Almost everyone aboard was fleeing. There were a few Dutch-American business men, and a few stiff racial snobs who ate and sat and gambled apart. The rest were Jews. Most of them had gone from Austria to Holland. Then, as things grew worse, they had finally managed to leave Holland for America. They were doctors, many of them, wondering how they could pass state examinations after thirty or forty years of practicing and sometimes months of cruel stagnation in labor camps.

In First Class they walked quietly up and down with little dictionaries, or stood, not speaking to anyone, watching the swift gray waters. There were a few who talked with me. One was a short tired old man, who shyly drank beer with me and asked about Texas, where he had a grandniece who might welcome him.

I helped him with his dictionary words, and the day we docked he said, "You must have children soon. Here is my address in Texas. I want to deliver them for you . . . free, for friendship."

The other was a lean white-haired editor from Berlin. He had owned one of those slick revues that after the last war made German photographic technique famous . . . especially pictures of nude girls with long jade cigaret holders, and apple blossoms trembling against spring skies. He prowled restlessly about the ship, like a man in great pain, and occasionally sat in the chair next to mine and talked very wittily in French about the reasons for the New Order in his country.

In Second Class the people were poorer and younger. They were less resigned, and their eyes, even while they played chess or deck tennis, were ferociously resentful. Most of them were doctors or lawyers, many with girls they had married in Holland. The blonde wives spoke quite freely and even calmly about their flight, but the dark repressed men said very little, and played games and smoked.

They had cameras and fine medical tools, which they hoped to sell in America because they were allowed to bring so little money with them. And like all the others, they must go to stay with unknown relatives. . . .

In Third Class (the differences were rigid on that ship, with luxury on top, plainness in the middle, and stark clean poverty below), the people were small, bent, furtive, true products of the pogrom and the ghetto. I knew that somewhere in them beauty and love and even hate still lived, but they were the Victims, malnourished for centuries into these silent shivering little creatures.

That voyage was the one that made me most mistrust myself, alone to face sea change. I was full of a slow misery of loathing for what was happening to make all the people around me act as they must. It mixed, there on that proud stiff-necked ship, with my own perturbation at the hurt I was causing people I loved, and with my realization that leaving Chexbres even for a few weeks was one of the stupidest things I had ever done.

I saw clearly for the first time that a woman traveling alone and behaving herself on a ship is an object of curiosity, among the passengers and even more so among the cynical and weary officers. I developed a pattern of behavior which I still follow, on ships and trains and in hotels everywhere, and which impresses and undoubtedly irritates some people who see me, but always succeeds in keeping me aloof from skulduggery.

There are many parts to it, but one of the most important is the way I eat; it not only surrounds me with a wall of awe, but makes my private life more interesting and keeps me from boredom.

I discovered, there on the staidly luxurious Dutch liner, that I could be very firm with pursers and stewards and such. I could have a table assigned to me in any part of the dining room I wanted, and, best of all, I could have that table to myself. I needed no longer be put with officers or predatory passengers, just because I was under ninety and predominantly female. It would never again matter to me that the purser looked oddly at me for my requests, and that people stared and whispered when I walked alone to my table; I had what I needed to bolster my own loneliness, a sense of strength.

And once seated, I could eat what I wanted, and drink what I wanted. I could spend all the time I needed over a piece of pâté, truly to savor its uncountable tastes; I could make a whole meal of little lettuce hearts and buttermilk, or ask for frogs' legs *provençale* and *pêches* Victoria—and get them.

And if I felt like it, I could invite another passenger to dine with me, and order an intelligent thoughtful meal, to please the chef and the wine steward. That was enjoyable occasionally, but in general I preferred to eat by myself, slowly, voluptuously, and with an independence that heartened me against the coldness of my cabin and my thoughts.

It has always been that way since, so that in a Hollywood "bachelor" with a pull-down bed, or on a plane pointed any which way, or even in my own hollow house with death at my shoulder, I can protect myself with that same gastronomic liberty, and eat quietly, calmly, and with a special dignity. It has often saved me, and my reason too, as it probably did when I first found it, on that trip away from Chexbres.

There was a great deal of whoring all about me. It had none of the perverted vileness I felt on the German ships, and was in general good-natured, except for the one fact that some of the most outspokenly anti-Semitic of the small group of business men in First Class were the hottest after the beautiful Jewish girls. It is equally unpleasant that they were very successful.

The two most discreet girls on board were what was spoken of quite casually by the officers as "water babies."

They were married, both of them, to men in concentration

camps. They seemed to have plenty of money, and for safety and probably from habit they had not set foot on land since they escaped from Germany. Instead, they went back and forth from Europe to America, sometimes for months on a single ship, making one trip as the First Officer's girl, the next as the Second's, and so on.

The men seemed genuinely fond of them, and apparently had a strict code of behavior in deciding whose turn was next and in respecting it.

The girls were pretty, and very well behaved. They danced and drank beautifully, and must have grown equally accomplished in more intimate matters. I asked one of them what she did while the ship was in port, and she said she read all the newspapers and then bought new clothes by telephone. Sometimes if she read that another ship was near by with one of her girl friends on it, they talked to each other and made plans for the next few voyages, always by 'phone.

I wondered if that strange sea-borne life was in its own way like the one I was evolving for myself, and if it protected them from thoughts of their men in Dachau as mine did shield me from my own grim dreamings. It was based on hungers, all of it. . . .

II

I went back to Switzerland as soon as I could. I found when I changed my reservations that the only other ship at that time was one with six hundred German youths and maidens on it, returning from a Good Will tour, of course. So I went Second on the *Ile de France*, probably the coldest, most unattractive luxury liner I ever saw.

My system of public independence was working well, partly because I was headed in the right direction and full therefore of secret joy. I ate alone usually, and well . . . but almost every night I went with two Frenchmen named Jacques and Pierre to First Class, where the officers were impressed with Jacques because of his title and all of us because we were actually traveling in Second.

They were bitter men, the officers, in a gruesome laughing way, and always spoke of the line they sailed on as *La Compagnie Générale Tragique*.

We would sit in the bleak fantastic bar, perhaps only ten of us or twelve awake on the whole ship, and at eleven the waiters would set up one of the most lushly extravagant buffets I have ever seen, and we would drink champagne and have the maître d'hôtel cut one sliver of breast from a grouse, or dig one spoonful of pâté from a great yellow terrine.

"Please accept more," he would beg, and piled caviar on our plates, while we talked quietly, wearily, against the rhythm of the great ship, about Laval and Blum and which way France would fall when she fell. . . .

III

About two years later Chexbres and I came back. We wanted to be on the *Champlain*, because he had often enjoyed it, but it was retired. The *De Grasse* was a sister ship, I think. There were only twenty passengers, and I was the only woman, which made the seating easy for the Captain's Dinner.

I don't know how we ever got to New York. Chexbres was dying, really, and in revolt at the whole cruel web of clinics and specialists and injections and rays we had run away from in Europe, as if we knew that nothing could be worse than what was happening there to us. We were without nurses, for the first time in months. It was a very rough crossing, and I still wake up shaking sometimes to remember how I prepared hypodermics between rolls of the ship. . . .

We were bolstered by the wine of freedom, really, and I don't think anything could have daunted us.

We went to meals whenever the motion permitted, and Chexbres would invent dances down the empty corridors on his one leg and the crutches, so that when we went into the dining room we were always laughing wildly.

The chef, bored almost insane, pounced on us via the wine steward, and we were sent dishes such as I had only read about before. We seldom did them justice; the motion perhaps and our state of mind made it hard to eat. But we were appreciative, and we heard that the chef was happy.

The only passenger I can remember was a tall fat man, ringed and heavily perfumed in spite of his Brooks Brothers tweeds, who ate by himself and flew into rages when he saw anything being served to us that was not on the menu. Finally he pulled off the linen and all the dishes, one day, and ran from the room crying.

After that his waiter, with many apologetic eyebrows at us, served him small editions of our masterpieces, always with a polite mockery about him that would have reduced me to more than tears. The fat man beamed and giggled with pleasure, and lifted his glass magnanimously to us. . . .

He was a milliner. "The most expensive chippies in New York wear my hats," he said candidly to us. He told Chexbres that he was in great demand socially, but that his deepest pleasure was to stay at home, take off all his clothes, and let his cat sleep on his naked stomach. The purring made him feel creative, he said. Chexbres had another drink.

The captain sent me flowers once or twice, because he knew Chexbres was so ill, and after I thanked him for having caviar at his dinner, he presented me with a large tin of it when we left the ship. He was always polite and impersonal, but the note with the caviar said, "Pain cannot touch the loving-hearted." I thought of his eyes, dark, tired, intelligent *French* eyes. *Compagnie Générale Tragique* . . .

IV

Then, in half a year or so, eleven and twelve.

I was with Chexbres. We knew what was happening, and how to cope with it as long as he lived, and we were like two happy ghosts, I really think. We were charmed, so that doors opened and people smiled shyly, and everywhere there was decency and cleanliness and light. It sounds fatuous to say that, but it was so.

We had to go back to Switzerland, to close our house forever and sell many of our goods, and to get medicine for him, figured coldly to last as long as he did. And that sounds, not fatuous, but grim and ugly. It never was . . . we were immune to everything, that summer, that could hurt us.

We went to France and back again on the *Normandie*, both times in the same beautiful room which was in First Class but right next to the door into Second. Second was easier for Chexbres, smaller and with fewer stairs and such.

The *Normandie* was the loveliest ship I ever saw. It wasn't a ship the way the little Dutch one had been, but at the same time there was nothing vulgar or pretentious or snobbish about it, like some of the others.

We spent the time either in bed (it was a big room with real beds in it, the first I had seen on a ship except in movies), or in the Smoking Room or Lounge or whatever it was called: an airy place, all glass walls but not frightening, with comfortable places to sit and a wonderful waiter. He reminded us with his sad hollow eyes of François, our Swiss houseman.

His dream was to save enough money to send himself to a mountain sanatorium, and there die. We knew the one he had picked out, a glum barracks in the Savoy Alps. But he had read fine things about it. We agreed with him that it would be a peaceful way to end. He was only about thirty, but his mind was made up and his lungs were obviously rotting.

We drank to his plan, the night before we landed back in New York . . . and then the next time the *Normandie* docked, it was to burn, and that poor man was cheated. He liked us very much, sensing perhaps a companionably fateful air about us, and he approved highly of our well-organized and thoughtful drinking.

We got up late, and went after bathings and shavings to the Lounge, where we sat in soft chairs by the glass wall and looked out past the people sunning themselves to the blue water. We drank champagne or sometimes beer, slowly, and talked and talked to each other because there was so much to say and so little time to say it.

I have probably talked more to Chexbres, and he to me, than to all the other people put together in both our lives. We often wondered about it: how we could talk so much and never bore each other. The wine served perhaps as a kind of delicate lubricant . . . but without it, it would have been the same.

Then we went slowly down to lunch. We had a table near the door, easy for Chexbres, and there we watched the people coming in and out, and drank more beer or a good wine . . . whatever we had started with. The *sommelier* liked us, of course, and stopped often to tell us strange things about people or his bottles.

We ate lightly but well; by then we knew just about what Chexbres needed and could stand, and although I ate more than he, it was in the same way, not grimly because we must still live, but with much enjoyment always.

After lunch we rested. That sounds silly . . . but the way we had to move about, and even sit down or sneeze, was a great deal of work for both of us. In order to stay self-controlled and blissful, the way we were, we had to rest a great deal.

About four o'clock we would go up to the Lounge again, and turn our backs on the ocean to watch a movie. We had never liked movies, but this time, sitting in the slowly rolling gently shaking body of the great ship, watching the artful foolery unwind on the screen, they seemed a natural part of the whole trance-like voyage we were making. We sat in great soft chaises-longues, with little tables beside us on a kind of private balcony, and for the first time in my life I drank Pernods.

If there was one film we each drank one, in small sips until the end, and if there were two films we drank two. I cannot imagine drinking them any place else, but then they were perfect, in a quiet comforting way, and very clean in the throat.

And before dinner we drank more champagne, watching the sun set through the thick glass walls, and after dinner, which we sometimes ordered at noon to please our waiter who was convinced we were starving to death, we drank still more, or sometimes cognac. Then we went to bed again, and two or three times in the night we would start talking, and eat a few of the little sand-

wiches the worried waiter sent down to us, and drink some hot
consommé or more brandy.

Even when New York loomed near us, we felt outward bound.
I bit gently at my numb fingers. I seemed beautiful, witty, truly
loved . . . the most fortunate of all women, past sea change and
with her hungers fed.

The Lemming to the Sea

1938

More often than not people who see me on trains and in ships, or in restaurants, feel a kind of resentment of me since I taught myself to enjoy being alone. Women are puzzled, which they hate to be, and jealous of the way I am served, with such agreeable courtesy, and of what I am eating and drinking, which is almost never the sort of thing they order for themselves. And men are puzzled too, in a more personal way. I anger them as males.

I am sorry. I do not like to do that, or puzzle the women either. But if I must be alone, I refuse to be alone as if it were something weak and distasteful, like convalescence. Men see me eating in public, and I look as if I "knew my way around"; and yet I make it plain that I know my way around without them, and that upsets them.

I know what I want, and I usually get it because I am adaptable to locales. I order meals that are more typically masculine than feminine, if feminine means whipped-cream-and-cherries. I like good wines, or good drinkin'-likka, and beers and ales. I like waiters; I think the woman who said that waiters are much nicer than people was right, and quite often waitresses are too. So they are always nice to me, which is a sure way to annoy other diners whose soup, quite often, they would like to spit in.

And all these reasons, and probably a thousand others, like the way I wear my hair and what shade my lipstick is, make people look strangely at me, resentfully, with a kind of hurt bafflement, when I dine alone.

Sometimes the results are more tangible. I think now of Jacques.

He was on the *Ile de France* when I went back to Switzerland. By then I had fairly well developed my system of public behavior, but the ship was a hard test, bleak, rattling, stuffy in Second, and heartbreakingly pretentious in First. Jacques and I were in Second.

I saw him soon, and enjoyed the way he moved quietly about the decks and halls, like a Spanish dancer, very self-contained. He was small and dark, and made me think of a fox, not because of the cunning a fox is supposed to have, but because of a smooth fine brown-eyed potency about him.

He was looking at me, and admiring me too, but I did not realize it: my whole reason for being lay ahead of me, on the lake near Vevey in the canton of Vaud, and I was hurrying there as irrevocably as an Arctic lemming hurries to the sea cliff, through poisoned fields and fire and flood to what he longs for.

Jacques watched me in the dining room, where I sat alone and ate judiciously, with amiable concentration. And he watched me in the Smoking Room, which was the only warm place to sit. I read, and drank without ever showing anything but a self-contained enjoyment, and seemed not to want better company than my own. All this was puzzling to Jacques, and because he was a man it was annoying too.

Finally we met, and when he told me his name and asked me teasingly if I could spell it, I amazed him by doing so, because I had learned it in a history course in Dijon, years before.

He was a Norman. There were seven sons and six daughters in his family. Some of the boys went to the colonies or to Canada, like Jacques, and some of the girls went into nunneries. There were a few of each sex in private insane asylums. The rest were very important in Paris, or the Foreign Service. Jacques showed me pictures of his home, a great grim place with its own church, its own village, and of his stubborn handsome mother.

He was a very simple man, almost childish, and did not talk much at a time. Sometimes we drank cognac together after dinner, and once he ate at my table, with a kind of charmed jealousy at the good meal we had, and the good wine.

He was very modest, but always there was in his bones, in every hair on his fine dark head, the assurance of his great name, so that one night when he was trembling with nervousness at having to officiate at the ship's concert, and I said, "Why not get someone else to, then?" he dismissed the idea and me with it by saying, very simply, "But it is expected of me."

That night, in honor of the concert and perhaps of taking me up to dine in First with the captain, he wore a beautiful little satin waistcoat, I remember, of the most delicate shell-pink, with flowers embroidered on it in petit-point. It was perfect on him, for some reason I cannot tell.

Only twice did he ever say anything personal to me. Once he said he liked to look across the dining room and watch me eating there, so thoughtfully and voluptuously, because I was the only woman he had ever seen except a Chinese, the wife of a great leader, who could do it. I knew very little about her, but I asked if it might not be our smooth hair. No, he said, and did not have words for more.

And another time, just before we landed, he stood twirling his beret on one finger, not confusedly but with real grace, and asked me if I had ever thought what it would be like to marry a trapper and live in the Canadian forests. I never had, but when I looked at him I realized he was planning something in his slow simple brain, and I said, "It would take strength."

"Yes," he said, looking impersonally at me, as if I were a horse.

I don't know how or why I told him what hotel I would stop at in Paris, on my way to Switzerland. Certainly I never thought to see him again. My mind was fixed on tomorrow, on being once more with Chexbres.

The boat train was late, and by the time I had tidied myself for dinner and got to Michaud's, a boy was putting up the shutters. I felt depressed and tired, and went past him anyway, thinking I could get a good glass of sherry, and then go to bed. But when Madame Rollo saw me she shrieked for her brother, and a dash to the kitchen proved that there was enough heat left in the ranges to make me a little omelet, and would I consider eating a few spiced mushrooms first, and yes, by God, there was one portion of *crème au kirsch* left, after a little salad. . . . and for this time of night and this cold month a small bottle of Montrachet '23, with my permission. . . .

It all made me feel warm and human, sitting there with those kind voluble quarrelsome people behind the shutters, knowing that tomorrow I would be with Chexbres again, and my long journey over.

When I got back to the hotel and saw Jacques sitting by the desk, I could hardly remember who he was. He was very nice, and asked me to forgive him for being importunate. . . but two of his brothers were in Paris, and anxious to meet me, and . . . and he looked so fine-boned and simple and honest that I left my key on its hook, and went out with him to a waiting car.

We went to the little upstairs-bar at Weber's. It was the first time I had been there. People were sitting quietly, drinking champagne and eating vanilla ice cream, which one of Jacques' brothers told me was chic at the moment.

They were taller than he, and handsomer, but they did not have his *good* look. They were much more intelligent, and treated him with a kind of affectionate scorn that older members of a large family often seem to feel for the young ones. He was a yokel home from Canada, and they were Paris diplomats, and even if he had been articulate he would have said very little.

They were politely startled when I ordered a very good cognac. One of them drank scotch, and the other champagne, and Jacques ordered a bottle of Perrier water.

I had told them when I first met them that I was very tired and must go back soon to the hotel, but as I listened to them I wanted to go even sooner. I was speaking good French that night, probably because their accents were so perfect, but very quickly I knew there was nothing I could say that would be truthful. They were the most cynically weary men I had ever met, like the young officers on the *Ile*, but with more force . . . not physically or religiously or sexually, but in their patriotism. They were complete defeatists.

I sat there listening to them, hardly able to swallow for the revolt and horror I felt. They were betraying France, two men as old as France herself, and strong and intelligent enough to fight for her. They were selling her, there in Weber's little bar, as surely as they were selling her on the Bourse and in the embassies.

I looked at Jacques, to see if he understood what had happened to his brothers, but it was impossible to tell. He was tired and obviously bored by them.

They kept on talking, charmingly, wittily, and I realized that all around me there was the same kind of conversation. Hitler and Tardieu and Laval: these aristocratic Frenchmen were discussing them blandly, as if they were unpleasant but humble menials, to be handled puppet-like at their own discretion.

I could stand no more of it, and asked to be taken to my hotel. I was shocked, so that I could hardly keep from shaking.

Jacques took me to the desk from their car, and when he kissed my hand he looked at me and said, "I should have stayed in Canada. I understand trapping animals better."

His poor simple mind was full of misery, I could tell, and I said goodnight gently, as if I would see him tomorrow, to comfort him.

A few weeks later I got a strange letter from him. "I am just back in Paris for a couple of days," he wrote. "I find the country place most depressing, dreary, and terribly damp. I can hardly tell you how much unpleasant it was to stay there, in consequence of the wet and my sister who has returned to the château after twenty-one years in a convent, to expect the world to have been stopped during that time. However, my dear, I shan't bother you with all that . . . how are you getting on, working hard, do you?"

Here Chexbres, who knew as much as I did about Jacques, said rather stuffily, "I thought you told me his English was good." I could only laugh. I thought the letter was funny.

He wrote about going south. He wanted to go to Corsica and buy an old farm. "I don't want to stay home too long. I will feel too depressed. Do you know Marie Françoise how happy I will be if it were possible for you to take that trip with me?"

"The bastard," Chexbres said softly.

The letter told me that it might help my writing to go on such a trip in that interesting island, and then, "Please let me know how foolish it all sound to you. I won't get *fâché*. Excuse this awful writing. The pen is a poem! Hoping to read you soon and have my life worth living, *à bientôt*."

I felt confused, to have to read this in front of Chexbres. He would think I had flirted. . . . Then I began to laugh again. It was such a simple proposition, just like Jacques.

But Chexbres, for a time, was almost hateful toward me, feeling a kind of brotherhood with Jacques against all women. "You can't do things like that to men," he said resentfully.

"But what?"

"Whatever it is that makes them write letters like that," he muttered, hating me. "That chap's suffering. . . ."

How could I say it was because I ate in a dark cold miserable ship as if I enjoyed myself, and drank without getting silly . . . because I behaved myself in public?

I wrote to Jacques and thanked him for his invitation, and told him that if ever he was near Lausanne, Chexbres and I would be so glad to see him. It was a very polite letter.

And in a few days I was called up to the village (it was before we had a telephone), to reverse a call to Evian from the Café de la Grappe, and it was Jacques. I had sat trembling, thinking awful thoughts of runaway relatives and such, and when it was only

Jacques, so matter of fact, I felt almost glad to hear him. He wanted to stop to see us on his way south.

I was rather ungracious, and told him our houseman had influenza, which was true, but he ignored that. I knew Chexbres would look grim, and he did.

Jacques came that afternoon, and that night we went to dinner at Cully and ate piles of perch filets on a big platter in the café. I don't think Jacques had ever eaten so simply that way, with a lady and gentleman in a common-man's place.

Later we dressed and went dancing at Montreux, and drank a lot of champagne. Jacques danced almost as well as Chexbres. And that night his only personal remark was, very close to my ear in a tango, "But who is Chexbres?"

I told him, as well as anyone could ever tell who that strange man was, and he said, "Oh."

The next day we went all over the neighboring vineyards with Jules, our own *vigneron*, and it was wonderful to see Jacques with those cautious careful Swiss.

They had always been cordial with us, and seemed to like us, but with him it was different. They frisked about like stiff colts in the spring, and I have never heard such delight and laughter from them. They boasted and sang, and brought out bottles of wine that we had only learned about in whispers, and invited us all to festivals months away. It was fun, although Chexbres and I felt a little jealous of what we had thought was our own solid friendship with the vineyardists.

That night we drove up through the snow to Châtel, and ate trout at the Treize Cantons. We had a nice enough time, but Jacques was really hard to be with for very long, because he was too simple. He had only a few reactions to things, and almost no words to describe them. And besides, there was the feeling underneath that he had written asking me to go to Corsica with him. . . .

We were glad when he said that he must leave the next day at two o'clock. He told us that a sister-in-law was staying at Glion, and that he was very anxious to have her meet me. Would that be all right with Chexbres? Chexbres looked strangely at me, and said of course.

So I drove Jacques up the winding road behind Montreux, and was presented to his sister-in-law, who as wife of the oldest son was representing the mother of the tribe. She was a beautiful thin Englishwoman, resting while her husband took one of his periodic vacations in a private asylum. She inspected me in a completely cold-blooded and charming way.

And then we drove down the mountain again. Jacques looked depressed.

"Denise is enchanted by you," he said glumly. "My mother will be enchanted by you too. It is very important that you go see her. She is old, and hates Paris now, or she would be glad to meet you in Paris."

I felt a little hysterical.

"Jacques, we have time before your train," I said. "Let's go eat something. We need some lunch."

"Undoubtedly you know just where you want to go," he said politely, and if I had not known his denseness I'd have suspected him of sarcasm.

We sat in the station restaurant, and ordered a fondue, because it was a cold day and Jacques said he had never tasted one.

It was not very good: too thin, and then suddenly stringy like cool rubber. Jacques ate two or three polite bites of it, and drank a little of the Dézaley and ate some bread crumbs.

We made conversation about regional dishes, and all the time he looked glummer and sadder. He wrote out his mother's address for me, and said, "I have showed you her picture, haven't I?"

"Yes, yes," I said. I didn't think I could stand much more.

"She will be enchanted by you," he said again.

We still had twenty minutes or so. I picked up a piece of bread, and dabbed at the cold gluey fondue on my plate. Suddenly Jacques began to speak very rapidly, standing up and reaching for his hat and coat on the station rack behind the table.

"Go on eating. Go on sitting there with your food and your

wine. I saw you first that way, alone, so goddamned sure of your-self. This is right. I'll leave now. Do this last thing and stay as you are, here at the table with the wine in your hand."

"Oh, Jacques, I'm so sorry," I said. I looked up at him, and his eyes were very black. Then he moved swiftly among the tables, like a dancer, and the door swung behind him.

I must get home, I thought. I feel awful, like crying or being sick. I must get back to Chexbres.

I drove as fast as I could. I didn't know what I would do when I got there, but I must get home. I wanted never to be alone again, in a restaurant or anywhere.

The house was full of a fine smell. Chexbres was in the kitchen.

"Hello," he said. "Did that poor bastard give you his address? He left his pajamas. I've invented a new way to make fondue. It's absolutely foolproof. Here . . ."

We sat by the fire for a long time, and the fondue was indeed de-licious, and by the time we had finished it and the bottle of wine and written the new recipe, Jacques was well on his way to Cor-sica, and I felt all right—sorry, but all right.

The Flaw

1939

There was a train, not a particularly good one, that stopped at Vevey about ten in the morning on the way to Italy. Chexbres and I used to take it to Milano.

It had a restaurant car, an old-fashioned one with the agreeable austerity of a third-class station café about it: brown wooden walls and seats, bare tables unless you ordered the highest-priced lunch, and a few faded advertisements for Aspirina Bayer and "*Visitez le Maroc*" permanently crooked above the windows.

There was one table, next to the galley, where the cooks and waiters sat. In the morning they would be talking and sorting greens for salad and cutting the tops off radishes for the hors d'oeuvres, and in the early afternoon they would eat enormously of some things that had been on the menu and some that certainly had not. There was always a big straw-wrapped flask of red wine with them.

Sometimes the head chef smoked while he drank, or read parts of a newspaper aloud, but usually he worked with his helpers. And if one of the two waiters sat there, he worked too.

We liked to go into the restaurant partly because of the cooks, who after a polite salute ignored us, and partly because of the waiters, who were always the same ones.

Of course, it is impossible that they were on every train that went to Milano through Vevey at ten in the morning. But they were on that train every time we took it, so that very soon they knew us and laughed and even patted Chexbres' shoulder delightedly when we appeared.

We always went into their car a few minutes after we started . . . after we had been seen by the conductor and what few travelers there were on the unfashionable train. The restaurant would be empty at that hour, of course, except for the table of amiably chattering cooks.

We would order a large bottle of Asti Spumanti. That delighted the waiters, whether it was the young smooth one or the old sour withered one. We would sit drinking it, slightly warm, from the thick train-goblets, talking and watching the flat floor of the Valais grow narrower and wilder, waiting as always with a kind of excited dread for the first plunge in to the Simplon.

The champagne would stay us, in that familiar ordeal. We'd drink gratefully, feeling the train sway, knowing a small taste of death and rebirth, as all men do in swift passage through a tunnel.

When we came out finally, into the light again and the high mountains, we'd lift our glasses silently to each other, and feel less foolish to see that the cooks too had known the same nameless stress as we.

Then people would begin to come in for lunch, and we'd go back to our compartment. The younger waiter would always call us when there were only a few more people to serve, in an hour or so.

Usually both waiters took care of us; they seemed to find us strange, and interesting enough to crack their cosmic ennui, and in some way fragile, so that they protected us. They would come swaying down the aisle as we ate, crying to us, "There will be a few bumps! Hold tight! Hold tight, M'sieu'-'dame! I will help you!"

Then they would grasp the wine, and usually my arm, and we would, it is true, make a few mild grating noises over some repairs in the road. Then they would gasp with relief, and scuttle away . . . one more crisis safely past.

It made us feel a little silly, as if we were imbeciles of royal blood, or perhaps children who only *thought* they had gray hairs and knew how to survive train trips alone. It was fun, too; almost everyone likes to feel pampered by public servants.

The young waiter with the smooth almond face was more given to the protective gestures, equally lavished on Chexbres or me to avoid any sexual misunderstandings, but the older one, whose body was bent and whose face was truly the most cynical I have ever seen, was the one who watched our eating.

He hovered like an evil-visaged hawk while we ordered, and we soon found that instead of advising changes then, he would simply substitute in the kitchen what he preferred to have us enjoy that day. After the first surprise it was fun, but we always kept up the bluff of looking at the menu and then watching him pretend to memorize our order.

One thing he permitted us: simplicity. The people who traveled on that train were the kind who liked plain food and plenty of it. The menu might or might not list meat or fish, but it always had *pasti* of some kind, and lentils or beans cooked with herbs, and of course fine honest garden salad. Then there would be one or two *antipasti*: the radishes we had watched being fixed, and butter for them in rather limp and sooty curls, and hardboiled eggs and sliced salami. There would be cheese for dessert, with fruit . . . fat cherries or peaches or grapes or oranges, according to the season, and always green almonds in the spring.

The people ate well, and even if they were very poor, and brought their own bread and wine into the restaurant, they ordered a plate of beans or a one-egg omelet with dignity which was no rebuke to the comparative prodigality around them. The two waiters served them with nonchalant skill, and everyone seemed to agree that Chexbres and I should be watched and fed and smiled at with extra care.

"Why are they like that? Why are they so good to us, all the people?" we would ask each other. I knew reasons for him, and he knew some for me, but for the two of us it was probably because we had a sort of palpable trust in each other.

Simple people are especially conscious of that. Sometimes it is called love, or good will. Whatever it was in us, the result was mysterious and warming, and we felt it very strongly in places like the restaurant car to Milano, always until the last time.

That was in the summer of 1939.

We were two ghosts, then. Our lives as normal living humans had ended in the winter, in Delaware, with Chexbres' illness. And when we got word that we should go back to our old home in Switzerland and save what we could before war started, we went not so much for salvage, because possessions had no meaning any more to us, but because we were helpless to do anything else. We returned to the life that had been so real like fog, or smoke, caught in a current of air.

We were very live ghosts, and drank and ate and saw and felt and made love better than ever before, with an intensity that seemed to detach us utterly from life.

Everywhere there was a little of that feeling; the only difference was that we were safely dead, and all the other people, that summer, were laughing and singing and drinking wine in a kind of catalepsy, or like cancerous patients made happy with a magic combination of opiate before going into the operating theatre. We had finished with all that business, and they had it still to go through.

They looked at us with a kind of envious respect, knowing that war was coming to them, but that we were past it; and everywhere we went, except the one time on the Milano train, we moved beatifically incommunicado, archangels on leave. None could touch us, just as none could be harmed by our knowledge of pain yet to be felt.

The train was the same. By then we had grown almost used to miracles, and when the young almond-faced waiter stood in the door of the compartment and gaped helplessly at us, we laughed at him. He stammered and sputtered, all the time shaking our hands and laughing too, and it was plain that he had buried us long since.

When he saw what had happened to Chexbres, he turned very red, and then said quickly, trying not to stare, "But the Asti! At once! It will be very chic to drink it here!"

And before we could tell him how much we wanted to drink it in the old restaurant car, and look once more at the faded aspirin signs and listen to the cooks, he was gone. It was necessary for him to disappear; we were used by then to having people do impetuous things when they first saw us, ghosts come back so far. . . . We sighed, and laughed, because even that seemed funny.

The boy brought the champagne, wrapped elegantly in a red-checked napkin for the first time. He was suave and mischievous again, and it was plain that he felt like something in a paper-bound novel, serving fair wine that way at eleven in the morning in a first-class compartment. He swayed with exaggerated grace to the rocking of the car, and flicked soot from the little wall table like the headwaiter at the Café de la Paix, at least, with his flat black eyes dancing.

We saluted him with our first taste, hiding our regret at having to be "gentry" and drink where it was chic. The wine was the same, warm and almost sickish, and we looked quietly at each other, with delight . . . one more miracle.

But at Sion, before the tunnel, three Strength-through-Joyers got on, bulbous with knapsacks and a kind of sweaty health that had nothing to do with us. We huddled against the windows, not invisible enough, and I wondered how we could ever get past all those strong brown hairy legs to the corridor.

But there in the doorway, almost before the train started again, stood the little waiter. His face was impassive, but his eyes twinkled and yet were motherly.

"*Pardon, pardon,*" he murmured. "*Entschuldigen Sie, bitte . . . bitte . . .*"

And before we knew it the German tourists were standing, trying to squeeze themselves small, and the boy was whisking us

expertly, nonchalantly, out of the compartment, down the rocking aisle, and into our familiar hard brown seats in the restaurant.

It was all the same. We looked about us with a kind of wonder.

The old waiter saw us from the end of the car. His face did not
change, but he put down his glass of wine and came to our table.
The boy started to say something to him in an Italian dialect . . . it
was like Niçois . . . but the old man motioned him bruskly aside.

His face was still the most cynical I had ever seen, but his eyes
were over-full of tears. They ran slowly down his cheeks for a few
minutes, into the evil old wrinkles, and he did not wipe them
away. He stood by the table, flicking his napkin and asking crankily if we had made a good trip and if we planned to stay long in Milano. We answered the same way . . . things about traveling and
the weather.

We were not embarrassed, any more than he was, by his tears;
like all ghosts, I suppose, we had grown used to seeing them in
other people's eyes, and along with them we saw almost always a
kind of gratitude, as if people were thanking us for coming back
and for being so trustful together. We seemed to reassure them, in
a mysterious way . . . that summer more than ever.

While the old man was standing there, talking with his own
gruff eagerness about crops and storms, flicking the table, he had
to step in behind my chair for a minute while three men walked
quickly through the car.

Two were big, not in uniform but with black shirts under their
hot mussy coats, and stubble on their faces. The man between
them was thinner and younger, and although they went single file
and close together, we saw that he was handcuffed to each of them.

Before that summer such a thing would have shocked us, so that
our faces would be paler and our eyes wider, but now we only
looked up at the old waiter. He nodded, and his own eyes got very
hot and dried all the tears.

"Political prisoner," he said, flicking the table, and his face was
no more bitter than usual. "Escaped. They are bringing him back
to Italy."

Then the chef with the highest bonnet saw us, and beamed and raised his glass, and the others turned around from their leafy table and saluted us too, and the door slammed behind the three dark men.

We got through the tunnel, that time, without feeling our palms grow sticky. It was the only difference: the train was the same, the people were the same. We were past the pain and travail, that was all. We were inviolate.

We drank the rest of the Asti, and as people began to come in to lunch, we made the signal to the suddenly active boy that we would be back later.

Just then there were shouts and thuds, and the sound of shattering glass. A kind of silence fell all about us, in spite of the steady rattle of the train. The old waiter ran down the car, not bumping a single table, and the door at the end closed sharply behind him. People looked strangely at one another.

Gradually the air settled, as if the motors inside all the travelers had started to hum again, and the young waiter took orders for lunch. When he got to us he said without looking at us, in his bad French, "I suggest that M'sieu'-'dame attend a moment . . . the restaurant is not crowded today."

As a suggestion it had the icy command of a policeman or a guardian angel about it, and we sat meekly. There was no more champagne. It did not really bother us.

Finally the old man came hurriedly back into the car. His face was furious, and he clutched his shoulder. The travelers stared at him, still chewing. He stopped for a minute by our table. He was panting, and his voice was very low.

"He tried to jump through the window," he said, and we knew he was talking about the refugee. "The bastards! They tore my coat! My only coat! The dirty bastards . . . look at that!"

He flapped the ripped shoulder of his greasy old black jacket at us, and then went madly down to the galley, muttering and trembling.

We stood up to go, and the smooth almond-faced waiter hurried toward us, swaying with the downhill rush of the train under a big tray of hot vegetables. "I am bringing M'sieu'-'dame's order at once," he called.

We sat down obediently. We were being bullied, but it was because he was trying to protect us, and it was kind of him. He brought two glasses of a dark vermouth, and as he put them in front of us he said confiding, "A special bottle we carry for the chef . . . very appetizing. There is a little muss on the platform. It will be swept up when M'sieu'-'dame have finished. *Santé!*"

As we lifted our glasses, willy-nilly, he cleared his throat, and then said in English, "Cheerio!" He smiled at us encouragingly, like an over-attentive nurse, and went back to serving the other people. The vermouth was bitterer than any we had ever tasted, almost like a Swiss gentian-drink, but it tasted good after the insipid wine.

When we went through to our compartment, there was indeed a neat pile of broken glass on the platform between the cars, and the window of the door that opened when the train stopped was only half filled: the top part of the pane was gone, and the edge of the rest curved like ice in a smooth fine line, almost invisible.

The Strength-through-Joyers leaped politely to attention when we got back to our compartment, and subsided in a series of small waves of questions in English . . . did smoke bother me, did we mind the door open, did we feel a draft. . . .

I forget the name of the town now where the train stops and the passport men come on. Is it Domodossola? How strange, not to know! It is as if I have deliberately wiped from my mind a great many names. Some of them I thought would stay there forever, whether I wanted them or not, like old telephone numbers that suddenly come between you and the sound of a new love's voice. I never thought to disremember this town, that man, such and such a river. Was it Domodossola?

That day we were there a long time. There seemed more policemen than usual, but it was always that way in Italy. We got the questions of visas and money straightened out; that used to upset me, and I'd feel like a blushing diamond-smuggler when the hardeyed customs man would look at me. This time it was easy, unimportant.

I kept thinking it would be a good idea to walk back to the restaurant car while the train was quiet, but Chexbres said no, we should wait for the boy to call us.

Finally we started, very slowly. We went past a lot of roadwork. Men were building beds for new tracks with great blocks of gray stone, and the Germans looked at them with a grudging fascination, leaning over us to see better and exclaiming softly.

We were glad when the young waiter came to the door. "Your table is ready, M'sieu'-'dame," he announced loftily, and the men stood up hastily to let us out.

When we got to the end of the car, the boy turned back. "Take care, please," he said to Chexbres. "There is a little humidity on the platform."

And the place was wet, right enough. The curved piece of glass was still in the window, but it and the walls and the floor were literally dripping with water. We went carefully through it, and into the almost empty restaurant.

The chef rested at the end, reading a paper, but got up and went back to the galley as we came in. Our table was nicely laid, with fresh linen, and there were two or three little square dishes of pickled onions and salami and butter. We felt very hungry, and quite gay.

The boy brought us some good wine, a fairly expensive red Chianti we always drank on that train, and we began to eat bread and salami with it. I remember there were some of those big white beans, the kind Italians peel and eat with salt when they are fresh and tender in the early summer. They tasted delicious, so fresh and cold. . . .

It was good to be eating and drinking there on that train, free forever from the trouble of life, surrounded with a kind of insulation of love. . . .

The old waiter came through the car. He was going to pass our

table without looking at us. Chexbres spoke to him. "Stop a minute," he said. "Your coat . . . how is it?"

The man turned without answering, so that we could see the
neat stitches that held his sleeve in place. I said something banal
about the sewing . . . how good it was . . . and Chexbres asked
quietly, "The man . . . the prisoner . . . did he get away?"

The old man suddenly looked at us, and his eyes were hateful, as
if he loathed us. He said something foul, and then spat, "It's none
of my business!" He hurried away, and we could not turn to watch
him.

It was so shocking that we sat without any movement for quite
a time. I could feel my heart beat heavily, and my throat was as if an
iron collar hung around it, the way it used to be when Chexbres
was first ill. Finally I looked at the few people still eating, and it
seemed to me as if they met my eyes with a kind of hatred too, not
as awful as the old man's but still crouching there. There was fear in
it, and fear all around me.

Chexbres' face was full of pain. It was the first time it had come
through for weeks, the first time since we started to drift like two
happy ghosts along the old current of our lives together. The iron
collar tightened to see it there. I tried to drink some wine, but I
couldn't swallow more than once.

The young waiter hurried past us without looking, and
Chexbres stopped him firmly. "Please," he said. "What is wrong?
What has happened?"

The boy looked impassively at us, and for a minute I thought he
was going to be rude. Then he whispered, still protecting us, "Eat,
M'sieu'-'dame. I will tell you in a minute." And he hurried off to
the galley, bending supplely under the last great tray of emptied
plates.

"Yes, you'd better eat something," Chexbres said coldly to me.
"You've drunk rather a lot, you know." He picked up his fork, and
I did too. The spaghetti was like ashes, because I felt myself com-
ing to life again, and knew he did.

When we were the only ones left in the car, the boy came back.

He stood leaning against the table across the aisle, still swaying with the motion of the train but now as if he were terribly tired, and talked to us so softly that we could hardly hear him. There was no friendliness in his voice, but not any hatred.

He said that when the train stopped at Domodossola, or wherever the border was, the political prisoner was being taken off, and suddenly he laughed and pressed his throat down on the edge of broken windowpane. The old waiter saw it.

"That was probably the plan in the first place," the boy said. "The poor bastard was chained to the cops. There was no escaping. It was a good job," he said. "The border police helped clean up the platform. That was why the train stopped so long.

"We're making up time now all right," the boy said, looking admiringly at the rocky valley flash past us. "The old man keeps fussing about his coat. He's nuts anyway."

By the time we got to Milano everything was almost all right again, but for a few minutes the shell cracked. The world seeped in. We were not two ghosts, safe in our own immunity from the pain of living. Chexbres was a man with one leg gone, the other and the two arms soon to go . . . a small wracked man with snowy hair and eyes large with suffering. And I was a woman condemned, plucked at by demons, watching her true love die too slowly.

There in the train, hurrying across the ripe fields, feeling the tranced waiting of the people everywhere, we knew for a few minutes that we had not escaped. We knew no knife of glass, no distillate of hatred, could keep the pain of war outside.

I felt illimitably old, there in the train, knowing that escape was not peace, ever.

The Measure
of My Powers

1941

I

For several months after Chexbres died I was in flight, not from
myself particularly nor of my own volition. I would be working
in my little office and suddenly go as fast as I could out the door and
up the road, until I had no breath left. Or my sister Anne would
look at me and say, judiciously, as if I were a vase of flowers to be
moved here and there, "You must go to Mexico." Then she would
buy a ticket for me, and a new hat, and she would take care of visas.
It seemed all right. I doubt if it did much good, except to pass the
time with as little damage as possible. But that too was all right.

People thought I was in a state of shock at the dying, but it was
more one of relieved exhaustion after the last three years. It dulled
parts of me, so that although I looked quite normal I walked into
chairs and doors, and was covered with dreadful bruises without
feeling any hurt.

But other senses were bright and alive in me. I saw things like
rocks and mouse-prints clearly at last. I heard almost too much. I
ate, with a rapt voluptuous concentration which had little to do
with bodily hunger, but seemed to nourish some other part of me.

"She needs people around her," the people themselves would say. It was not they, but the chance to feed them that was good for me. I planned and cooked really beautiful meals for them, and when I was alone I did the same thing for myself, with perhaps even more satisfaction. Sometimes I would go to the best restaurant I knew about, and order dishes and good wines as if I were a guest of myself, to be treated with infinite courtesy.

I still kept walking into things, though, and after I side-swiped a parked car with the same cold immunity to violence, Anne said, "Mexico." That was all right. All I needed was time, and while it was passing I could look and hear and taste in Jalisco as well as California, and with my new acuteness.

I was late getting to Guadalajara, where Norah and David and his new wife Sarah were to meet me. The plane was to stop overnight at Mazatlan, the officials told us at three in the morning: the fog was too thick, and ice would form on the wings. I didn't care.

I stood aimlessly about for a few more minutes with the other passengers in the drear shoddiness of the airport offices. Then we went our twelve or thirteen separate ways to benches and folded overcoats and even one or two hotel beds. I rented a room, and turned down the bed, and then spent the rest of the night riding up and down in the elevator with the Filipino boy who ran it. We said very little, but he seemed to enjoy my sitting there with him, and we ate Lifesavers and smoked amicably now and then. It was quite a natural thing to do, although it seems a little strange now, in the telling.

At five or six we were back at the port again. The plane would perhaps take off in two hours. Some of us sagged back, bag-eyed and grimly polite, onto the benches; and others stumbled toward the newly lighted coffee shop, where a pale waitress flicked last night's crumbs off the counters and laid out last year's menu cards.

I saw four of the middle-aged men-passengers brighten as they dug into their eggs and meat and toast, and sucked their coffee. It was queer, in that gray waiting room, to look in past the shrouded cigaret counter to the harsh glare of the eating place, and watch the sleepy men revive. It was like watching a speeded-up movie of flowers opening, or of a foetus changing into a human in nine minutes instead of nine months.

I felt almost indecent, looking at them, and walked away toward the baggage office, where two colored men were chatting and snoozing on the pile of suitcases. I stood near them for a few minutes, listening to their soft snickering voices and feeling comfortable, the way I had in the elevator with the tiny clean brown boy. Then maybe I went into a little dream standing up, because when I awoke we were flying over puckered hills and unnaturally straight rivers without apparent banks, and I realized that everybody on the plane but me was eating breakfast. Especially the men who had eaten breakfast in the coffee shop were eating breakfast.

Of course, I could see only the two people across from me (I knew already that he was a dentist from Monrovia), and maybe one-third each of three people in front of me, but I watched the little dapper steward flicking his tail up and down the aisle, carrying trays and trays.

The women were for the most part drinking cups of coffee and eating one piece each of dry toast and then, a far as I could see, devouring everything their husbands would let them snatch from the more robust masculine trays, saying as they did so, "Just one bite!" Sometimes, but not often they said, "Just one bite, dear!"

The men, though, paid small attention. They looked beamingly at their well-filled laps, their brimming knees. It would not have mattered much if the air were rough, for not only was every cup and plate sunk into its own well in the tray, but each tray was clutched as if the poor men had never seen such good food before.

There was coffee, of course. It was properly steaming. There was orange juice. Besides that there was a large orange rolling slightly between the two cups, with more than enough publicity stamped on the skin in purple ink to make us realize that the state fruit-exchange was only too glad to add to the happiness of the airline's passengers by this little added surprise.

On the less liquid side there was, tucked among the expected array of stiff cardboard cutlery and paper napkins, a pair of oddly obscene envelopes made of cellophane. They were printed in bright blue ink with the name of a caterer, and his trademark of jolly little Dutch girls and windmills masked too inadequately the hot limp contents.

In one envelope was a generous slice of grilled ham, complete with its juice and what looked like an overgenerous supply of condensed steam. The men speared impotently for a minute at the horrid containers, and then their paper forks went in, and the whole inside slipped onto the plates. It must have looked good to them, because someone behind me said, "Oh boy!" Or maybe it was, "Golly, that looks fine, all right!"

The other of the two envelopes was filled with pale yellow, creamy, hot scrambled eggs.

I felt unusually well. There were purplish clouds underneath us, that really had no color at all when I looked down on them and thought about them. I had pulled out the little aircock above me, and thin sweet air poured in on my face, and made my eyes feel cool. Perhaps I needed food. But I thought that those limp cellophane envelopes of hot egg and meat were the most disgusting things I had ever seen. I kept watching the clouds and feeling a little ashamed for acting snobbish or persnickety, while the steward looked resignedly at me, sure that I had made up my mind to be sick, and the other men and most of the women tucked into their good hot food and enjoyed themselves in their own ways, as I was doing.

Lunch, which followed almost immediately, was very interesting. It was already packed in paper boxes, which folded open and back into trays. Of course, there were two or three cups of water and fruit punch and hot consommé and such, and the paper and napkins, and an enormous pear and an enormous apple tucked into little couches of shaved lavender paper.

Then there were two closed paper cups, each with a little spoon sticking out of it like a stiff umbilical cord. One held a canned pear with cottage cheese under it, and was undoubtedly called a salad, and the other was filled with fruit jelly, the kind that is bright yellow and has pieces of banana and pineapple in it.

Then there were three sandwiches, each wrapped and sealed separately in cellophane: one chicken on white bread, one cheese on white bread, one ham on rye. The fillings were generous, and there was good butter between them and the bread, which was perfect and tasteless, being American.

I called the neat lizard-like little steward and asked him to empty most of my drinking water. He looked puzzled, but almost before I could shift my tray enough to lean down to the floor for my handbag he was back with the half-filled cup. I poured in a good shot of bourbon from my flask, looked out of the window and toasted a cloud that had a big nose much like my father's, and almost at once felt even better than I had before.

The dentist and his wife looked queerly at me, or perhaps jealously. I sipped at my drink until there was one swallow left, and then went to work on the tray.

The cheese in one sandwich was the processed gluey kind, cut from a block, and I ignored it. I undid the ham and the chicken packages, and put all the insides of one sandwich on all the insides of another, and then telescoped the outsides, so that I had a thick ham-and-chicken sandwich put together with half white and half rye bread.

Then I poked around among the napkins and fruit wrappings and sandwich papers until, sure enough, I found a minute pair of salt and pepper shakers, and I fairly well plastered the chicken with salt and the ham with fine black pepper. Then I put the two pieces together, and ate them.

It turned out very well. It was a pleasant lunch, small yet nourishing, and I concocted it with a neatness and intense dispatch impossible anywhere but high above the earth, so that it was not ridiculous or gross or even finicky while I did it.

When I had finished I drank the *bonne bouche* of water and bourbon in my cup, rolled up all the odds and ends of paper into a little plug for one of the elaborate number of holes in the tray, and put all the cups and plates and uneaten things of food as best I could into the remaining places. Then I asked the steward if I might steal the tiny shakers, black for pepper and white for salt.

He looked completely thrown off the track of his Berlitz lessons for a minute, and then flushed and giggled and said, "Oh, but of course it will be serious jail for the Señora, with your permission!" He disappeared down the aisle, staggering slightly under the impact of his own waggery, and I put the shakers in my purse and as far as I can remember never saw them again.

Underneath there were dry black mountains, sharper than pins. Around me people sat back, literally full, eased by the action in their bellies from the secret fears of all men in the air. Their glands ticked on, whipped by the altitude and occupied and preoccupied by digestion, so that even if the plane had faltered and hiccuped they would not have minded.

The shadows on the black mountains grew impossibly acute, with the going down of the sun. Before long we would land. The flying was rougher . . . the cooling air flowing up or down the hot earth, maybe.

The little steward pretended to adjust the thermometer, forward in the cabin, and gave us all a sharp look. And before we knew it he was putting queer cellophane hat boxes on our laps, tied with bright blue rayon ribbon like something for Easter; and inside each one, very pretty indeed, were waxy pears and fine grapes and little packages of extra-fancy raisins and I think a few nuts, the washed-looking kind that come in gift packages.

In a moment what pale cheeks there were had flushed, and the fretting women were gay, and the tired men looked more mildly at the dour savage land beneath us, or forgot it entirely. People munched and exclaimed, like happy infants.

I took out my flask, drank a mature-sized sip, and opened my little hat box dutifully as the steward looked obliquely at me.

There was a slip of imitation vellum laid across the top of the beautiful fruit, which two hungry people might have eaten during a whole day, and on the slip was printed in old Gothic the name of the company so happy to donate this small token to the airline. Then it said, still in Gothic, "You may eat this with carefree abandon, for it has been washed and scrubbed and rub-a-dub-dubbed."

Good, I thought. That's fine. Me too.

I ate a few grapes, which were tasteless but enjoyable, and then carefully tied the bright ribbon about the box again and asked the steward to give it to me when we landed. It would be a nice little surprise for Norah and Sarah and David: they must be hungry for fruit that had not been dipped in anti-typhoid anti-malaria antidysentery water. This had been rub-a-dub-dubbed.

We were almost at Mazatlán. I saw coconut trees, poisonously impossibly green in the last sunlight, and then the blank silver bay and the black boats on it. We sloped over the port, and as I tightened my landing belt I suddenly felt very hungry, especially for something not wrapped or bedded or boxed in cellophane. And at the same time I was grateful to the air company for trying to take my mind off the troubled certainty that for several hours I, a little wingless human, had been much higher than a kite. A kite in flight, I thought, and the earth moved up to touch my foot . . .

II

It seemed as if we made a lot of noise when we walked into the high darkening coolness of the hotel. The Mexicans at the doorway, sitting under the arcade, talking and watching the sea across the road, looked curiously at us, thinking perhaps that we had been rescued from a plane accident; and the people inside bustled softly about, allotting rooms and carrying bags and being temporarily energetic.

All the other passengers stood in a clot by the desk, asking for the best. I leaned against a pillar, not caring whether my room had a view, nor if I had a room at all. The hotel smelled nice, and I could see a great sloping staircase without steps going up one side of the patio, and a mighty splash of purple flowers clinging to the stone wall. I felt good.

A pleasantly aloof man, an American-German Jew who ran a

clothing factory in Mexico and flew a great deal, asked me if I would have a drink with him, while we waited until the other passengers stopped being sure that on this, their first stop in a foreign country, they were not robbed, cheated, and insulted. It seemed like a fine idea.

He knew his way to the bar, a dim quiet room behind the *cantina* that opened off the street. The barman knew him, too, and with my permission the man said, "Two of the same, Charlie," in Mexican slang.

The same was a tall cool drink with rum in it. The man was nice, because he was so impersonal and seemed to enjoy the same thing in me. We talked about smuggling, and rum, and a drink made with tequila and tomato juice called, appropriately, *un sangre*. Then I thanked him and we went into the hall again, feeling better.

At the desk the three or four men behind it exclaimed "Ah!" loudly and with a kind of coy theatrical relief, and a little boy laden with four bags and an enormous ring of keys trotted ahead of us up the long incline of the stairless stairs and through some halls, and after a bit of breathless finagling flung open a door. It was a beautiful room, with two great double beds, as high and four-postered as something in *David Copperfield*, and the sound of the sea everywhere.

The boy put the bags inside. I stood there without any embarrassment, waiting to be alone, smelling the air and feeling light and warm.

The man flushed a dark red. "These bags are mine," he said quickly to the boy.

He put his hand on the knob of the door, bowed with a stiff movement never learned since he left Germany, and said very quietly, "I hope you will forgive this. It is a stupid mistake."

I looked at him, and his nice brown eyes were full of misery. But before I could tell him how little it mattered to me, and how sorry I was for his confusion, he had closed the door. He must have dined away from the hotel, because I saw him only on the plane the next morning, and then he did not speak.

The room was wonderful, austere and airy the way I like a bedroom to be. I decided which of the two beds I would climb into, later, and put my slippers beside it and my nightgown on it, with the waist pinched in the way the maids used to do at the Ritz, or at the Trois Couronnes in Vevey.

The bathroom was like a big box of hand-made tiles, colored a vile yellow that seemed lovely to me, with occasional smears of purple under the glaze, as if the people in the pottery work had grown bored with one color and plainness. There was, besides the washbowl and moderately regal throne, a fine large tub. And one corner of the floor sloped a little, with a grill in it and a pipe overhead, and that was the shower.

It is fine to take a bath standing up with no tight walls around, when the room is warm. I felt fresh and self-contained, in spite of sleeplessness and being up so high, but still it was pleasant to bathe again. I dressed slowly, wandering about in a kind of distracted contentment, leaning every now and then on the deep sill of the open window.

A sunset breeze pushed the long white curtains back against me, and filled my nostrils with the male smell of kelp on tide-rocks. Underneath, in the arcade of the hotel and on the roadway, people talked and walked softly, and past the low wall the waves broke, like the regular breathing of something known, familiar. The water in the harbor, beneath the fading brashness of the sunset, was as hard and colorless as gunmetal, or an old engraving.

Finally I was dressed, in a clean blouse under my gray jacket, but without a hat. I went down slowly, stilted in my high heels along the steep slope of the stairway, like a horse trotting downhill.

I went out on the quai or esplanade or whatever it was. Under the arcade of the hotel lights were on over the café-tables, but along the sea-wall it was dark now, and cool. Couples already strolled silently, or young men alone, looking at me and murmuring.

I went back, and five or six of the passengers at a table asked me to sit and have a drink with them. I was surprised, in a dispassionate way. Probably they felt sorry for me, all alone: most people are so afraid of that for themselves that they assume it is the same for others. I ordered a tequila and a small beer, and listened to them talking about the exchange and tipping and how you had to watch the Mexicans every minute. They were not bad people, but shy and on guard against everything, especially everything that did not speak good American.

Then I asked if they would not have a drink with me. They said no, no, one was plenty thank you, and laughed daringly. I was sorry to be obligated to them but there was nothing to do about it.

They were making plans for "seeing the town" after dinner, and asked me to go with them. I said I was going to bed, and they looked strangely at me. "You've been here before, then?" they asked, and when I said no, they laughed again, daringly, and said *they* weren't going to waste any time in bed; *they* weren't going to miss a trick. Then one of the women asked me if I'd sit with them at dinner, after I'd got my hat, and I told them I was very tired, and thanked them for the drink and went into the hotel. I knew they felt hurt and snubbed, and in a blind way angry at me for being alone and hatless and self-sufficient enough to go to bed when I was tired. But there was nothing to do about it that seemed worth the changes I would have to make, even for a few minutes, in the way I was.

The dining room, like hotel dining rooms all over the world, was large, bleak, dull. I walked through it as far as I could, past a few tables of almost silent people who stared for a second and then dropped their eyes to their food again.

A waiter appeared at the end of the room, chewing and looking surprised to see me so far from the safe company of the other diners. I smiled at him, and he smiled back, and I sat down at a little table by the open door into the patio, dark and strange now like a cave.

I ordered a bottle of beer, and drank slowly at the first little glass of it until the food started coming. I asked for only a few things on the pretentious menu, but even they were too many. The stuff was abominable: a tasteless *sopa de pasta*, a salad of lukewarm fish and bottled dressing, some pale meat . . .

I felt very sorry, but I simply could not eat it. And all the time delicious smells came from the kitchen when the waiters went past me, not from what they carried but from something they had just left. And I could hear laughing and talking, so that the stilted silence of the dining room was painful.

Finally the waiter brought me a little dish of bread pudding . . . *poudingue inglesa*, the menu said. There must have been something about my face that broke him then, in spite of my being an uninvited unexpected diner there. He leaned over me and whispered something very rapidly. I understood only, "There is an American kitchen and there is a country kitchen, side by side out there . . ."

Then he disappeared. It seemed to me the smells got better as I waited for what would happen next. They were like a farm kitchen in the south of France, but with less garlic and more pepper. I was almost alone, waiting peacefully, sipping my beer. The passengers who had bought me a drink came and went, stiffly looking away from me. I felt mildly sorry to have hurt them by staying apart.

Then the waiter came back, and he was smiling and breathing hard in a pleasant excitement. He brought me what he and the others were eating in the kitchen, and it was even sitting in their dishes: a brown clay bowl and plate, with green and white birds under the thin glaze.

The bowl had beans in it, large light-tan beans cooked with some tomato and onion and many herbs. I ate them with a big spoon, and now and then rolled up a tortilla from the plate and ate it sopped in the beans.

And the feeling of that hot strong food going down into my stomach was one of the finest I have ever had. I think it was the first thing I had really tasted since Chexbres died, the first thing that fed me, in spite of my sensuous meals always. I ate everything . . . enough for three or four probably . . . and finished the beer while the waiter peered paternally at me occasionally from the kitchen door.

Then I paid him, and thanked him more than he could know, and went up to my sea-filled room. I slept like a cat all night, dreaming good dreams in my well-being, but hearing the waves when I wanted to through the dreams.

III

The little house in the fishing village was fairly new, built to rent to summer-people who came for the lake and the quiet. It had a bathroom upstairs, fed from a tank on the roof which a man came every night to fill by the hand-pump in the tiny patio. The tub did not work, but that was all right because Norah and Sarah and I were helping David paint murals in the municipal baths, and spent several hours every day neck-deep in the clear running water of the pools, walking cautiously on the sandy bottoms with pie-plates full of tempera held up, and paint-brushes stuck in our hair.

(The lavatory and toilet worked well, though, except occasionally when the water-man did not feel strong enough to come, after a fiesta. Then David would go next door to the bar, and Norah and Sarah and I would have a convenient beer in the lobby of the Hotel Nido on the plaza, where there was plumbing almost as good as ours.)

Our house was about thirty steps from the little square, which was very correct, with a wooden bandstand in the middle and a double promenade around it under the thick green trees, so that the boys could walk one way to the music and the girls the other . . . until the boys found courage or centavos enough to buy flowers and join their loves.

The flower-women sat at one end of the plaza on concert nights, the dark end, and candles or little lamps shone like magic on the blossoms lying on clean cloths in front of them. There were camelias and tiny gardenias, and sometimes spidery jewel-like orchids, and plainer garden-flowers, all glowing in the soft light on the earth while the women crouched darkly behind, deep in their shawls, and the band wheezed bravely for the innocent concupiscent strollers on the paths.

There were two or three bars, with juke-boxes when the orchestra got tired, and a little kiosk sold bright pink and yellow ices and Coca-Cola.

In the other direction from our house, and around the corner was the market. It was a sprawling wandering collection of stands, some of them elaborate, with counters for eating and stoves in the center, and some of them a piece of cloth on the ground with two little heaps of dried peppers and a bruised yam or a pot of stew waiting to be bought. Of course there were *serape* merchants and sandal-makers on Sundays, and piles of thin pottery everywhere and always because it broke easily after it was bought.

There were hungry dogs and cats near the one meat-stand, where flies buzzed so thickly over the strange strips of hanging bony flesh that we could hear them before we even turned the corner.

Some days, and perhaps for a week at a time, there would be almost nothing to buy except one thing, like tomatoes, at every stand . . . little pungent tomatoes no bigger than pigeon eggs. It was the wrong season for avocados when I was there, but now and then we found string beans, or a rotting papaya.

It was hard to get enough food for our meals, even though we probably had more money than most of the marketers. I'd have liked to take bowls to the open kitchens, the way the people did, and buy them full of hot beans to eat with a stack of tortillas . . . but perhaps that was because I had not been in Mexico as long as my sisters and brother. Perhaps it was because I remembered the beans in Mazatlan, too.

Whenever any of us went to Guadalajara we bought lettuces and butter and bread there, and whatever else we saw.

The little house, besides the bathroom, had three sleeping rooms upstairs and two rooms and a kitchen downstairs. I wanted very much to cook something, to fold myself in the comfortable cloud of mix-baste-and-boil. But there seemed very little to cook, and the kitchen itself was baffling. I think I could soon have learned to handle myself in it. But I was a guest.

The room was very small, with a window and door into the stub-end of the patio, by the pump, and another door into the shelf-lined hallway to the dining room. There was a small table, almost a tabouret, with a deep clay pot of supposedly sterile water in it, for drinking and rinsing vegetables, and on the long side of the room a kind of ledge of red tile, waist-high.

I can't remember whether there was a little sink in the ledge, with a cold-water tap. I think so. Then there was a sunken place for a charcoal fire, with a grill over it, and room for the little two-burner kerosene stove David had bought in Guadalajara after all of them had tried miserably to learn how to fan charcoal enough to cook anything in less than several hours. Above the ledge there were five or six clay pots and an iron saucepan on a shelf, and some wooden spoons and a knife hung above the grate.

In the little hallway one of the shelves had a screen door to keep flies away from food, and there was a tiny ramshackle icebox, that held about four kilos of ice when there was any to be had.

And that was where we got our meals, when we got them.

A square ageless woman, not quite a dwarf, came every morning to get breakfast and do the cleaning. For some reason we made a point of not knowing her name. I think it may have been because we were all so big and she was so little, and she did all the dirty work for us, so that we felt basically ashamed of ourselves and tried to hide it by keeping her anonymous. David ordered her to be called Big Lige, as if her name were Elijah. Little Lige was her daughter, who worked there before I came and did our laundering, and she was almost normal in size.

Big Lige worked harder than her child, and had a very strong unpleasant smell, not foul but stifling. She was one of the most courteous people I have ever been with. When we left she wore her Sunday *rebozo*, and wept. I would like to have her near always, like a little dark stone to anchor me, except for that smell.

She admired the kerosene stove deeply but always used the charcoal one. When she worked it, it made a nice thin smoke, not at all like the black clouds we could draw from it so easily, and the toast had the same delicate smokiness to it, delicious with butter. She learned quickly how to make coffee the way my family liked it, and seemed especially happy when Sarah or David would ask her to go to the corner for an egg to boil for them. Canned tomato juice was more than she felt worthy of coping with, though, and David always had to open and pour that himself, while she held her shawl over her eyes shyly.

We used to sit in the little dining room a long time at breakfast, eating and talking and listening to Big Lige fan patiently at the embers, waiting for us to command her.

At noon, when we collected from the baths or walks or our own workings, we could sit in the small high living room on the floor, because there were only a few stiff chairs, and drink for a time . . . beer or tequila. The others liked Coca-Cola for a mixer, and a little lime juice, but I liked tequila alone, and then beer afterwards.

The room was like a glorified bath, all of stone and tile, so that our voices echoed wonderfully, and sounded full and rich, and clearer than ever before. David played his guitar, and sometimes Norah, and we sang in our various ways, but all beautifully because of the resonant walls and the tequila we were drinking. I heard myself doing *vocalizes* that amaze me even to think on . . . like a robust flute I was.

Then Sarah or Norah or I, or all of us, would go to the kitchen while David kept on like a rooster, strumming and crowing until the hens came back.

We ate bread and butter and what we wanted from a plate as big as a table-top covered with tomatoes and hard eggs and whatever other things like radishes we had been able to find. Sometimes we had a jar of red caviar from the grocery in Guadalajara. We drank some more, and ate and sang.

At night we usually went to one of the little restaurants. They were very plain, and it was best to stop by in the afternoon and ask what there would be for four people. Most of the people ate in them or ordered food to be cooked there and taken home, even if they were quite poor. It was because the kitchens were so bad, I suppose, and charcoal and water and food so scarce. Always at meal times boys would be walking through the streets with food on their heads, from the little eating-places . . . pots of stew and beans, piles of tacos, sometimes a boiled chicken steaming naked on a platter if it was for a family feast-day.

We would order little white lake-fish if we could: they were like the perch I used to eat at Cully, on the Lac Léman, but not so knowingly prepared. Then there were thick porridges of rice and herbs, "not running and not standing," like Elizabethan soups. And tortillas.

And unless you liked beans, which none of my family seemed to, that was all: the meats were repulsive and poorly cooked; there were no salads and almost no vegetables; none of us liked the violently colored stiff sweet pastes that were called desserts.

There was one place, a bare room with two tables in it and a stove at the end, that made nothing but tacos. I liked them very much . . . hot limp tortillas filled with chopped herbs and lettuces or whatever you wanted. We went there often, and watched the pretty woman swirl two big oval pans slowly over the embers, just enough to wilt the tortillas without burning them.

Always the *mariachi* players would find us, whether we had any pesos left for them or not, while little children squatted listening delightedly on the sidewalk, and cats waited under the table for our crumbs. The music followed us everywhere, like something in a dream.

A few times, in spite of my shyness about the kitchen, I made supper. It took a long time, and involved scuttling all over the village for supplies, the way I used to in Dijon before I learned how to market there. I found there was very little I could cook, partly because of the lack of food and partly because I could do nothing with it but boil it.

I scrambled eggs a few times. But it was hard to find more than two or three at once, and there was no cream or cheese in the village.

One night I produced a very fine sauce, which we ate with toasted tortillas. It used up most of the kerosene to cook it enough, and took almost a day, and kept me occupied agreeably. I stirred and stirred, there in the little kitchen.

I remember it was after dark when I heard the pump clanking. I looked out the window, past the steam from my pot of sauce, and saw the white eyes of the water-man going up and down, up and down, never leaving my face as he rode the stiff handle. His face was very thin.

I tasted the sauce, and stirred, and put in more things, and all the time the man looked at me, but so that I could not tell if he saw me.

Finally I got a little glass of tequila and rolled some of the dark rich juice in a tortilla, and took it out to him. I knew that it was more work to start the pump once it had stopped, but I felt wrong there in the light and flavor and comfort, unless I took some of it to him. It was always like that in Mexico: I felt wrong to be clean and nourished among those fine people who could not be . . .

He was very nice about it, and stood holding the glass and the taco while the pump slowed itself silent.

We exchanged a few phrases, the kind printed in conversation-books which people really say by instinct in every language, and then I went into the kitchen again, feeling a little foolish before his poised gentility.

I started to take a drink. The man tapped on the window, waiting for that, and held up his little nip, bowing to me from the darkness. I bowed to him. We smiled. Finally he ate the taco, politely, in three bites instead of one. I felt a little better about stirring all that sauce . . . but not much.

One morning we were sitting after breakfast around the big cluttered table, when there was a strange dreadful sound outside on the street, and a wailing cry.

We looked silently at one another, pale because of the sickening finality of the noise, and before David got up unwillingly to see what had happened, I thought of a book I'd read long ago in France, in which a pregnant girl jumped from a window and "split open on the pavement like a ripe melon." It sounded like that.

When he came back he said, with a kind of relief but mournfully too, that a woman from the hills with a big pot of boiled beans on her head had stumbled, there in front of our house on her way to sell them in the market. She had probably walked most of the night. And they were probably her whole crop, David said.

He moved restlessly about, and we all got up and went away from one another, in a kind of pain.

I looked down from Norah's room. The beans, pale and nasty, were spread on the stones, all mixed with broken pottery and already half-eaten by the starved dogs of the village and a few beggar-children. People walking to market made a wide silent circle, or hurried past sadly, impotently. And the hill-woman sat folded into her shawl, with her face on her knees, never making any sound after her first wail.

She sat there all day, not moving even her shoulders, with one closed hand beside her on the cobbles.

The beans were soon gone, and someone picked up the broken clay into a little pile, so that the street looked cleaner than before, where the dogs had licked around her.

At lunch we could not eat or sing or talk. We did not speak of the woman sitting there, but each of us would go secretly from the others to the upper windows, on tiptoe, and peek to see her. None of us knew what to do, in the face of such absolute stillness.

David told me, long after we were all in California again, that he tried once to put some money into her hand, and shook her a little. He had a very gentle way with women when he wanted to, or thought he was alone with one, but she did not hear his voice at all, and the money rolled away from her fingers. The man who ran the bar next to us saw, and said, "It's no use, Señor. Come in and have a drink."

And at sundown she was gone. None of us saw her go. She took all the pieces of clay with her, back to the hills. We could go out past the place where she had been, then, to eat some supper. We went to the Nido, and spent a lot of money, and drank cocktails first by the lake, still feeling shocked by the sound of the pot falling on the stones, and her long silence. It was her own kind of flight, as good perhaps as mine . . .

Feminine Ending

1941

I

How can I write the love story of a woman I don't know? There must be more than cerebration, more than the skillful plotting of my thoughts. A song, a drunken look, a light remembered along Juanito's fingers . . . but will the blended brew have flavor?

Recollection is not enough. Perhaps I must pound the table, be harsh, be loud-tongued, to make what never happened assume its own reality.

What shall I hate, then? Shall I hate something beyond hatred, something like the Church, the tawdrily solid Church in that village on the Mexican lake, where the young long-nosed priest wore his cassock short, as if his trousers' virile proof would reassure him?

Shall I hate myself, as part of the life that molded us all, my brother, my sister Norah, the sloe-eyed Sarah, so that we went there in our white skins, with our vocabularies of suffering and hunger and our soft light hair, and lived among the courteous people of Jalisco as if anyone could live anywhere in such pale immunity?

Shall I get drunk on hatred, or sit back tranquilly, listening to the quiet voices of the long and newly dead, peacefully now as I should have been on the lake?

I heard Juanito singing almost as soon as I came to earth in Mexico. I did not know it at first. I was like a sea-plant, with a thousand ears out on little stalks, but only to hear what I was listening for.

Norah and David met my plane at Guadalajara. How tall, how insolently beautiful they were, moving within their fine skins and their clothing and the world about them like creatures from another planet, and yet shyly. We drove through the edge of the city and then out over the long gaunt plains, talking a great deal and listening tentatively to one another, not asking questions for a time. Then we came to a break in the wavering flatness, and started to go down, with the lake below us and the air changing. The little car stopped rattling and swooped smoothly toward the shore.

Norah got out at the gates of a place where her picture was being painted, and walked with a kind of cool assurance along the path toward the villa, as if she liked going there. David and I stopped talking. The road was very bad. And we were thinking of the next stop, where I would meet Sarah, my new sister-in-law, all three of us nervous and educated not to show it, all three wanting things to be easy and friendly long before we'd had the time to make them so.

I was the oldest child, and David was the youngest, and between us there were years of dependence and resentment and love and ruthlessness, and now the knowledge that he had married sooner than we'd hoped for him, and in a far country, to an unknown girl. It was a cautious moment . . .

We stopped in front of a door a few steps off the leafy plaza, and David beeped the horn and jumped out to fuss at the back of the car, in self-protection.

Sarah came out. She had a true share of dignity. I liked that and her fine unlacquered fingernails and the sloping contours of her very quiet face. I suppose she was nervous, like me, but probably neither of us showed it much. We went into the little house, and soon she left, without any fuss or explanation, to market or sit by the lake, and to leave David and me to get used to each other. It was well done.

The house was a good one, with simple bones to it. A stair went up two sides of the living room to the bedrooms, so that the ceiling was high. It was wonderful for singing, or for any sounds from the street, which rang clear and full and rich. There was almost no furniture, and the tile floor looked as clean as a plate.

David took me up to my room: I felt foolish in high heels and a hat and a flannel suit, with jet in my ears and my traveling face still on. The room for me had a wide window, with white curtains tied back with pink candy-box ribbons, and there were two narrow beds in it, one soft and lumpy and the other a real Mexican bed with boards instead of a mattress. After one or two nights, I always slept on that one. There were beautiful *serapes* for blankets, and some of David's pictures on the wall, and the three children had bought me a little silver comb, and a pair of Spanish *alpargatos*. David said they had been imported for the refugees, but the refugees liked leather sandals better.

I put on slacks, and the soft blue cotton shoes, and the comb in my hair, and went down the stairs again. It was like going down into a clear white well, and David was at the bottom, sitting on the floor, with a guitar on his knees and a drink on either side of him. We talked for a while, not about Sarah, nor anything that had happened to any of us. The drink was very good.

I was glad to be there. I felt welcome, but not as if it would have mattered if I had flown north instead of south, and that was the way I wanted to feel.

David was waiting for something. Maybe it was Sarah, I thought. He tapped on his glass and on the belly of the guitar, and I noticed how his knuckles had thickened in his long pale hands. His face had changed too, but I could not yet tell how, except that it looked much older than he was.

"Why don't you play?" I asked.

"No, wait," he said, and his eyes were mischievous, and wary, far back in his skull. "Wait. You'll hear some real music pretty soon."

So we went on drinking, and I told him about our parents, and he asked me if people at home were wondering much about war . . . things like that.

Then, far away, I began to hear the music. It came upon us quickly, so that before I could think about it the whole tall white room was full of sound, beating insistently like an excited heart all around us. David's worn look vanished, and he stared delightedly at me, but with a sideways slant to his vision, as if he were seeing the music, too. It was the first time I ever heard such sounds. I knew there were musicians outside in the street, but I had no idea yet of what they looked like, or how they could make such wild nagging sounds. There was a steady strumming, but it had no *thump* to it, no *plunkety-plunk*. There was some sort of wind instrument, but I didn't know what. And the men were singing, in a kind of rollicking wail.

"It's a *mariachi*," David said, under the beat of the music. "There are two bands here, in spite of the god-damned juke-boxes. They're disappearing, though. This one is Juanito's, the good one. Juanito is the falsetto. You'll hear."

The men kept on playing, about three songs, I think, and then they began one that made David lean back voluptuously against the cool wall. It was a kind of duet with sometimes one or two or three singing against all the rest, and always the chorus in a high single voice, piercing and sweet, with the strings beating against it. It was a passionate song, and at the end the two male voices singing under the high one sobbed like children, in thirds.

Then the band went away, and we could hear it faintly at the far end of the plaza. It seemed, though, as if the whole house, and we in it, were still throbbing, almost with fatigue. I felt shaken. Perhaps it was because I had been so high in the air that morning, then drunk the long good drink: I knew that, but still I felt strange.

David finally stood up, and stood looking down at me tenderly. "The high one was Juanito," he said. "That was *La Malagueña*. There's a good *mariachi* band at the hotel bar in Guadalajara, but nobody can sing like Juanito. It gets you, doesn't it?"

He stood leaning against the wall, as if he wanted to say more.

"I thought I'd heard plenty of recordings," I said, "but I never heard Mexican music like that."

"There are some records . . . but it's Jalisco music, and there aren't good recording stations down here, maybe. Or the *mariachi* bands don't like to leave their own villages. I don't know. They're getting scarcer. God-damned juke-boxes . . ."

Norah came in then, and Sarah just after her, with a big purple eggplant in her hands.

"I see you had some music. We met them," Norah said in her noncommittal way.

She and Sarah stood looking at me, so that suddenly I felt awkward and asked, "Is it all right to wear slacks here?"

"Of course," Norah said.

"You look fine in them," David said, as if he were soothing me. "You look fine in slacks. I don't like slacks on women, but you . . ."

"Did she see Juanito?" Norah interrupted. I felt like a backward child, or like a hermit who has forgotten how other people communicate with one another.

"No, I didn't see him," I said impatiently. "He's the falsetto, though. Did you want me to see him?"

"Well," Norah said, "you will. Tonight, probably. He plays all the time . . . if Dave's there."

"Yes," Sarah said in her soft light voice, "Juanito is so young to have his own band."

Then David said, "Let's have a little drink before lunch, shall we?" And that was really the only thing I understood in the whole conversation.

They all stopped looking at me with their blue and brown and green eyes, big and little and flat and deep eyes, speculating eyes, cool and full of question. I sat there on the floor, waiting for lunch, and waiting too, for the next time I would hear that music, and not the ghost of it that still throbbed in my head.

II

There was a bar on the lake, under a kind of roof. It was too expensive for the village people, but enough tourists and weekenders from Guadalajara came to keep fine silk dresses and heavy bracelets on the fat widow who ran it. She was a white-faced woman with a sly flashing smile, and welcomed me warmly. I ordered the kind of cocktail the children told me they always drank there, and I could see her smiling toward a prosperous future as she stirred the liquors.

It was beautiful and peaceful under the roof by the quiet water. Little islands of hyacinths nudged and drifted against the half-flooded quai, and across the lake a few lights winked already in the clear darkness of November twilight. The air was warm and sweet. I thought of another lake, with Saint Gingolphe under the shadow of the Savoy Alps, cold and familiar, instead of these lower, stranger Mexican highlands. But the lake was the same. All lakes are alike when they are quiet . . .

The widow called to David, and then snapped on the lights under the roof, so that we were walled in from the darkness suddenly, and as suddenly were glad to be secure against it.

I looked at my fine-boned brother walk with the wary slouch of a tall man to the bar and pick up the tray of drinks, and I saw that there was a man on the other side of the bar, who fell silent as David approached, and watched as I was doing.

He was a small man in a tight Spanish beret and thickly horn-rimmed spectacles, with the thin shoulders and half-fed bravado of a ghetto-boy. It was almost startling to see, as my eyes got used to the hard light, that he wore a very short priest's cassock, so that his trousers and brightly striped socks in brown shoes showed below the hem. It was plain that he and David knew each other, although they did not speak, but as David came back silently toward us I was thinking more of the trousers than of that.

The only frocked priests that I saw much in my life were in Dijon, and there they wore long underwear and on very cold days flannel petticoats. If there were ordinary trousers anywhere, they were well-hidden by the long full cassocks, even on windy days. And now these flagrant inches of pin-striped masculinity astonished me. I was still pondering when David put the four glasses gingerly on the table.

We all toasted each other, and my coming, and the invisible lake so near us. The drink was good, like a Martini in Southern France, with a strong taste of herbs to it. The widow stopped her quiet laughing talk with the priest to put a waltz on her phonograph, and Sarah and David danced silently to it. They danced well. David bent over the small blonde woman with a drowsy smile.

"Norah," I said, touching my glass to hers as if I could reach her more quickly that way, "the little priest keeps staring at us. Don't you know him?"

She looked slowly at me with her large brown eyes, as if she were thinking. Oh yes, I remember you . . . Sometimes there is not even that recognition in them, which must be more disconcerting to men who love her than it is to me, who also love her and rubbed olive oil on her before she even had a navel.

She turned toward the bar without answering me, and bowed cordially to the priest. He bowed to her, and his face was very sweet and kind when he smiled. I saw the widow whisper something to him and then they both looked at me, still smiling. So I bowed too.

"Why doesn't he come over here?" I asked Norah. I was still warm from the way his face changed, and thought I would like to talk with him.

It was almost the end of the waltz. Norah said quickly to me, "It's because of Dave. I'll tell you . . ." And then Sarah and David were back again, and he said, "What about ordering another drink and I'll go up to the hotel and tell them ten more minutes."

The widow was delighted when David told her we wanted more, as he walked past the bar, but the priest was looking the other way.

The whole thing was so queer and rude and exciting, there in the little pavilion by the Mexican lake, with everything so new around me, that I stopped treading lightly, and said, "What's going on? Tell me. Is Dave fighting a one-man battle against the Mother Church?"

But Sarah looked cautiously at me from her tilted myopic eyes, and Norah said, "Not exactly. You know Dave. He shoots off his mouth a lot about what the Church has done here in Mexico. But it really isn't that. It's about Juanito."

I could hardly believe the thoughts in my head. But I had to ask more: our little house was like an echoing cave, impossible for confidences, and I felt I must know why my brother was so discourteous to a little Jewish priest, and what Norah meant about the *mariachi* singer.

"But Norah," I said angrily, "are you saying that Dave and this man are in love with . . . are having an affair with . . . I mean jealous of . . ."

It was such a strange thing to ask in front of the unknown little silky woman David had just married that I floundered clumsily, until both girls began to laugh at me, Sarah blushing under her mop of yellow hair.

"Oh, *no*," Norah said. "It's not that at all! We'll tell you about it. But you must see Juanito first."

"Yes," Sarah said earnestly, "we want you to see Juanito."

Just then the widow brought us the new drinks, and the priest walked past our table toward the village. He bowed again, but not smiling, and we answered him silently.

David came padding back on his big silent feet grinning at us. He loved ordering dinners.

"Everything is ready! The entire hotel holds its breath. To-night," he said, turning to me, "you're going to eat *pescados blancos* from the lake and wild hill-birds no bigger than a fig, as many as you want . . ."

"*Salud, pesetas, y amor,*" we all said, and the second drink tasted better than the first, and we felt very happy to be there together, the four of us alone in the brightness beside the still lake, while the woman watched casually and any other lives seemed far away.

III

The other *mariachi* band, not Juanito's, came to the inside door of the hotel while we were eating, and played three or four songs. The big plastered room, which went up to the glass ceiling, with bed-rooms opening onto galleries around it, and the tables at the bot-tom like pebbles, made the music almost unbearably loud. But still I liked it.

"Yes, it's good," the others said. "But not as good as Juanito's. We'd better go back to the widow's for a while . . . this is a party, anyway . . ."

There was a wind blowing from the water, when we had fin-ished our long dinner. Under the widow's roof the lights on long cords swung a little, so that strange shadows jumped and stretched around the tables. There were a few people now, drinking beer or coffee, and the phonograph played loudly from somewhere under the bar. We drank little glasses of a poor brandy.

"They'll stop the music when Juanito comes," David said.

"How are you so sure he'll come?" Norah asked, but there was no more malice in her voice than there was smugness in his when he answered.

"Oh, everybody in the village knows where we are. He'll be here."

I was beginning to feel bored with the whole noncommittal mystery. All right, *mariachi* music was fine. All right, I loved my family for entertaining me. But it had been a long day, and suddenly I wished I were all alone somewhere, maybe back at Mazatlán with the sea in my ears and a big white bed for me and nobody in the world to wait for.

Then the music came to the end of a record, and the widow did not put on another one, because up near the plaza was the sound of the band, whuddering in the wind, but with the underbeat strong and sturdy, like a pounding heart.

More people came silently in from the darkness where they had been watching us and listening to the records. They sat against the steps, so that the widow would not serve them anything, and waited, and while the music got nearer a few beggar-children flitted toward us, and then obediently away as David waved his long hand at them and said, "Later."

I felt that he liked them, maybe for being citizens in the world already, feeding themselves in their own way . . . so tiny, so big-eyed . . .

Then the band was there, standing in a little group on the street at the edge of the light. There were eight or nine men, some short and old-looking, a few big fat-bellied ones. The fattest man played a cornet, in a harsh, triumphant way, and when he played the others sang in unison, letting it take the melody to their thirds. Other times they all sang, always in thirds, and the insistent beat of the music was six-eight time, I guess. It never stopped. There were two violins, and two guitars and the rest plucked and strummed at big curved things like cellos or flat ones like mandolins.

The horn-player wore a pink silk shirt, but he and all the other men had their small *serapes* over one shoulder, and their straw hats with the embroidered bands and the wide black strings knotted at the back and hanging down like pigtails.

David and two or three others gave pesos to the fattest one after songs, but Norah whispered to me, "Juanito's the boss. He's there at the back. He won't come out because of David."

As if she had dropped a stone in a pool, people all around us began to say, "Juanito, Juanito," and finally call and clap and whistle.

David called too, and Sarah put her hand quickly on his arm in protest, and when he did not notice her, but went on with the other people, she and Norah looked strangely at each other, in a kind of female amazement.

Finally a small figure stepped out from behind the men, and while everyone shouted names of songs, and Juanito smiled a little and waited, his eyes cast down, touching the strings of his instrument, I solved the mystery for myself.

I knew that the three others were looking at me, even David in spite of his absorption in the band, and I kept my face as still as plaster. I was remembering, while I looked at the stooped slender little man who was the leader.

He had a pale dirty skin and hair that was rusty black, like a half-breed's, and there was a dry old look about him, as if he slept in the dust. His hair was almost shaved off, under the Jalisco hat, and his face was young and very weary. His hands on the guitar and his sandaled feet were like claws.

He stood waiting in the light, and then began to sing one song alone, without his men, a raw wild yelling song like Flamenco music, but with the *mariachi*-beat to it.

I was hearing it all, and watching him, and I was remembering one day when I was maybe sixteen. I was filled with eagerness, then, partly romantic and partly hereditary, to know more about my father's newspaper office. He humored me, but only a little: I was a woman, and he wanted to save all that for David. One day, though, he took me through the Back Room, and I watched the linotypists and then went over to the job-presses. The men did not seem to mind my watching their finicky work, but Father was in a hurry, and we went on through to his office.

At supper that night we were talking about the little presses, and Father said, "There's one chap there . . . I should have pointed him out to you. He does the finest work in the shop. He made a little trouble a few years ago . . . tried his hand at agitating. All right now. But he spends all his spare time illuminating . . . the real thing. Churches and big companies wanting rolls of honor . . . that sort of thing. I should have pointed him out. He uses real gold leaf."

"Do you mean the short fat one, with white hair?"

Father stared at me. "That's the one. Always has a cigaret in his mouth. He never says much, but he's the best man in the shop."

Before I thought, I said, "But, Father . . . that's not a man! It's a woman!"

Father was really upset. He was sure I was teasing him for some obscure reason: the chap had been there for years, he used the men's toilets, he'd even been in some labor-scare, he had a good reputation. And anyway, how in hell did I know?

I tried to tell Father that I had looked at the worker, and suddenly she had looked right into my eyes, and I had known . . . but that was no answer to him.

And the next day he was so disturbed by this strange thing that might have been going on for so long in his own place that he called his foreman, who laughed in his face. So Father called the worker, and she said, "Yes. Do you want me to quit?"

He didn't, but she stopped work for a few days, and talked to a minister, and after that she worked all week as a man, and then on Sundays she dressed in tailored dresses and went to church. I always felt badly about it, although the minister's wife said things were much happier for her. And once in a while at home Father would shake his head and say to me, "You certainly called the trick . . . I don't see . . ."

I knew, while I sat listening to the harsh music, with the shadows jumping in the wind, with my brother and sister and even Sarah watching me. I felt bewildered and timid. If they already had the answer, why did they wait for my confirmation? Was I going to hurt anything?

I saw the young priest on the edge of the light. He was watching me, too. I could not see his eyes behind their thick glasses, but his big nose and all the lines of his thin face were sneering, sardonic.

Then Juanito finished, and melted in among the men again,

smaller than even the bent old fiddlers, and the priest disappeared. People started to leave.

"How about one more song? How about *La Malagueña*?" David's eyes were bright, and his face fresher and younger than I had seen it for years, as if the music had filled him, just under the skin, with some kind of magic wax.

But Norah said, "No!" very sharply, and we all stood up. We said goodnight and thank you to the band, and they bowed so that the front fringes of their *serapes* touched the ground.

The streets were dark and uneven, and we walked arm in arm. I felt so tired I could hardly move my legs. I was full of little roasted birds and alcohol and a kind of heavy impatience with the world, so that when David said, "Well, what about Juanito?" I could hardly drag an answer through my lips.

"Well?" I said angrily. "Why 'o'? Why this bluff? It's Juanita, of course, feminine ending . . .'a.'"

David laughed delightedly, as if he had pulled off some sort of *coup*, and I knew he had been boasting to Sarah, just the way Father might have, about the time I saw the woman at the job-press.

"What of it, what of it?" Norah murmured wearily, and I felt her fingers tighten on my arm as if she were comforting me in some way that must for a time more be wordless.

IV

It took a long time for me to find out more about Juanito than I discovered that first day. Once the three children had it settled for them that I knew the little worn boy was a girl, they seemed to avoid talking about her.

It was impossible for me to question David: he was, in those last months of his life, turned in upon himself with a concentration I had seldom seen, in a hard, furious devotion that was at once tragic and admirable. It was beyond selfishness, beyond cruelty, so that his marriage, his imperious gentleness with Sarah and his sisters, even the intensity of his eating and drinking had a remoteness about them impossible to assault.

The only thing that seemed to reach him, and then as a kind of reassurance, was the *mariachi* music. It had a visible effect on him, so that while he listened to it, I could see his skin change from a strange jaded gray to the fresh firmness rightful in a young man. No. I could not ask him questions.

And, as I say, once he knew that I recognized the little musician, his interest in the whole thing stopped, and she was simply a part of the *mariachi* band. Even when she sang *La Malagueña*, she was not Juanito, a mysterious human with a passionate voice: she was a voice, passionate because David willed it, singing to David for David. At least, that is the way it seemed to me, and I withdrew in a kind of timidity from such ferocious self-concentration.

With Sarah and my sister the reasons were different, but it was hard still to ask about Juanito. Sarah I did not know well, and behind her soft dignity I sensed a kind of resignation that would make such questions seem impertinent. Gradually from Norah I learned what she could tell me, but there was an unwillingness about her, as if she too felt mixed up with Juanito, and resented it.

I used to walk along the rutted road to the villa with her, and sit under the queer heavy twisted trees while her picture was being painted, and on the way back to the village again and our house she would talk sometimes.

Once we met a handsome man in a black suit. He looked like a lawyer in a provincial French town, with sad eyes and a smirking dissipation in his face.

"That's the doctor," Norah said. "He's a snob, and thinks he is condemned to this village because in a bigger place people would look down on him for his Indian wife. But he says he's a liberal. He and the priest are the intellectuals. He pierced my ears for me. We both got a little drunk. I was scared and I don't think he'd ever touched a white woman's ears before. He did a bad job. He was with the priest the night David and Sarah came back from their honeymoon."

That was the way she talked, but before I came back to California I knew all there was for me to know about Juanito. And what I knew made me sorry that any of us had ever gone to that village, and ashamed that we were so big, so pale, so incautiously alive.

If we had gone somewhere else, though, it might have been the same . . . not for Juanito, but for some other creature. Or, if stars and bodies had been different, it might have been Juanito who with an innocence even greater than ours could blast our lives . . . But how can you know, when you walk through a room, that you have made such havoc? Must you hide always, for fear of the damage you may or may not cause?

Juanito came down from the hills as a boy, alone. That was not strange: there were many children who lived that way, begging when they had to, running errands, sleeping where there was the most shelter. Some of them disappeared, into another village, or into the lake, like stray cats, but Juanito stayed because that village still had real *mariachi* music in it.

He used to go everywhere with the bands, and finally he was singing with them in his wild cracked voice, and playing the instruments with his claw-fingers while the men rested between songs. In a year or so he was the leader: all the best men went with him, and his band was the one people called for when they got married or wanted to go out onto the summery lake for eating and singing and love-making.

Juanito grew a little, but not much, and lived with the children of the cornet-player. After the priests could wear cassocks again in that part of Mexico, and the young Jewish Father came to the village to stay, Juanito went regularly to confession . . . but only the two of them ever knew that he was anything but a proud local possession, a fifteen-year-old boy who had his own band, and could play and sing for three days running, at fiestas.

That is how it was when David and Norah came.

They were odd strangers to the small dark village-people, as they moved with their naïve insolent assurance through the stony streets. Everywhere they went eyes watched them politely, acutely, and as soon as it was seen how they smiled and looked peaceful when the bands played, they lived in an almost constant storm of music. It beat and whimpered and nagged insistently outside their home, whether they paid for it or not, and at night when they ate in the little open restaurants, the men seemed to know where they would go before they did themselves. They loved it.

David got Juanito to come to the house sometimes, to teach him new words to the songs, and better ways to hold his fingers. Perhaps that is what started Juanito to change, but I doubt it. Juanito's eyes, downcast and far back under his wide-brimmed hat, saw every time he played how David's queerly exhausted face grew younger, and Juanito saw that as a woman would see it, with tenderness and probably a purely physical stirring inside.

And then, instead of going away to do it, she changed right there in the village into a girl.

She had to stop playing with her men, and stop wearing trousers. The cornet-player's wife got her a dress, which hung slackly on her thin body, but no more so than it would have on any other malnourished girl there in that hungry village. She let her hair grow, but it kept its dusty spiked look, and hung incongruously over her large eyes in her small sallow face, like a monkey's.

She went to church with the other women, instead of all alone to confession, and the young priest watched over her anxiously, gently. Perhaps he felt that religion had brought Juanita to her true life at last. Perhaps he simply felt relieved that someone he knew to be female was no longer living as a male.

As for the villagers, they seemed to accept the change without much surprise. Keeping themselves alive took most of their energies, and what little was left over they spent, with native wisdom, on fiestas to make them forget their hungers and sicknesses. They missed Juanito the *mariachi*-leader; there was no doubt of that.

Two or three men tried to hold the band together, and then it melted slowly into the rival one or went to other parts of Jalisco.

Norah told the doctor how much she and David missed the good music, one day when she was having the little holes in her earlobes disinfected, and he smiled and said the priest would be interested to hear that. Had she heard, he asked her, swabbing and poking, that in Guadalajara there was a *mariachi* band much better than the little Juanito's had been? It played in a few bars . . .

My brother and sister began to go oftener to the city, especially after Sarah came.

Then David and Sarah were married, and went away on their honeymoon, and Norah went to stay at the villa with the big gates until they came back. She said she saw Juanito in her ugly dress a few times in the market, and they always smiled shyly at each other, the way women do when they have nothing to say but feel friendly.

The Saturday David was to bring his new wife home, Norah moved back to the house to have it ready for them and ordered a fine dinner at the hotel, and warned the widow to have the cold drinks waiting.

Everybody in the village knew about it, and there was an almost visible shimmer of excitement behind the courteous faces everywhere: the young American was coming back with a wife . . . not a friend, a *wife* . . .

Things went off beautifully. The flowers in the little house did not wilt much, and the flies under the high dome in the hotel dining room did not settle as hungrily as usual on the dinner Norah had commanded. And afterwards at the widow's the brandy seemed almost as good as the cocktails had before, and a moon spread smooth over the windless waters of the lake.

The little beggar-children came giggling and grinning to look at Sarah, and when the lone *mariachi* band rolled up to play, people came as always from the shadows and smiled and even nodded timidly as they watched the three strangers and listened to the music.

Norah saw the priest on the edge of the light that night. He seemed searching, and soon hurried off, without bowing to her. There were a lot of people still on the streets when the three went home, because it was Saturday, and on the plaza the little tequila-joints were full. Norah said that on a bench outside of one of them, the worst one, which was often closed for days while its proprietor lay drunk on the floor, the priest was sitting.

She was surprised to see him. Even though he was so young, and wore striped sport socks under his short cassock, he was still a priest, and Saturday night on the plaza was not right for him.

Then she saw . . . they all saw . . . that he was holding up Juanito.

Juanito was a boy again, since that very morning. His hair was shaved roughly from his head, and his white face and closed eyes made him look like a saint, somehow. He was drunk, dead-drunk, and the little priest was holding him around the shoulders, like a mother, to keep him from rolling to the ground.

Norah said they walked over, shocked, intuitively thinking they could help. David was big . . . maybe he thought he could carry the little unconscious Juanito away from the foul air in front of the bar. But when the priest saw who it was coming toward him, the three tall compassionate strangers, David and his pale-haired wife and his grave-eyed sister, he stood up slowly.

Juanito felt softly along the bench. The priest took off his thickly rimmed glasses. He kept staring at David, and Norah thought, "There's trouble! There's trouble!" And then the little man, with a look of complete scorn on his pinched, pale, hook-nosed face, spat in the dust in front of him.

"Hey!" David said in the slow way big men say it when their stomachs are tightening and they are going to fight.

There were some people watching, but not with much interest, and all the time music from the juke-boxes in the bars whined and bellowed, three or four tunes at once, while the two men stared at each other and the boy Juanito lay on the bench, dead-drunk.

As I think about it now, I feel almost as if David and the priest were the same man. Even their bodies were alike: tired, big-nosed, sunken-eyed. One had grown higher and fuller, because of good food and freedom from oppression. One had grown wiser, perhaps from hunger and slavery. And they met, there in the plaza.

The doctor came swiftly down from his pharmacy on the corner. Maybe someone had told him . . . one of the beggar-children. He said in a fast low voice, almost without stopping as he passed my family, "Go home. Hurry. This is not your affair."

The priest stared for a few seconds longer up into David's eyes, and then he put on his glasses again, and as the three strangers turned and walked toward their house, they saw him help the doctor lift Juanito, and head toward the church with her.

It took a long time for me to find out what had happened, and instead of feeling that it had stopped, to me it was still going on. I knew it whenever I saw the priest. He always walked past the widow's, or the restaurants, when Juanito was playing and we were listening. If David was not there he bowed to us, and I wanted to know him better, and knew that I never would.

And I knew something was still going on when I watched the faces of my family, and saw how David's always grew younger and simpler to the music, and how sometimes Sarah's and Norah's looked tight under the smooth beautiful well-bred skin. Sometimes when David would call out "*La Malagueña*," and clap and smile, Sarah would permit herself one small movement of protest, as if she had been jabbed with a goad, or she and Norah would look at each other in a kind of wonder, as if David were beloved but imbecilic.

I was the one who would say, "No more, I'm tired. No more tonight." It was because sometimes I felt as if I could not stand another note to beat into my body, the way they all did in those insistent *mariachi* songs, until they were like blood in a fever, or a wild heart.

The strangest thing, maybe, was that after Juanito came back, David took it for granted the lessons would go on. He asked her one night why she had not come as usual on the set day, to finish teaching him a song interrupted when she left her band. She said she would come the next afternoon, and David was annoyed when she did not.

One of the cornet-player's children tapped on the window, and shouted in that Juanito was sick, but would come in two more days. Perhaps Juanito got drunk again. When she finally came, she looked more than ever like a little monkey, or a ghost.

Norah and Sarah went away that afternoon, and every time the lessons happened, and I stayed up in my room, lying in a kind of helplessness on my wooden bed, listening to David and the singer in the patio. The stone house sent their voices up to me with a clear intensity.

David treated him as if he were the boy who led the *mariachi* band, and who was giving him lessons at so much per hour. I think what had happened about Juanito, and my brother's knowledge that she was really a girl, had gone completely from his strange mind. He was too concentrated on his own existence to be conscious of any others, except as they could help him. I am sure, certain-sure, that it never occurred to him that he had anything to do with Juanito's behavior. He thought of her, if he thought at all, as an instrument who played music that pleased him.

It was the priest who thought of Juanito as a human, the priest who seems mixed now in my mind with David, as if they were parts of a whole.

V

Finally it was time for us to go. Norah and I were going to fly, from Guadalajara, and we all went up there for a few days before the plane left. Then David and Sarah were starting out in the little car.

We went to the bull fights, and took showerbaths and drank beer. There were many Germans in the city then: they seemed to own all the big groceries and pharmacies and such, and the best restaurants were very much like ill-kept beer-halls. People ate sauerkraut and sausages around the big tables, and played backgammon or read old Berlin newspapers. But there was good Mexican food, too. It goes well with beer, bottled or in steins.

We would rest after the bull fights, and bathe, and then in the twilight, ride in a carriage to an oyster-bar, and eat pink oysters, black oysters. Sarah hated that part, but she was patient. Then we would go to a plaza where there was a restaurant named, I think, Valencia's. Valencia was the chef, and he fixed chicken with herbs and oil, the way I have often eaten it in Italy. We would sit under the trees in the plaza, while other swells in carriages ate all around us, and the drivers flicked goodnaturedly at ragamuffins with their whips.

Or we would have a drink or two in the bar of the hotel, where the good *mariachi* band played high up against the ceiling in a little alcove, and go afterward to one of the beer-halls for supper.

The night before Norah and I were to leave, we decided to do that.

We went into the noisy little bar, where most of the local bloods crowded about six at night and a few hard-faced genial American business men were well known by the barman. He was a eunuch. By now he knew us, too, and he greeted us shrilly, and made us each a double-Gibson with a special flourish. We felt gay and taut, the way you always do when you know you are ending one part of your life on a high note.

Men and a few women were talking all around us, and the band was beating it out up near the roof, yowling in thirds that would never sound anything but exciting to us. I think we had finished the drink and started another when we looked at each other and knew that Juanito was singing up there. It made us all feel strange. The village was behind us, we had thought . . .

David got up and asked the barman, and came back looking as pleased as a child. It was Juanito, all right. He was well known, and any time he wanted to, the barman said, he could leave his own band for this one. He came in just before the music started. We could not see up into the alcove, but his voice was as familiar as our own.

I felt disturbed, in a passive way. There was nothing to do or say about it. Sarah seemed as withdrawn and silky as ever, and Norah would not look at me, and David was obviously happy. To him it was probably one more bit of good luck, one more augur of the gods' special interest in him, in David . . .

We went on to the beer-hall. I forget its name. It was a good one, dark and smelly, with old Coca-Cola ads on the walls and an agreeable disinterested hum from all the other people. We had a table in a kind of booth. We had often sat there, and the waiter was pleased to see us. We started in drinking dark beer, from fine big steins.

When the food came, it was delicious. We ate of lot of enchiladas, some with herbs and cheese in them and some with chicken. Then there were beans, of course, and a rather despondent guacamole in our honor, though it was long past time for avocados.

I think all of us but David were deliberately liking everything, the way people do when they are trying to push down in their minds the insistent knowledge that never again, never again will they be together and young and free and all the other things they may think they are at that moment. No matter how many times you have said goodbye to yourself in the presence of others you will assume something of the same resolute gaiety. It is a form of armor.

We were perhaps half-finished with our supper, eating slowly because it was the last one, when a little *mariachi* band came in. The men were tired and tipsy, but they were playing like demons, and Juanito was leading them, not singing far back as at the bar. He stood boldly in front of his few recruits, and struck at the guitar slung over his suddenly strong-looking little shoulders with a vigor that was uncompromising. He looked straight at us, not shyly any more, and his eyes were all black, like a squirrel's . . . no pupils, no whites.

We listened, while they played for us and then moved slowly around to other tables. When they came back, David asked them if they would not like a drink. Juanito bowed, and said in his cracked sweet voice that they would come back soon, and then if the Señoras permitted . . . He bowed smilingly again to us and marched out, tiny in front of his tired meek band.

We kept on rolling tortillas into pencils and dipping them in a bowl of hot brown sauce, and drinking beer. Sarah wanted to go back to the hotel. But we felt we must stay a little longer, in case Juanito came back. The chairs were hard.

Finally the music came again, and Juanito was standing by our table, with his men swaying from weariness and a few more shots of tequila, and playing as I have never heard a band play anywhere. They were hoarse by now, but they sang with a muted savagery, and Juanito's clear wailing rose and fell against the strumming like a voice from a dream.

It did not matter that we were too full of beer, too full of regrets and presentiments: we sat there like dry trees in the rain. The music washed over us, and it hurt, but it was good.

The men drank some more, and Juanito too, and then Sarah said, "I'm going."

She said it almost violently, and slapped her hand on the table. It was the first time I had ever known her to be like that, and I was glad to see it. Her oval face with its odd oblique blue eyes was flushed, and she started to stand up.

Norah said, "Yes."

But David said, "Wait. One more thing. Let me ask them one more thing. I want to see. . ."

He spoke to Juanito, before we could protest. "Señor," he said in his fluent bad Spanish, "will you do us the favor of playing for us the song you think is the most beautiful in Jalisco?"

Juanito looked at him for a moment, as if to decide something in a language never spoken. The men straightened, waiting, with their hands on their bows and strings. And Juanito, with his full black eyes moving easily from one face to another, in a new assurance, sang *La Malagueña*.

It was so beautiful, and the high passionate woman's voice rose so wildly above the whimpering men, and the strings beat so rhythmically into our hearts, that all over the beer-hall people fell silent, and put down their steins and their newspapers, and turned to watch, as if that could make them understand what the music was meaning.

It was a different song for each of us, of course. Sarah looked very peaceful, suddenly, and there were the same tears in Norah's brown deep eyes that I had seen there when the first bull dropped proudly to his knees, that afternoon in the arena. David's face was calm and drowsy, remotely voluptuous, like a Chinese carving.

And for myself, as Juanito sang the last bars to us and the weeping voices rose against hers over the rhythm, I felt a kind of humility and a thankfulness that we were leaving. Juanito would be free again, as much as anyone can be who has once known hunger and gone unfed . . .